THE MEDIEVAL SCRIPTORIUM

The Medieval Scriptorium

Making Books in the Middle Ages

SARA J. CHARLES

REAKTION BOOKS

To my family

Published by
Reaktion Books Ltd
Unit 32, Waterside
44–48 Wharf Road
London N1 7UX, UK
www.reaktionbooks.co.uk

First published 2024

Printed and bound in India by Replika Press Pvt. Ltd

A catalogue record for this book is available from the British Library

ISBN 978 1 78914 916 6

CONTENTS

Sites of medieval manuscript production in Britain and Ireland.

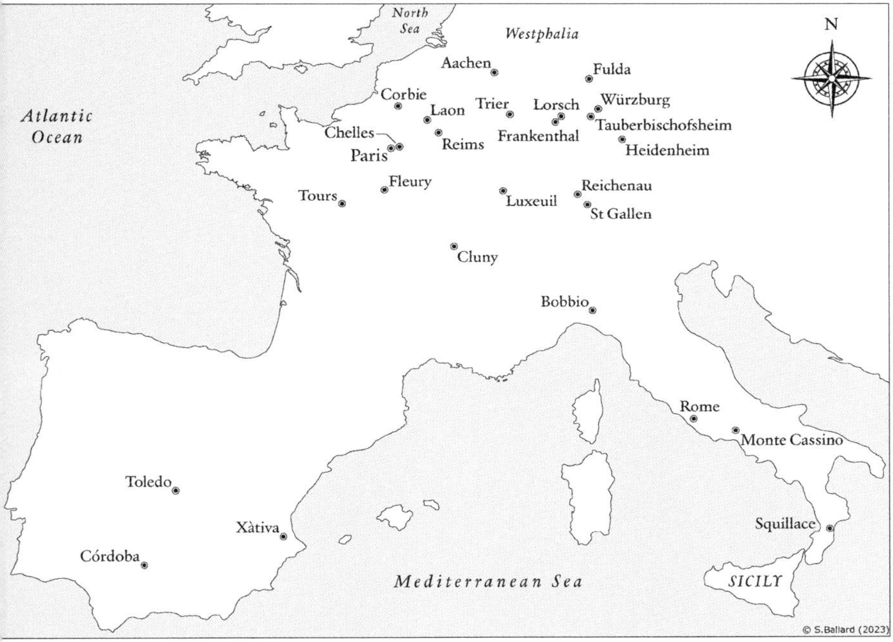

Sites of medieval manuscript production in Europe referred to in this book.

An enemy ended my life, took away
my bodily strength; then he dipped me
in water and drew me out again,
and put me in the sun where I soon shed
all my hair. The knife's sharp edge
bit into me once my blemishes had been scraped away;
fingers folded me and the bird's feather
often moved across my brown surface,
sprinkling useful drops; it swallowed the wood-dye
(part of the stream) and again travelled over me,
leaving black tracks. Then a man bound me,
he stretched skin over me and adorned me
with gold; thus I am enriched by the wondrous work
of smiths, wound about with shining metal.

RIDDLE 26, Exeter Book, tenth century
(translation Kevin Crossley-Holland)

Introduction

Take a moment and, in your mind's eye, conjure up an image of a medieval scriptorium. What do you see? The chances are, there will be cowled monks, hunched over rows of wooden desks, leaning forward in concentration. There may be hushed silence, or the muted sound of Gregorian chanting in the background. Possibly the sound of quills scratching laboriously over the parchment. Brilliant sunlight might stream down from the upper windows or maybe a multitude of candles light the shadows of a cold stone room. You may envisage rolls of fresh parchment, arranged onto shelves by size, lining the corners of the room. Perhaps a stern librarian sits at the head of the room overseeing the scribal activity, with a pot of feathered quills on their desk. You may imagine painters and illuminators working in a different part of the room from the scribes, perhaps in some orderly production line, with the freshly scribed parchment being passed onto the illuminator to decorate with gold.

All of this, some of this or none of this may be historically accurate. The truth is, we do not really know. There are no surviving pictorial representations of a defined monastic scriptorium. We have plenty of images of individual scribes, but very few images of groups of scribes, and none that specifically relate to the common image we have in mind when we think of a medieval scriptorium. So where does this stereotype come from?

Television and film adaptations have helped create this image, based on fictional narratives. It feeds into our fascination with the medieval monastic world, a world dominated by the Church, and a strictly cloistered society. It may be that the idea of working silently and calmly, steadily forming letter shapes, speaks to us amid the cacophony of modern life. A perfectly still environment, with no mobile phones or computers to complicate our lives, no aircraft buzzing overhead or sirens or alarms. Perhaps, even, there is something reminiscent of bygone schooldays when life was simpler, being instructed by the teacher to write out lines of spellings in the cocoon of a classroom.

In reality, the making of a medieval manuscript was dirty, smelly, often boring and certainly back-breaking. It involved blood, urine, excrement and earwax. From the visceral process of preparing animal skin, to the wrist-straining tedium of endless writing, to the foul-smelling ingredients of illumination, to the finger-numbing effort of sewing tough parchment together – making a manuscript was an act of hard labour. Consider all the work hours that would have gone into the production of one single medieval book in Europe. First, you would need good-quality animal skin for the parchment. For a manuscript of reasonable length (say 120 folios/240 pages), you would need about twenty animal skins that were not scarred or covered in holes from the flayer's blade. Then you would need to prepare the parchment, which would take a good few weeks. For the ink, you would need oak galls, either foraged from local oak trees or bought at the market, plus ferrous sulphate (which would have been relatively easy to source in Europe). The last ingredient, gum arabic, would require sophisticated trade links, to import the gum from Africa or Asia. Alternatively you could use a local plant gum as substitute. The quills you would collect in the months of June and July, when the geese and swans shed their feathers, and store them to naturally harden over the year.

Then consider the time it took to physically copy out the book by hand. As a scribe, you would first have to be trained to write a decent-looking script, in the style of the religious house you belonged to. Then, hour after hour bent over a desk, you would meticulously form words, with hands, back and eyes aching and intestines constantly cramped. It's no wonder that some scribes could not keep their misery from spilling onto the page, complaining bitterly of their lot in added notes in the margins.

But still the manuscript was far from done, even with the writing finished. The coloured initials would need to be added, and the images sketched out before adding the ingredient that would make it truly precious – gold. First, you would need to prepare a mixture of gesso, as a base for the gold. The gesso is full of unpleasant-smelling ingredients, such as egg glair, fish glue and garlic juice, and you need to apply it quickly before it sets. If the gesso had too many bubbles in it, you would simply add some earwax to smooth it out. Even though it sets quickly, you then need to wait at least twelve hours for the gesso to harden thoroughly before applying wafer-thin sheets of gold. This is a skilled and delicate operation that requires complete stillness and concentration, otherwise you end up losing most of it by the slightest air current.

Only when the gold has settled and been polished to a shine with a dog or boar tooth is it ready for the next stage. The medieval palette consisted partly of locally grown or easily made pigments, but also of incredibly dangerous substances and metamorphic rocks from far across the sea. The time, skill and networks needed to source the variety of pigments were immense. For example, madder – a plant grown easily in Europe – needs at least three years in the soil to develop its roots, and another year to let the roots dry out. Only then can you extract a decent reddish pigment. And lapis lazuli (otherwise known as ultramarine) needs to travel all the way from Afghanistan, traded from merchant to merchant, before finding its way into monasteries on the western side of the known world. Orpiment, otherwise known as *auripigmentum* (gold paint), was understood to be deadly, yet continued to be prized for its golden hue. So, once you have sourced all your pigments, you grind them into powder with a stone, then mix with a binder before pouring them into pots or shells. You would then select a paintbrush made from the hair of a squirrel or badger or cat, and now, finally, you are ready to paint.

Even though you now have your text, your shining gold and your beautiful images, it is still not complete, for it needs to be bound together. The text block is first sewn onto alum-tawed leather supports with a thick needle piercing through the tough parchment. Once sewn together, you need wooden boards for the covers. The wood has to be a hard wood, such as oak or cherry, and shaped into the right thickness. Small channels then need to be carved in the boards for the alum-tawed leather supports to thread through, joining the text block to the wood.

But it's pretty dull just having wooden boards as covers, so you might want to dress it up a bit in leather or cloth, or even jewels or embroidery. If you want leather, it might mean a trip to the smelliest part of town where the tanner worked. Buckets of dog excrement collected freely from the streets would be lying around there, ready to be used to soften the animal skins, and the stench would greet you long before you arrived. But – you've now got a nice red leather cover over your boards and the manuscript is nearly finished. The problem with parchment, though, is that it doesn't want to lie flat; it wants to spring open (even between thick wooden boards), so it needs something to keep it shut. The last step in the process is a trip to the blacksmith to fashion an iron book clasp or two. Once they are attached to your boards and snapped into place – that's it! You have a medieval manuscript.

Just consider that book in your hand and its utter uniqueness in a multitude of ways. No other manuscript will ever be made of the same parchment. It came from animals that were once grazing in a field, and the parchment will still contain traces of the living being, with skin imperfections, pores and veins often still visible. No other manuscript will be written with the same quill and very few will be written with the same batch of ink and by the same scribe. No other manuscript will have the same pattern of mistakes, erasures, wax drips and squashed insects. No other manuscript will be painted in exactly the same way, using exactly the same pigments. No other manuscript will be sewn together and attached to its covers in precisely the same way as yours. No matter how sophisticated book production became in the medieval period, there would never be two identical manuscripts. Every medieval manuscript is a single unique object, largely sourced from natural products and produced completely by human hands, and containing a wealth of physical information about the time in which it was produced. Think of all the other hands that have been involved in its creation – from the parchment maker, to the scribe, to the illuminator, to the painter, to the bookbinder, to the woodcutter – before it is held in your hands. The physical structure of any book means that all its secrets are hidden away between its covers, only to be revealed when you open it. This is even truer of a medieval manuscript, and the reason why the written words and images remain so vibrant today is because they are preserved in this ideal packaging.

Now that you have an idea of the reality of manuscript production, this book will take you further on a journey through medieval bookmaking in Europe, describing the sights, sounds and smells that medieval makers would have experienced. We will look at the development of monastic manuscript culture and the rise and fall of centres of book production through the early and late medieval period. Starting with a brief overview of the history of text production and materials up to the classical period, the first chapter also explores the beginnings of Christianity, and how the drive to spread the word of God made text production an intrinsic part of it. The second chapter covers manuscript production in the early medieval period in Europe, up to the mid-eleventh century. It looks at the Insular style of script and decoration from the seventh and eighth centuries, and then the influence of the Holy Roman Emperor, Charlemagne, who in the ninth century promoted Caroline minuscule as a universal script. The Ottonian era in the tenth century then saw new developments in artistic style.

The third chapter deals with the main question of this book – did our romantic image of the scriptorium actually exist? Looking at evidence from medieval texts, manuscript images and architectural remains, what can we tell about the writing places of monastic houses. Who were the scribes and what was life like for a medieval copyist? The fourth chapter focuses on the materials that the scribe used – parchment, quills and ink – and describes the processes of writing. Similarly, the fifth chapter looks at illumination, painting and bookbinding – pigments used and artistic techniques. The sixth chapter picks up the chronological thread started in Chapter Two, covering the Romanesque period from the late eleventh to the early thirteenth century. There was an explosion in manuscript production in this period, with many of the finest books being produced, thanks to a blending of monastic and secular collaboration. The seventh chapter signals a shift in manuscript production, as universities and towns led to a commercial industry being more suited to the sharp rise in demand for books. Paper increasingly started to replace parchment. By the end of the fifteenth century, the printing press was beginning to be recognized as a superior technology for book production, and manuscript production declined.

The world we live in now, with mass-produced books, print on demand, home printers and 3D printers, is a far cry from the viscerality of the medieval period. Parchment is a material many people will not be familiar with, compared to the ubiquitous paper. And some of us may remember writing with a fountain pen, even filling up from an ink pot – yet apart from professional calligraphers, very few people today actually use a quill to write. But have we lost something in our sanitized culture? Is that link with the natural world meant to be broken? Many of the processes of manuscript production meant working with, and understanding, the environment – taking what you needed at the right time of the year, being able to think ahead and plan. The parchment may have come from a monastery's own livestock, the quills from their local geese and swans. The ink may have been made from galls collected in their local woodlands, and some of the pigments from plants harvested from their own gardens, sown years previously as a long-term investment. And so, these connections to the natural world and to their immediate surroundings must have formed an incredibly strong bond between manuscripts and their creators. We may have a favourite pen or a favourite book but imagine how much stronger that connection would be if it were a quill from a domestic goose or parchment from the calf of a favourite cow. Although the use of animal skin (particularly from young animals) may seem cruel, animals slaughtered one or even two millennia ago now live on through ancient manuscripts. This was a society in which nothing went to waste, and every bit of the slaughtered animal was put to good use.

Manuscript style changed dramatically over hundreds of years, from its rise in the third century to its gradual eclipse by the printing press after the fifteenth century. But in those centuries, we see it change from basic lines of text and somewhat crude illustration to the intricate interlacing and beautiful script of the early medieval period (as seen in the Lindisfarne Gospels), to the staggering three-dimensional beauty of fifteenth-century illuminated Books of Hours. We see developments in parchment making, resulting in parchment in the thirteenth century so thin as to be almost translucent. The range of pigments expanded as new manufacturing techniques were developed and more trade routes opened. Bookbinding improved dramatically, creating such strong structures to hold the text block that many still survive today. And all of this was done because of the simple desire to learn and to share knowledge. No matter how long and arduous the process, it was all worth it to have the finished product. Manuscripts became not just carriers of knowledge, but physical objects in their own right – and so monastic book production took off in medieval Europe, with experiments and developments in writing and decorating styles showcasing the beauty of the written word.

One

The Beginnings

Bethlehem, fourth century CE

Paula rises just before dawn, putting her rush sleeping mat to one side in the grey light. Wearing a simple tunic, already patched in several places, she draws back the blanket across the entrance to her rickety wooden hut and steps out as the sun is rising. Shivering slightly, she inhales the early morning air, smelling the dust mingled with the spicy scent of the wild irises. She says her thanks to God for this morning and enjoys a moment of perfect stillness before walking serenely towards the communal prayer courtyard. Signs of the day beginning are all around her, and as she walks down the central path of the women's quarters, she hears her fellow sisters in their shared rooms talking quietly, gently laughing or humming. Despite the buzz of activity, there is an air of calm tranquillity that encompasses the whole monastery. They chose this site specifically, herself and Jerome, to be near to the birthplace of the Lord. What better way to keep God's message in their hearts than by basing themselves in the very place that it all began, and with the Church of the Nativity so close, their double monastery was becoming a beacon, not just for pilgrims, but those curious of the new religion.

All the residents of the monastery come together every morning for the dawn recital of the psalms. As they file into the courtyard lined with palm trees, the sun creeps over the stone buildings and wooden huts of their humble community, chasing the shadows away. The courtyard reverberates with voices blending together, male and female, old and young, faces turned heavenward in their morning song.

Once the morning psalms have been sung, Paula gathers her equipment into a small leather bag, including meagre rations for her lunch. She leaves her instructions for the day with her daughter Eustochium, reminding her to prepare the rooms for the weary pilgrims on their way to Jerusalem. She sets off to her private cell on the hillside, away from the familiar hum of the monastery so that she can have perfect silence to absorb herself in her writing. As she walks down the street, she watches the monastic labourers going about their daily tasks purposefully, the ploughman tilling the soil and singing alleluia in a low, resonant tone, the reaper wiping the sweat off his brow while chanting the psalms, and the vinedresser carefully pruning the leaves with his curved blade while singing the Song of David. The sounds of the compound gradually fade away, leaving her only with the sounds of the birds, her feet slapping on the bare ground and her steady breathing. The heat of the sun intensifies as she walks alone along the scrubby path and she concentrates on the beauty of the reds and golds of the desert hills on the horizon to distract her from her growing thirst. She reaches her small square hut, her scriptorium for the day, and is grateful for the shade.

She starts to unpack her bag and lays out her materials on the dusty floor – a wooden board to use as a desk, blank sheets of papyrus rolled up in a bundle, a sealed terracotta pot of ink, a reed pen and a knife. She remembers the beautiful books she saw when she lived in Rome, made of purple-stained parchment and glittering with gold letters and jewels, but now she prefers the humbler papyrus. Like Jerome, she thinks it is the words that are important – no need for unnecessary decoration. The folded-book format, rather than the scroll, and the iron gall ink, are still new to her as writing materials; she was taught as a girl to write on papyrus scrolls with carbon ink. The older ones at the monastery still frown upon this new technology, but she believes a new religion needs a new way to express itself. The folded papyrus codex is much easier to use, with no endless rolling and unrolling of the scroll to find a certain passage. And the oak galls used by her grandfather to dye his hair black now have a new use as a long-lasting ink. Lastly, she pulls out the wax tablets, with Bible passages crammed with Jerome's notes scratched by his stylus into the soft wax surface. These words are like alchemy to her – from God himself, captured first in Hebrew on the holy scrolls of the old Bible and then into Greek, flowing from one mind to another through stylus and wax, pen and ink, papyrus and parchment. Now Jerome and Paula are transforming them into an everyday Latin text, to allow a greater audience to witness the word of God and understand His message.

Sitting on the floor and using the wall of the hut as a backrest, she flattens the first sheet of papyrus on the wooden board, propped up by her knees. She takes a small drink of water and a morsel of bread to sustain her. The sunlight streams through the open doorway, and she will measure the day by the shadows shifting across the room. Closing her eyes in prayer, she asks God to assist her with her writing, her understanding of His words and her interpretation of them. Then, dipping her pen into the pot of ink at her side, she leans over her makeshift desk and begins to scratch the first words: 'In principio creavit Deus caelum et terram'.

Paula works silently and steadily, the ink forming neat lines of shapes, woven together by her dextrous hand. She is totally absorbed in her task, her mind focused on how the words fit together, flowing from her stream of consciousness, through her hand, onto the page. She does not stop at the third hour, the sixth hour and the ninth hour to recite the psalter – this, then, is her prayer to God, the worship of His words, word made flesh. The sun makes its familiar journey across the sky, insects scuttle in and out of her hut and flies buzz lazily through the dry air, yet Paula is oblivious to all worldly things, lost in the reverie of holy words. When the shadows start to lengthen and the heat starts to go out of the day, Paula brings herself back to her earthly surroundings. She lays down her reed pen and rotates her aching hand, then stretches her neck from side to side. She lays out the text before her, examining the script she has written, checking for any mistakes. Tomorrow she will show this text to Jerome, and then pass it onto her group of women scribes at the monastery to copy, instructing them to write neatly and quickly. She is driven by the need to spread the word of God to the Latin-speaking Christians, so they can understand the power of His words in their own language.

Sensing the coolness of the early evening air, Paula packs up her writing materials and gets to her feet. Stretching and yawning, she feels the satisfaction of a day given to God's work. Stepping out into the desert, she once again attunes to her surroundings, noticing a lizard standing on a pile of rocks, skin shimmering gold and green in the evening sun before darting through a gap in the stones. She smiles at his hasty retreat, and hiking her bag up over her shoulder, she heads back to the monastery with her heart singing.

To begin with, let's think about the word *scriptorium* (plural *scriptoria*). It is a Latin word: the first part, *scriptor*, means writer, and the suffix *-ium* denotes a grouping, so literally it means a group of writers. In classical times the term referred to a writing room or writing desk. So, if we take that definition, there are many situations through history to which the term 'scriptorium' could be applied – children writing in a classroom, people working in a private study at home, accountants jotting down figures in a ledger, customs officials checking goods at the docks or clerks copying letters to be sent out to customers. Yet the word 'scriptorium' conjures up so much more than the indifferent movements of hands dutifully scratching words on paper. The term is intrinsically bound up with the medieval monastery, where the inhabitants would copy religious texts in the belief that knowledge should be disseminated. The definition given in the *Oxford English Dictionary* is: 'A room or area in a monastery set apart for writing, esp. one used by scribes copying and illuminating manuscripts.'

In the early days of Christianity, the idea of sharing knowledge was crucial to the spread of the new religion. The word 'gospel' means 'good news', and so copying the gospel texts and sending them far and wide to share the news of the kingdom of God became a vital part of the mission. This spirit of sharing knowledge was also intrinsic to the notion of the scriptorium, and this book shall explore its development in the medieval period. We have evidence of government clerics and bureaucrats clustered in writing rooms, copying records and accounts from the earliest times up until relatively recently, but it is not the purpose of this book to examine those kinds of writing rooms. We are looking specifically at the medieval Christian period in Western Europe and the growth of manuscript production. The dissemination of knowledge is the very essence of the term 'scriptorium', with texts that are copied for a higher religious purpose, and with the intention of keeping sacred words alive. As we will explore, evidence for a physical writing room within a monastery is hard to find, so 'scriptorium' in this book is generally defined as 'a centre of manuscript production', rather than a specific room within a monastery. While the focus of this book is medieval scriptoria, we first need a brief overview of the history of writing.

The Evolution of Writing

Between 12,000 and 8,000 years ago, a shift occurred in the hunter-gatherer mindset. Tribes started to swap nomadic lifestyles for a settled, agricultural existence, growing and harvesting crops and domesticating animals. One of the earliest places this happened (if not the earliest) was in Mesopotamia, a region in west Asia. As these settlements grew and developed, trade became a vital part of the functioning society. At a certain point, about 3200 BCE, the number of accounts and transactions needed to govern a society increased beyond human capability. To aid our insufficient little brains, a system evolved of recording transactions with pictographs on a piece of clay with a stylus – and just like that, writing was invented. This type of writing became known as cuneiform, wedge-shaped marks pressed into a slab of wet clay from the riverbank with a reed stylus, used by the Mesopotamian people up to the first century CE. The Mesopotamians were fiercely proud of the writing system they had developed, worshipping their own scribal gods, Nabu and Nisaba, and passing down myths about the invention of writing. It was common for scribes to include a dedication to Nabu and Nisaba in their work. Scribes were held in high regard in the Mesopotamian world, writing down hymns, prophecies and scientific and astrological texts. Their role was to copy sacred texts to pass down to later generations, thus preserving their heritage.

Scribes prepared their own clay tablets – using wet clay collected from the riverbank, then kneading and shaping it into the size they needed. Once the correct shape had been moulded (mainly rectangular, but it could be circular, square or cylindrical), the tablet would have been held in the left hand while a reed stylus was held in the right, pressing it gently into the damp clay to form a wedge shape. The text was written from left to right, with no spaces between words. Cuneiform symbols are made up of a combination of three strokes – a vertical wedge, a horizontal wedge and a slanting wedge. The scribe would have been against the clock, trying to finish the text before the belting Mesopotamian sun dried out the clay.

Wax tablets were also used for writing by the Mesopotamians, although few have survived due to natural decay. These wooden or ivory boards were flat with a recess carved out of the middle to hold the wax. The recess was scored with diagonal lines to allow the wax to adhere to the surface. Molten wax was then poured into the recess and left to set. Like clay, the wax also made a soft and impressionable writing surface, but it had the advantage of being more portable and easier to take notes on – unlike clay, it would not dry out. It was also much more forgiving, as mistakes could be easily erased and rewritten, and if you wanted to start afresh, you could just scrape out all the wax, melt it down again and refill it. A pointed stylus made of wood, bone or metal was used to write in the wax, often with a flattened end to smooth over any mistakes made. The flat boards were often joined together with a hinge, allowing the tablet to be opened and closed like a book, with the soft writing surface on the inside protected. It was even possible to join several boards together, creating a concertina effect. The wax tablet was such an effective tool for note-taking that it survived for millennia across many different cultures, and we shall see it often.

Not far from Mesopotamia, Egypt was developing its own form of writing around the same time. Like cuneiform, the Egyptian writing system started with a form of pictographs that became known as hieroglyphics. Hieroglyphics means 'holy writing' in Greek, translated from the ancient Egyptian phrase *medu netjer*, meaning 'the word of god', indicating its sacred properties. Unlike the Mesopotamian cuneiform on clay, the Egyptians used rush brushes dipped in ink to create hieroglyphs on papyrus sheets pasted together (papyrus is where the word 'paper' comes from). The sheets were then rolled up in a scroll.

The Egyptians also had their own scribal gods: Thoth, and his female counterpart, Seshat. Egyptian culture embraced the idea of the immortality of the scribe, understanding that even though the scribe had died, the written word would live on: 'a man has perished and his corpse has become dust . . . but writings cause him to be remembered in the mouth of the reciter.'[1] Egyptian scribes enjoyed a high status with a choice of many different specialisms, such as royal scribe, inspector of scribes or military scribe, and often had dual roles, such as scribe/judge or scribe/priest.[2]

Writing surfaces in Egypt included papyrus (the most widely used), ostraca (pieces of pottery), wooden boards, leather and even linen. Papyrus (*Cyperus papyrus*) is a native African aquatic plant that grows in shallow water and was abundant along the banks of the Nile. Unfortunately we don't know exactly what type of subspecies of *Cyperus papyrus* was used to make ancient Egyptian papyrus, as the reed ceased to grow in Egypt by the late eighteenth century, but from studying existing papyri and from classical accounts such as Pliny the Elder's *Natural History* (*c.* 77 CE), we can work out how papyrus was made.[3] The green outer layer of the plant was removed and the white inner core cut into even strips. The strips were then aligned in a vertical layer, with another layer put over the top horizontally. Once the strips were laid over each other, they were pressed together or beaten with a mallet, and allowed to dry. The side with the horizontal strips outermost was called the recto, and the vertical side the verso. When dry, the sheets were pasted together to form a roll. Generally, only the recto side was written on, with the verso left blank – the vertical side was harder to write on as you were going against the direction of the fibres.

The early scribes constantly drew on their environment to create materials – the rushes and reeds that grew in plentiful supply by the fertile rivers were easily adapted into writing implements. Egyptian scribes used a thin rush (*Juncus acutus*) with a width of just 1–2 millimetres to write on papyrus. These rushes have an internal fibrous structure and chewing or hammering on the end of the rush splays it out to create a brush-like tip. The rush was held about 5 centimetres away from the end – much more like a paintbrush than a pen.[4] So, since writing on cuneiform tablets may more accurately be described as printing on damp clay with a stylus, writing on papyrus may more accurately be described as painting on papyrus with a brush. By about the fourth century BCE, thicker reed pens started to be used. They were made from a piece of dried reed (*Phragmites communis*) about 20 centimetres long, with one end shaped into a nib with a slit at the top to hold the ink. The reed pen would have been held much the same way we hold pens today.

The Egyptians used a black carbon ink made of soot, another readily available material that had been used for thousands of years. Soot was collected from burning wood or bone and ground up with water and a binder, such as the sticky resin from a plant.[5] The binder helps the ink to attach to the surface of the papyrus and not brush off when dry. Egyptian scribes wrote both left to right and right to left. They are commonly depicted sitting cross-legged, sometimes with one leg raised with their kilt stretched taut to act as a 'desk' for the papyrus.

Alongside cuneiform and hieroglyphics, another writing system emerged around 1900–1700 BCE, which used letters to represent consonants. This proto-alphabet spread out and developed into other alphabet systems, including the Phoenician alphabet (*c.* 1400–1000 BCE). The Greeks, influenced by Phoenician traders from the Levant, created their own alphabet system circa 800 BCE. Crucially, they added vowels to the consonants to make an alphabet of 24 letters, and it is from this Greek alphabet that all modern European alphabets descend.

Greek scribes would have written on papyrus imported from Egypt, with a reed pen (*kalamos*) dipped in carbon ink. Wax tablets were also used, as was ostraca (and this is where the word 'ostracize' comes from – Greek citizens could vote to have a person exiled by scratching their name onto a pottery shard). Classical scribes were not revered in the same way that Mesopotamian and Egyptian scribes were – there was a clear distinction between 'writers' as the creators of intellectual works (citizens/free men), and 'scribes' who did the actual physical labour of writing or copying (the majority of whom were enslaved people or formerly enslaved people working as freelancers). Some enslaved scribes were highly educated, but generally held a low status in Greek society, with writing regarded as mere manual labour.

Although papyrus was the most common writing material throughout the ancient world, in the first century CE Pliny the Elder, the Roman author, naturalist and natural philosopher, makes this comment on the rise of parchment in the second century BCE:

> owing to the rivalry between King Ptolemy and King Eumenes about their libraries, Ptolemy suppressed the export of paper [papyrus], parchmenta was invented at Pergamum; and afterwards the employment of the material on which the immortality of human beings depends spread indiscriminately.[6]

This is quite misleading – parchment (animal skin) was definitely not 'invented' at Pergamum (a city in Turkey), but was already used as a writing surface throughout the Mesopotamian and Egyptian world. It is much more likely that papyrus was expensive to import (especially with the Egyptians having the monopoly on the market) and the abundance of goats and sheep in the landscape made parchment a much more feasible option. Yet Pliny highlights an important shift from papyrus to parchment, and it is quite possible that the process of parchment manufacture was significantly improved at Pergamum. Also, he is not wrong when he says that parchment, which gave humans the ability to live on through its recording of deeds and stories, spread rapidly throughout the ancient world. Papyrus continued to be used, certainly in the Eastern Mediterranean, until about 1100 CE, but parchment grew in popularity and became the standard writing surface across Western Europe until the introduction of paper towards the later medieval period.

The Romans (as usual) copied the customs of the Greeks, using enslaved people or hired hands as copyists. Yet plenty of citizens were able to write – we see many depictions of writing equipment on surviving wall paintings, and many physical objects (like styli) have survived, indicating the pervasiveness of the written word. Also like the Greeks, the Romans continued to write on papyrus with a reed pen. They would have used a carbon ink, or a metal-based ink made from oak galls, often stored in beautifully designed inkwells made of terracotta or metal. Pens and inkwells were stored in leather cases. Ink could be dehydrated into pellets and rewetted when needed, to allow easy transportation. Red ink was used for titles and headings, and was made from either cinnabar or red lead (minium) pigment. Wax tablets were a popular tool for everyday writing, with styli of metal, wood or bone. Writing accessories for the scribe around town included a wax spatula to smooth or scrape out wax, a stone to sharpen the stylus and a portable stylus case.[7] Leaf tablets (like the Vindolanda letters) were made of thin sheets of wood, written with ink, and laced together with notches and string. Ostraca continued to be used. Parchment was also used in folded notebook form (*pugillares membranei*) – although parchment seems to have been regarded by the Romans as an alternative to wax merely for notetaking and jotting down thoughts, rather than being considered a suitable medium for permanent texts.

The Latin alphabet evolved circa 700–600 BCE, from a version of the Greek alphabet that was used by the Etruscans. By the classical period, there were several different Latin writing scripts – square capitals, based on the angular letterforms used in monument inscriptions; rustic capitals, a more undulating script used for literary works; and old Roman cursive, an everyday script (cursive comes from the Latin word *currere*, which means to run – so literally the pen runs over the page). The formal scripts were written without any spaces between the words (*scriptura continua*) and no punctuation, which makes for difficult reading. There was a hierarchy within the professional scribal system – calligraphers were expert at writing beautifully, whereas notaries were trained for more bureaucratic purposes. While the majority of scribes seem to have been male, it was not unusual to have female scribes, particularly serving the female upper class. Suetonius' *Lives of the Caesars* (*c.* 121 CE) makes a reference to Vespasian's mistress, Caenis, who is described as a 'freedwoman and copyist of Antonia'.[8]

Jewish scribes had their own significant scribal culture, but unfortunately there is not as much surviving evidence from the ancient era. There were two types of professional Jewish scribes – those who recorded official documents and court records, and those who copied religious texts (called sofers). Jewish writing culture seems to have developed significantly after the Babylonian exile in the sixth century BCE, when there was a greater need to cement their identity in a permanent format. Most of the books of the Hebrew Bible were written down in this period, rather than just being passed on through oral tradition – the Torah (the first five books of the Bible – Genesis, Exodus, Leviticus, Numbers and Deuteronomy) was probably completed by the fourth century BCE. Hebrew script is made up of 22 letters using an abjad system, which means that there are no vowels, only consonants, and it reads right to left.

Jewish religious scribes were held in high regard, being learned in the Law of Moses (the Torah), and therefore having a direct link to him. Scribal status is mentioned frequently in the Bible – King David is described as a scholar and a scribe and Ezra (*fl.* 480–440 BCE) as a priest and scribe. Ancient Jewish scribes were not necessarily mere copyists, but could fulfil many different editorial roles, expanding and adapting texts as necessary – so they would have been highly educated. Little evidence survives, but they probably learnt their scribal craft in the temple school, or perhaps from their father, as it was often a family profession. Scribal access to the scriptures, and their role to read, understand and interpret the text, gave them a respected status in Jewish society.[9]

The oldest known Hebrew manuscripts are the Qumran Caves Scrolls (also known as the Dead Sea Scrolls), which date from the third century BCE to the first century CE, providing fascinating evidence of Jewish scribal history. They are scrolls of religious texts written in Hebrew, Aramaic and Greek, mainly on parchment, but also papyrus and even copper. Scribes used a carbon-based black ink, written with a reed pen, and the few examples of red ink have been identified as cinnabar.[10] These materials were typical of the time and culture.

In the ancient world, a strong relationship between writing and religion was established by the Mesopotamians and Egyptians, and scribes were revered for their intellect. In the classical world, literacy spread further, although the scribal craft lost its high status and many were regarded as mere copyists (apart from Jewish scribes). Writing surfaces varied from clay tablets to papyrus to parchment but were always accompanied with a stylus of one form or another, with the wax tablet remaining a constant aid to notetaking. The Mesopotamians and Egyptians had scribal gods with myths surrounding the invention of writing, and the Egyptians regarded hieroglyphics as coming from the mouth of god, which tells us just how much importance they placed upon the written word. This is a central theme that we will see again in the medieval world. Let us now move forward to the beginnings of Christianity and see how the concept of the scriptorium developed alongside the rise of the Christian faith in the medieval world.

The Beginnings of Christianity and the Codex

In the first century CE, a man proclaimed to be the son of God was crucified near Jerusalem. The story of this man, known as Jesus Christ, spread throughout the Roman empire and gave rise to the most-practised religion in the world – Christianity. An important part of early Christian doctrine was to go out and spread the word of Jesus. His teachings were recorded in the New Testament, including the four canonical gospels of Matthew, Mark, Luke and John, which told the life of Jesus. The word 'gospel' comes originally from the Greek word *evangelion* (good news), which became *evangelium* in Latin and *godspel* in Old English (*god* means good and *spel* means news). So, spreading the good news of Jesus and the coming of the kingdom of God was a fundamental mission of the early Christians – it was expected all to happen imminently, which really mobilized the movement. The teachings were first spread orally, but as those in living memory of Jesus and his apostles started to die out, it became important to create written records.

Christianity and the codex are inextricably bound together. From about the second century onwards, the book format that we are so familiar with today (the codex) – with pages folded in half, sewn together and sandwiched between two covers – started to be used by the early Christians (although the format

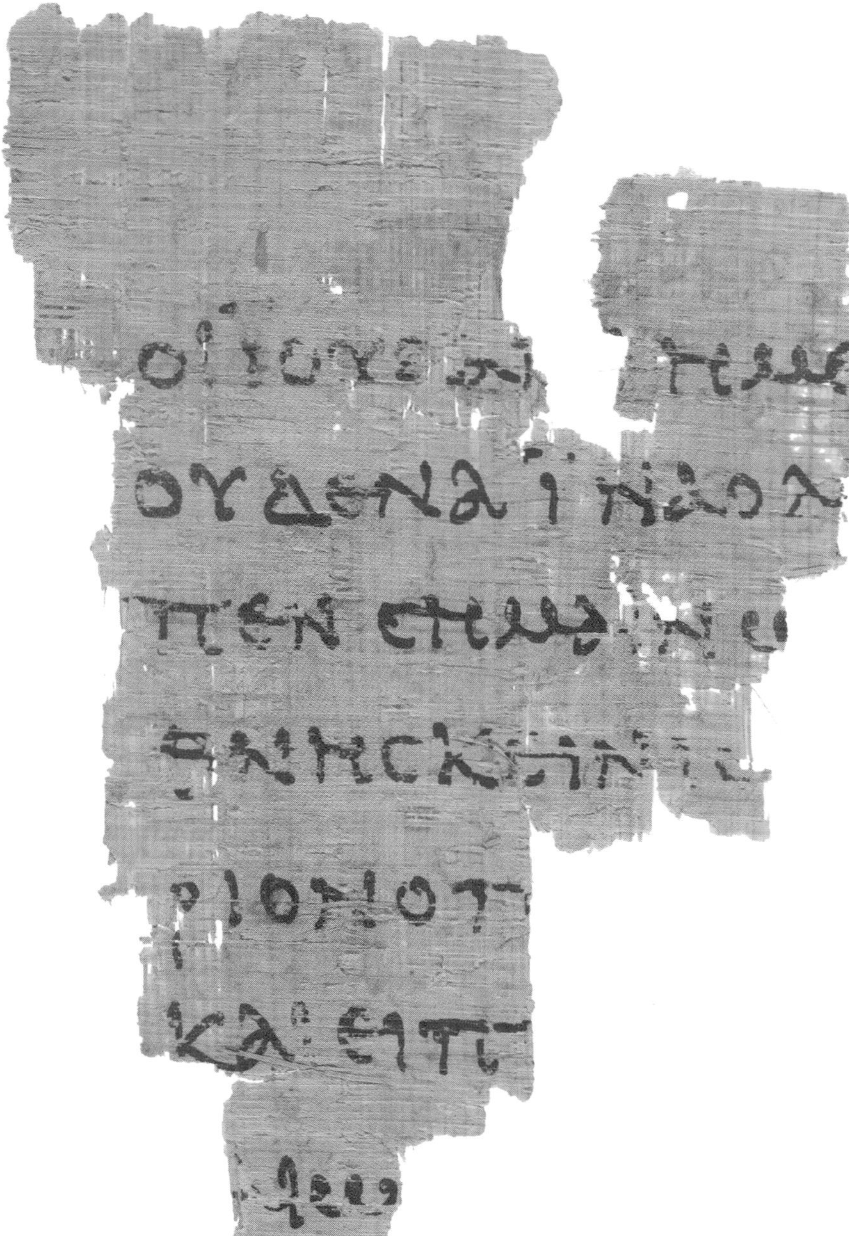

Fragment of the Gospel of John (recto), 2nd century CE.

did not gain widespread popularity in the Roman empire until the fourth century). In a belief reminiscent of the early Egyptians, Christians also believed that copying out religious texts was a sacred duty and that these words were literally the 'words of God', a power within themselves. The early Christians first used codices made of folded papyrus – for example, a fragment of the Gospel of St John dating from the second century was written on both sides of the papyrus, indicating it was from a codex rather than a scroll (Rylands Library Papyrus P52). There are many other examples of early Christian papyrus codices, including the Nag Hammadi library – Christian and Gnostic texts that were written on papyrus codices around the fourth century, bound in leather and secured with straps wound around them. Most of the surviving Christian papyrus codices have been found in Egypt, probably because of the ubiquity of the plant material and the right conditions for text preservation (that is, extremely dry).

These early Christian texts were not particularly polished or professional looking, indicating that the people probably copied them themselves, among their communities. As it was thought that Judgement Day was at hand, there was a real urgency to the movement. The priority of the early Christians would have been to circulate their texts among their communities, rather than producing lavish documents. Also, early Christianity was very much an underground movement, so ostentatious volumes would not only have gone against the basic principles of Jesus's teachings but could well have invited unnecessary attention.

It is not entirely clear why the Christians embraced the codex format so enthusiastically, rather than continuing with the traditional Roman/Jewish scroll format. There could be a number of reasons, including transportability and easier navigation of the text. Substantially more text can fit into a codex than a scroll, making it ideal for longer works (such as all four gospels of the New Testament). The codex format allowed compilations of different texts to be bound together, whereas the classical scroll tended to be one work by a single author. Also, there's a lot to be said for the easier navigation of a codex compared to a scroll. You need to find something quickly in a book? Flip it open in your hands, leaf through the pages. Easy. You need to find something quickly in a scroll? Unroll the twenty papyrus sheets stuck together and quite literally scroll through the columns. Not so easy. Another thing in the codex's favour is its design – having the precious inner text clasped between two hard protective covers immediately creates an outer shell for preservation.

There may have been a more personal reason for the early Christians to use the codex – as a form of identity. It was a new movement, starting out, so perhaps they wanted to distance themselves from the Roman/Jewish traditions of the classical world and use a different medium that would be associated with their new religion. The papyrus scroll was still used for less important, non-canonical Christian texts, but almost all surviving examples of the Old Testament and all surviving examples of the New Testament were written in codices.[11] A significant number of fragmented Christian texts from the second and third centuries have been found in ancient rubbish pits just outside Oxyrhynchus (el-Bahnasa) in Egypt, an early hub of Christian activity and book production.[12] These discarded papyri include many fragments from Christian codices – with all of the New Testament material in the codex format, giving a sense of identity to these new texts.

By about the fourth century, parchment codices started to replace papyrus codices. Papyrus does not actually lend itself so well to the codex format, where the custom is to write on both sides of the page. As we saw in the Egyptian scrolls, scribes preferred to write on just the recto side of the papyrus, as the vertical fibres running down the verso side made writing difficult. Also, papyrus is quite a fragile structure, so folding it in two creates a weakness in the crease, as does stitching the leaves together through the crease – which over time leads to the papyrus pages splitting and detaching. Parchment is hardwearing and flexible; therefore, it gradually became established as the preferred medium for the codex. It was easy to write on both sides and many more sheets could be sewn together. Crucially – although making parchment was much more labour-intensive than cutting down a few papyrus reeds and pressing them together – papyrus only grew in specific areas along the Nile, which allowed the Egyptians monopoly on the market and control of the supply of exported papyrus. In contrast, the supply of parchment merely required livestock (which was everywhere) and someone handy with a knife.

We know that at least by the mid-fourth century there was a conscious effort to transfer Christian papyrus texts to parchment, as Christian scholar Jerome mentions that Euzoius took on the task of copying 'the already damaged library of Origen and Pamphilus' onto parchment (*in membranis instauere*).[13] However, papyrus carried on being used in some parts of the Mediterranean until around 1100, and parchment scrolls and papyrus codices were also used as valid forms of recording information throughout the medieval period, so the parchment codex did not completely usurp other formats.

Parchment may have been preferred over papyrus as a space-saving device (because using both sides meant you could write double the amount) – yet the examples we have of early manuscripts don't seem that keen on saving space, as they have generous margins and widely spaced text. Early Christian texts were often written in a script now known as 'reformed documentary' or 'informal uncial'. This was an everyday, cursive script rather than a highly trained calligraphic hand.[14] This informal script probably reflects the social status of early Christians – many came from lower social groups, such as artisans and clerks, so this may have been the script they were familiar with.[15] This may also explain the generous spacing on the manuscript page (unlike the *scriptura continua* text, with no word separation, familiar in classical texts), rendering the texts more accessible to those less educated and reflecting the inclusive attitude among the early Christians and the socio-economic status of the newly converted.

Early Christian scribes copied a variety of texts. The 27 canonical texts of the New Testament were affirmed by the Church around the end of the fourth century, comprising four gospels (Matthew, Mark, Luke and John), the Acts of the Apostles, fourteen Pauline epistles (letters), seven general epistles and the Book of Revelation. There were many other texts about Jesus in circulation (known as Apocrypha) that did not make it into the official canon, but they continued to be copied and disseminated anyway. This is just as well because many of these stories are highly entertaining. The Infancy Gospel of St Thomas, for example, depicts a volatile young Jesus who indiscriminately kills his playmates when they irritate him, including withering one poor boy into a corpse. The Acts of Paul and Thecla relate the adventures of the young noblewoman Thecla, who follows the apostle Paul on his missionary work. At one point she is sentenced to be thrown to the beasts by the Roman governor but is protected from death by a lioness in the arena. Then Thecla decides to baptize herself by plunging herself into a vat of water filled with hungry seals, but before the seals can attack her, they are killed by heavenly lightning. Thecla then rises triumphantly from the water, surrounded by a cloud of fire and dead sea-creatures. This version of Thecla sounds magnificent, and the fact that these texts continued to be copied by scribes indicates the fluidity of early Christianity and shows just how much the early and medieval Christians loved a good story.

Christianity and scribal culture developed alongside each other. The early Church was dominated by the Church Fathers, religious men whose teachings shaped Christianity (women have largely been written out of the story, but that is not to exclude them from their important role in the development of the religion). Eusebius of Caesarea (260/265–*c.* 339 CE) is known as the father of Church history and thanks to his *Ecclesiastical History* we have a chronology of the development of Christianity from the first to the fourth century. In his account of Origen of Alexandria (Christian scholar and ascetic, *c.* 185–*c.* 253 CE), Eusebius tells us that Origen dictated his commentaries on the divine scriptures to 'more than seven shorthand writers . . . and as many copyists, as well as girls trained for beautiful writing'.[16] As lovely as this sounds, it is probable that these girls were enslaved – this description fits into the hierarchy of the scribe system in Roman society.

However, we soon start to see a shift in attitude from classical snobbery towards copying to a desire for Christians to copy texts as a form of religious devotion. Pamphilus (d. 309 CE) was a biblical scholar who developed the theological school and library at Caesarea Palaestina (also known as Caesarea Maritima, now modern-day Israel) and collected a great number of Christian texts. Jerome wrote that Pamphilus was 'so inflamed with love of sacred literature, that he transcribed the greater part of the works of Origen with his own hand and these are still preserved in the library at Caesarea. I have twenty-five volumes of Commentaries of Origen, written in his hand.'[17]

Yet Eusebius, a pupil of Pamphilus, conformed to the traditional hierarchy. In 331 he was commissioned by Emperor Constantine I (306–337 CE) to produce

> fifty copies of the sacred Scriptures, the provision and use of which you know to be most needful for the instruction of the Church, to be written on prepared parchment in a legible manner, and in a convenient, portable form, by professional transcribers thoroughly practised in their art.[18]

Eusebius was affiliated with Pamphilus' library – which probably also housed a centre of manuscript production capable of carrying out Constantine's demands. Eusebius tells us that Constantine's order was followed by 'the immediate execution of the work itself, which we sent him in magnificent and elaborately bound volumes'. So, not only was the task able to be done quickly, but attention was paid to the binding of the codices to produce attractive volumes with fine covers. This demand for high-quality copies saw a shift from simple codices being produced ad hoc by small communities to a considered push to create valuable documents. Certainly the emperor had the finances to back up this particular commission, but when he acknowledged Christianity as a religion in 313, he created the conditions for an influx of new converts and for a whole new audience. The Christian book starts to emerge as a sacred object – rather than merely a carrier for the text – made sacrosanct by the fact that it contains the word of God. Thus greater attention starts to be paid to the decoration, inside and out. Admittedly, it was not just the early Christians who adopted the codex format in the classical world, but the enthusiasm with which they embraced it drove forward the development of the codex, and by the fourth century it became increasingly popular among non-Christians too.

ANYTHING that holds text can be a 'book' – a clay tablet, a papyrus scroll, a wax tablet, a bamboo slip – but the codex is the format that is familiar to most of us today, and what we best understand by the term 'book'. The word 'codex' comes from the Latin *caudex*, meaning block of wood – a nod to its development from folded wooden wax tablets and of the early wooden manuscript covers.

The pages of the codex were made by folding sheets of parchment inside each other. A single sheet was called a bifolium, which when folded in half became two folios (or four pages). Like the papyrus, there is a recto and verso side to the folio, with the recto being the right or front page and the verso being the reverse side. In an open book, the left side is the verso and the right side is the recto. 'Folio' comes from the Latin *folium*, meaning leaf. To avoid the bulkiness of folding multiple sheets of parchment (or papyrus, or paper) inside each other, it was usual to create 'gatherings' or 'quires' instead – by folding four bifolia inside each other to create eight folios or sixteen pages (although the number of bifolia can vary from one to ten, or more). The individual quire was then stacked on top of other quires and sewn together along the spine to form a text block. The text block was then often (but not always) attached to a front and a back cover of wood, or parchment or leather.

There were also some features that came to be identified specifically with the text of early Christian codices. As mentioned, the early Christians wrote in a script called reformed documentary, a slightly more refined version of the everyday script used for administrative, bureaucratic purposes. (However, it should be noted that there is a huge range within the reformed documentary script, with many Christian hands coming in at the higher end of this range, and many classical hands coming in at the lower end.[19]) This script was often written with gaps between words, rather than the *scriptura continua* used in classical literary texts, and the text was written in one single column (known as longlines), rather than a multi-column layout.[20] These created immediate visual differences between classical and Christian texts.

Structure of a manuscript.

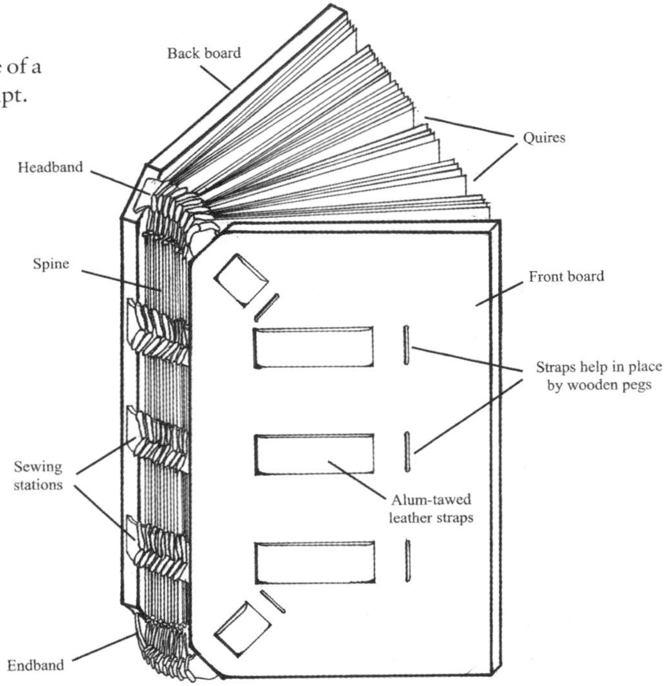

Quire structure.

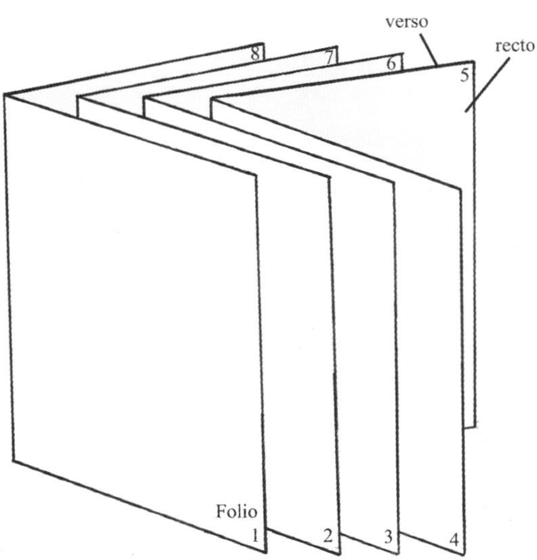

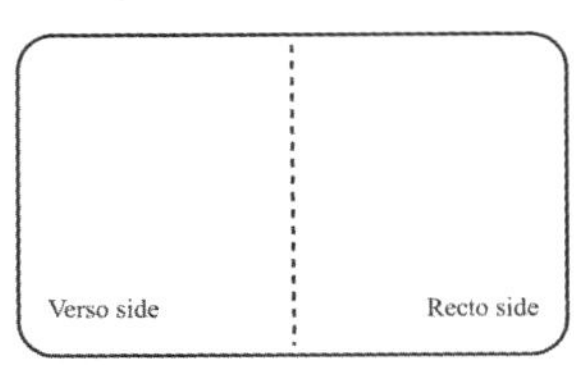

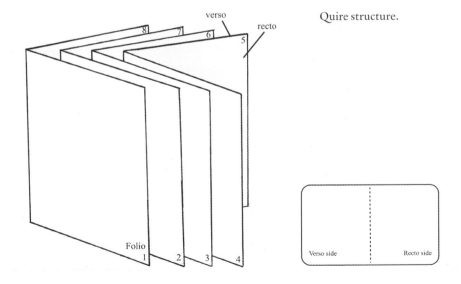

Another feature of Christian texts were the *nomina sacra*, the abbreviations of sacred words, such as Jesus, God, Lord and Christ, into two or more letters with a horizontal line over the top. Jesus Christ in Greek is ΙΗΣΟΥΣ ΧΡΙΣΤΟΣ and so this was abbreviated to $\overline{\text{ΙΗ}}$ $\overline{\text{ΧΡ}}$, a practice that carried on through the medieval period. Although these words were abbreviated, it was not intended initially as a space-saving device, but as a way to signify the sanctity of these words, and seems to have been employed fairly regularly throughout the early Christian world, indicating an early standardized scribal practice.[21]

The reformed documentary script was common in Christian texts up to the fourth century, until it was replaced by an 'uncial' script. It is likely that this uncial script developed out of square capitals, the formal script for carved inscriptions, and the rustic capitals used for literary texts, both of which were quite angular, with each line formed by a single stroke. Uncial script must have come as a bit of a relief then for scribes, as it is all gorgeously rounded and therefore much easier to write a whole letter with one stroke of the pen. An uncial 'm' has a lovely, fluid curviness, compared to the four sharp single strokes needed to make a rustic capital 'M'. Uncial is a majuscule script, which means the letters are mainly capitals and fit between two parallel lines, with no ascenders or descenders above or below. The rounded uncial letters don't touch, so they need a lot of room on the page. Uncial manuscripts tended to be written in *scriptura continua* but separated into paragraph-like chunks. At this point of manuscript development, there is not much decoration or illustration in Christian manuscripts, but red ink (either red lead or cinnabar) was often used for the beginning of a new section.

An early example of uncial script is in the *Codex Sinaiticus*, a Greek copy of the Bible produced in the mid-fourth century. This was once thought to have been one of the fifty Bibles mentioned earlier that Constantine commissioned Eusebius to produce, and while there is no direct evidence for this, nonetheless it is representative of the type of books the early Christians were capable of producing. The *Codex Sinaiticus* is a large volume, written on parchment and measuring 38 by 34.5 centimetres. It contains part of the Old Testament (including the Septuagent), the New Testament, the Epistle of Barnabas and parts of the *Shepherd of Hermas*. (The *Shepherd of Hermas* was a very popular early Christian allegorical text composed in the second century. The work recounts five visions of Hermas, followed by twelve commandments and ten parables.) The *Codex Sinaiticus* was written by three, possibly four scribes, and it has an unusual format of four columns per page, suggesting it may have been imitating the scroll format. Many examples of *nomina sacra* can be found, and there are also many corrections to the text marked up in the margins, indicating it was checked by a senior scribe at the point of production. It comprises over four hundred folios (so eight hundred pages) and was made from both sheep and calf parchment, written with iron gall ink. The high quality of the parchment and overall book production shows just how far manuscript making had come in a few hundred years, from the papyrus codices of the early days of Christianity to this impressive volume.

This uncial script, like the parchment codex, was not unique to Christianity, but again became something that was closely associated with Christianity. Uncial was adopted throughout the Greek and Western world by the fourth century and was the script used in notable early medieval English manuscripts, such as the *Codex Amiatinus* and the St Cuthbert Gospel, both produced in the early eighth century. A slightly more informal 'half-uncial' script also developed alongside uncial. This was a minuscule script – which means that some letters had ascenders and descenders, such as the ascenders of *b* and *l* that rise above the topline of the text and the descender *p* that carries on below

Folio from the *Codex Sinaiticus*, 4th century.

the baseline (see, for example, Biblioteca Apostolica Vaticana, Vat. Lat. 3375, fol. 11v).

Although Christianity was pushing forward, it is important to point out that fine texts were still being produced in late antiquity by non-Christian Romans. The *Vergilius Vaticanus* (Biblioteca Apostolica Vaticana, Vat. Lat. 3225) and the *Vergilius Romanus* (Biblioteca Apostolica Vaticana, Vat. Lat. 3867) are fifth-century deluxe copies of the works of the Roman epic poet Virgil, written on high-quality parchment codices. The *Vergilius Vaticanus*, written in the early fifth century, may have been one of the first copies of Virgil that was copied from a scroll into a codex format, indicating the move from the older technology to new technology in the wider Latin world.[22] It is 22.5 centimetres high by 20 centimetres wide, so of a size that could comfortably fit in your hand. It is estimated it would have originally had 440 folios and 280 illustrations, although today only 76 folios remain intact. It is written in rustic capitals in brown ink in longlines, with the first line (or lines) of a new section written in a red pigment (probably cinnabar). The codex is illustrated with colourful images showing scenes from Virgil's *Georgics* and *Aeneid*, in text or sometimes taking up a full page. The pigments used were probably the same ones found in classical wall paintings, which include Egyptian blue, red ochre, cinnabar, green ochre, yellow ochre and calcium carbonate (white).[23] There is even some gold illumination decorating the frames surrounding the images and gold highlighting on costumes, trees and ships. This new codex format may have also been more suited to adding illustrations – the constant handling of a scroll would have placed extra stress on heavy applications of pigment, making it more likely to crack and flake off – whereas the structure of a codex naturally protects the flat page.

The *Vergilius Romanus* was written slightly later during the fifth century and is less accomplished artistically. It differs from the *Vergilius Vaticanus* in that it is much larger, originally measuring 33.5 by 32.5 centimetres, so would probably have been read from a stand rather than handheld.[24] It might also suggest an element of conspicuous consumption – this was a display object intended to be looked at and admired, perhaps more so than being read studiously. The illumination has developed into complete frames of gold around the images. Silver illumination is also present, for example, on the spear tip of a Trojan soldier on fol. 106r. So, while the early Christians adopted the codex as their preferred form of written communication, by circa 400 non-Christians were also transitioning to parchment codices, and clearly had sophisticated workshops to produce these items – although the culture of Roman society suggests that these continued to be enslaved people or hired scribes and artists.

In the years that followed, it's worth remembering that the late antique and early medieval period was a world in flux, particularly in Western Europe. The decline of the Western Roman empire led to much destabilization, with warring factions carving up the land and dismantling the systems of government. Christianity did not suddenly appear and fit neatly into the vacuum. Apart from anything else, there wasn't even a single 'Christianity' – there were many different interpretations of it. So, while this book may follow a trajectory of Christian development and book culture, in reality things were not that straightforward, and many splinters of Christianity and other religious beliefs existed alongside the version of Christianity we recognize today.

Early Christian Monasticism

In the early days of Christianity, the religion gained popularity among those with less of a voice in the classical world, such as women and enslaved people. The idea that eternal salvation was available to anyone who believed in Jesus was a powerful incentive; it was open to all, regardless of social status. Christianity promoted a universal family of God (the term 'catholic' originally meant universal), and men and women following Christ were responsible for spreading the word. The religion first grew underground, with informal church meetings in households up to about the mid-third century. The vast expanse of the Roman empire was extremely beneficial to the new movement, as it meant that preachers could travel along established routes to teach people about Jesus (as the apostle Paul did). Copies of the second-century Christian text the *Shepherd of Hermas* composed in Rome were found at the archaeological site of Oxyrhynchus, Egypt, dating from the late second/early third century, which gives an idea of just how quickly ideas and texts could spread throughout the classical world.[25]

There was also a movement among early Christians to embrace a more reclusive and ascetic way of life, living as a hermit in a small cell or setting up communities in secluded places such as the Egyptian desert. The early days of monasticism were undefined, but they were united in a common ideal to live a simple, celibate life devoted to the worship of Christ. The ascetic lifestyle was not something unique to Christianity, it evolved from Eastern and Greek religious and philosophical traditions, but like the codex, Christianity adopted it wholeheartedly and fashioned it to its own purpose. From these early Christians choosing to live a life of spiritual contemplation in the desert grew a monastic way of life that became widespread across medieval Europe, with women and men either living alone or in groups in cloistered communities, away from society, following daily rituals of prayer, study and work. The solitary, hermetic type of monasticism is known as eremitic, and communal monasticism is known as coenobitic. Due to the emphasis on study, over time Christian monasteries became natural centres of learning, education and book production.

Around 320, a coenobitic community was founded in Egypt by Pachomius, a conscripted Roman soldier who converted to Christianity. Pachomius' community was the first known organized monastic dwelling, with connected male and female houses following a set of rules that encouraged asceticism, learning and teaching, and working together for the sake of the community.[26] Pachomius also placed heavy emphasis on the importance of studying – insisting that all members must be literate. If any new members came in unable to read, they had lessons three times a day until they had mastered the skill (Rule of Pachomius, 139, 140). There also seems to have been an ample supply of books, as Rule 25 states *codicem si ad legendum petierint* (if they ask for a book to read, they may receive it), and Rule 100 specifies that members could not go to worship or to the refectory with a book that was not fastened (*codicem non ligatum*). These little comments give an insight into the daily life of books and their bindings within the monastery. Rule 100 also goes on to say that books should be returned to the alcove in the wall, which, as we shall see later, remained a popular storage place for medieval manuscripts. So, these examples from the *Rule of Pachomius* in the early fourth century already outline how intrinsic books and learning were to monastic life. Although the *Rule of Pachomius* was soon superseded by the *Rule of St Basil*, the central principles of monastic life remained the same: community life, study and prayer, and manual labour.

Women were just as active in the foundation of monasteries, and some become known as the Desert Mothers. Melania the Elder (*c.* 350–*c.* 410) was a wealthy young widow who moved from Rome to establish two monasteries on the Mount of Olives, Jerusalem, in the 370s. Her granddaughter, Melania the Younger (383–439), was also an important founder of monasteries and famed for producing her own books. An account of her life relates how she studied the scriptures, then 'copied them herself and furnished copies to the saints by her own hand'.[27] Like Pamphilus, the act of copying scripture in her own hand is seen as an act of religious devotion, rather than a low-status task, and it is significant to see this positive reference to female book production in the early days of monasticism.

Informal Christian communities also existed, such as the female monastery set up by Marcella (*c.* 325–410) in her house on the Aventine Hill in Rome. Marcella retired to her (very large) house after the death of her husband, and led a life of seclusion, devoted to prayer, study and charitable works. Marcella's establishment drew many other female Christians, influenced by the ascetic ideal of the East, who would meet at Marcella's house to discuss scripture. One of these women was Paula of Rome (347–404), who, like Marcella, came from a wealthy noble Roman family, and became increasingly involved in the Christian movement after her husband died. They soon became acquainted with Jerome (*c.* 347–420), a rising Christian scholar and secretary of Pope Damascus, who had made a name for himself translating the gospels and psalms from Greek into Latin. While staying in Rome, Jerome became part of this network largely consisting of wealthy female widows, whose status gave them a certain amount of autonomy in Roman society. However, not everyone in Rome was impressed with the pope's star pupil, and others suspected him of preying on wealthy women, imposing on them a too-strict ascetic regime and possibly having improper relations with them. When things got too uncomfortable for Jerome in 385, he was forced to flee from Rome to the Christian East.

Jerome, even by his own account, was difficult and hot-headed, and quick to press his opinions on others (particularly women). However, an intense friendship developed between Jerome and Paula and her daughter, Eustochium. In his correspondence, he praised Paula endlessly for her intellect and asceticism, claiming that 'of all the ladies in Rome but one had power to subdue me, and that one was Paula' (Letter 45). Disillusioned with the hedonism in Rome and drawn to the ascetic lifestyle in the East, Paula and Eustochium followed Jerome to Antioch, to begin a pilgrimage to the holy lands. After visiting Melania the Elder's monastery in Jerusalem and the monasteries in Egypt, Paula and Jerome settled in Bethlehem, the believed birthplace of Jesus. Here the Desert Mother Paula founded (and funded) a female and male monastery, and a hostelry for pilgrims. Having these single-sex monasteries meant that the women and men lived, ate and worked separately in their respective establishments, but would come together for prayer and chanting psalms.[28] Paula in particular embraced a life of severe ascetism, including strict fasting and a fastidious application to studying scripture. She was also fluent in Greek and Hebrew.

Jerome believed that fully immersing himself in his monastery in the land of Judea led to a greater understanding of the scriptures (that he learned to study in the original Hebrew). He produced many of his most famous works during his time in Bethlehem, including the *Biblia Vulgata* (the Vulgate Bible), a translation of the Bible intended for the everyday Latin speaker that would eventually become the official Catholic version. Jerome updated the existing Latin translations of the New Testament from Greek versions and, radically, included a translation of the Jewish Bible from the original Hebrew (rather than from Greek). As the patron and founder of Jerome's monastery, Paula was fundamental in the production of this Latin version of the Bible, financing the materials needed.[29] However, it is possible that Paula, as Jerome's equal and an educated woman in her own right, co-authored or at least co-edited the Vulgate with Jerome. Jerome himself referred to Paula's superior grasp of Hebrew, saying that once she decided to learn it, 'she succeeded so well that she could chant the psalms in Hebrew and could speak the language without a trace of the pronunciation peculiar to Latin' (Letter 108). Jerome records in his works that Paula was the driving force behind many of his works, and he dedicated many of them to her and Eustochium.[30]

Christianity was definitely the latest fad in Roman settlements, attracting wealthy patrons keen to support the new religion. However, this created tension between those who devoted themselves to emulating the humble life of Jesus and those who liked to throw money about. Jerome drew a line between simple and accurate book production from a monastery and the sumptuous tomes that were being produced for the 'metropolitan elites' in Rome. In a letter to Eustochium that thoroughly disapproves of the lavish lifestyles of the women in Rome, Jerome is also appalled that 'parchments are dyed purple, gold is melted into lettering, manuscripts are decked with jewels, while Christ lies at the door naked and dying' (Letter 22). He picks up this theme again in his prologue to Job, grumbling, 'Let those who will keep the old books with their gold and silver letters on purple skins . . . if only they will leave for me and mine, our poor pages and copies which are less remarkable for beauty than for accuracy.' Jerome also implies that papyrus, rather than parchment, was used at the monasteries in Bethlehem – in Letter 71, he checks copies that have been transcribed for a friend at his monastery *in charteceis codices* (on papyrus codices).[31] Although parchment was becoming increasingly popular by the fourth century, we can see that at least in Paula and Jerome's monasteries, the emphasis was on the humble and simple papyrus codex, rather than the 'magnificent and elaborately bound volumes' that Eusebius produced for Constantine. There are also disparaging mentions from Christian intellectual heavyweights John Chrysostom (347–407 CE) and Augustine of Hippo (354–430 CE), the former railing against those who boast of the gold letters in their books rather than the textual content, the latter condemning 'parchment and fancy covers fashioned from beautiful leather'.[32]

Yet the desire for fancy books persisted, and it is worth examining here the books of purple parchment and letters of gold that Jerome and John Chrysostom found so abhorrent. Purple, particularly when combined with gold, has always been associated with the highest echelons of society – such as Roman emperors. The architect and author Vitruvius (d. 15 BCE) wrote in the first century that purple 'above all other colours, has a delightful effect, not less from its rarity than from its excellence'.[33] The association with opulence and prestige came about because creating a rich purple dye was a complicated and labour-intensive process in the classical world. Pliny tells us that 'Tyrian' purple or imperial purple came from sea snails (*Murex trunculus*) that were harvested in great numbers and crushed to remove their glands, which were then boiled to create a deep, long-lasting purple. Purple also became the ideal colour to represent the majesty of Christ, and Christians soon embraced the use of purple in the codex. Despite Jerome's disapproval, Christian biblical texts continued to be produced in this way well into the medieval period. To add to the opulence, these purple dyed pages were written in beautiful uncial script in gold and/or silver. The *Codex Veronensis*, a fifth-century Latin gospel, and the *Codex Petropolitanus Purpureus* (St Petersburg, National Library of Russia, MS Gr. 537), a sixth-century Greek gospel, are wonderful examples of this style. As Tyrian purple was so expensive, it is likely that a more affordable purple pigment was used, such as orchil or folium, with possibly a thin overlay of Tyrian purple. It is not certain how the purple dye was applied, but from recent experiments it is suggested that the parchment was prepared in the normal way on a frame, removed and soaked in a purple dye bath, and then re-stretched afterwards (parchment needs to dry under tension to give a smooth surface).[34] The letters were made with finely ground gold or silver mixed with a binder, and probably written with a copper stylus, as a reed pen was not suited for applying thicker-grained metal inks.[35]

The new texts that Jerome produced in the fourth century were laid out in a format that was easier to read. In his prologue to Ezekiel, Jerome explains that his text, broken into short sections and 'written in words with spaces . . . gives a clearer meaning to readers'.[36] This was a type of punctuation known as *per cola et commata* – not invented by Jerome, but promoted by him – where each clause or phrase is divided into chunks. Think of it like the reverse to our modern paragraphs: we start a new paragraph with an indentation on the first line with the lines that follow flush to the margin; *per cola et commata* starts each new section with the first line flush to the margin and then the lines underneath are all indented to the right (see BL, Harley MS 1775). Even though it is the opposite layout to our paragraphs, the design clearly gives a visual signal for the beginning of each section, and makes it easier to digest – although many texts were still written without spaces between the words. The *per cola et commata* system was based on older texts to indicate when a breath should be taken when reading out loud.[37] Presenting the text in this way certainly makes it easier to read, but also to absorb the meaning. The spaces between the sections allows for a mental pause, to reflect and internalize the words before moving on to the next section.

IT MIGHT SEEM that all the exciting monastic innovation was happening in the Christian East, but it didn't take long for the West to follow suit and establish their own monasteries. Rufinus of Aquileia (344/5–411), companion of Melania the Elder, was a key figure in straddling the Christian East and

West. He translated the *Rule of St Basil* into Latin, and in the prologue informs us he wrote it at the request of Ursacius, abbot of the monastery in Pinetum, Italy, who wanted the monasteries in the West to follow the Rule. Rufinus tells Ursacius that now he has fulfilled his promise 'make it your task to provide copies also for other monasteries, so that, after the likeness of Cappadocia [Basil's monastery], all the monasteries may live not by different, but by the same institutes and observances.'[38] This seems to indicate that the monastery at Pinetum had the facilities to copy manuscripts on a large scale and disseminate them throughout the Latin-speaking West.

There is also evidence of scribal practice in the monastery founded in Marmoutier, France, by Martin of Tours around 372. Martin was a Roman soldier stationed near Amiens, who became one of the first Christians to establish a monastic way of life in the western reaches of the empire. His life was written by his hagiographer, Sulpicius Severus, who describes the monastery as full of eighty men who gave up all possessions to devote their lives to prayer and fasting. They lived in separate cells made of wood or carved out of the rock and were much more aligned to the eremitic way of monastic life – living in isolation, with no communal activities. Severus goes on to say 'no craft was practised there, with the exception of the scribe's, and even this was entrusted to the younger men, while the older ones remained free for prayer.'[39] So even in this northwestern corner of the Roman empire, by the end of the fourth century monasticism was not just establishing a presence, but anchoring the scribe's duty as a key role, even when no other duties were undertaken. Across the Christian world, from East to West, we see these gatherings of ideas and resources, centring upon communal houses devoted to work, prayer and study. And absolutely embedded in this movement was the need for books, to produce them, to study them and to share them.

Another person credited with introducing the monastic system to the West is John Cassian (360–*c.* 435), Christian monk and theologian. He had lived in a hermitage in Bethlehem and had visited many monasteries in Egypt before founding two monasteries in Marseilles, France – the Abbey of St Victor for men and the Abbey of St Sauveur for women. Unlike Martin's establishment in Tours, the emphasis here was on the communal life that Cassian had seen operating in Egypt. He wrote his *Institutes of the Coenobia* in 420, a guide to monastic life that highlighted the importance of routine and order and coming together at set times of day to recite the psalms – in contrast to the unstructured life of Martin's monks at Tours. This is where we see the beginnings of the canonical hours (regular hours of prayer) set down, which were to become so definitive of monastic life. Cassian's *Institutes* promotes manual labour, although makes no mention of scribal work. However, there is a mention of book production. Referring to the *Institutes*, Cassian says 'these little books, which we are now arranging with the Lord's help to write' (Book 2, ch. 9). It seems here that Cassian was organizing some push to distribute his works among the monastic communities.

So, by the fifth century, monasticism was starting to be established in the Christian West. With the parchment codex now fully integrated into the Christian religion, and scribal practice an accepted part of religious life, the seeds were sown for centres of manuscript production to flourish at monastic foundations. One wonders if those early Christians clandestinely meeting in their houses, swapping ragged sheets of papyrus about the life of Jesus, would have any idea how those words would spread, going on to influence the furthest reaches of the Roman empire. Would they have imagined that their hastily scribbled notes would become the foundation stones for the skilfully scribed, highly decorated volumes that would be produced by men and women in houses built for the worship of God?

Two

Monasticism and Manuscript Production in the West, 500–1050

Francia, *c.* 600 CE

'Brother Ciarán! The Lord does not reward idleness!' the senior monk reprimanded the new scribe, who had been staring dreamily into space. 'Sorry, Brother Eoghan,' said Ciarán humbly. He shifted uncomfortably on his wooden bench, laid his quill down carefully next to his parchment and flexed his stiff hand. He sighed heavily and leant back on the cool stone wall, looking out at the unfamiliar Frankish landscape. He had only arrived at Luxeuil monastery a few days ago, having been sent from his hometown of Bangor Abbey after Abbot Columbán requested Abbot Comgall send his finest scribes to join him at Luxeuil. Abbot Columbán, in his quest to spread the good news to heathen tribes in the Merovingian kingdoms, needed to produce Bibles and the texts of the Church Fathers to distribute among his new foundations. Many monks desired to travel to distant places to spread the good news and to convert pagans to the way of the Lord, but not Ciarán. Ciarán had been quite happy where he was at Bangor, surrounded by his books and copying out the words of God in his neat and practised hand. He had been raised at the abbey, taken into the monks' care as a young boy when he had been suddenly orphaned, and knew no other life. The monks had given him a home and an education, and though strict, they had cared for him too, showing him kindness and patience.

Here, everything was different. He missed the fresh, bracing air of home, and the lush green fields with the cattle gently lowing. Oh,

Hibernia! At the far end of the ocean, with its huge mountains of waves and white foamy seashores. He missed the everyday sounds of his monastery, with his fellow brothers reciting the psalms in their familiar timbre. He even missed his heavy woollen robe and thick stockings, and writing in the open air, only stopping when his ink froze in the pot. He found the inland air here strange, and he did not recognize the trees and the plants – he could not even identify the birdsong that he had heard on the way to morning prayers.

At Bangor, Ciarán's skill as a scribe had been well-known – the older monks would show their pupils his writing as an example of beautiful script and urge them to shape their letters the same way. As a young boy, he himself had been entranced by how the strange lines and curves of the letters suddenly began to make sense, how he began to recognize their sounds and put them together to form words, and suddenly a whole new world opened up to him. He was a diligent pupil, forming letters in the wax tablets over and over until his hand cramped up and was stiff and sore, but the years of practice had paid off and his beautiful writing was praised often by the abbot, who would display books full of his script to visiting dignitaries.

Here, though, everything he did was wrong. It was like being a young boy again, with no knowledge of the unspoken rules and habits of a different community. On his first morning, he had been severely reprimanded because he had gathered his quire of parchment skin together in the wrong way. At home, it was usual to have the yellower, hair side of the skin facing the creamier, flesh side – but here – oh no, no, no! Hair to hair side, flesh to flesh side. Well, how was he supposed to know that? Brother Eoghan had pulled him up sharply, leaving him feeling foolish and unworldly. It had been ten years since the brothers had left Bangor Abbey to travel to the Continent and set up new foundations – and here they were acting like the Irish methods that they themselves had learnt as boys were old-fashioned and unsophisticated. And the script he had seen some of the young French monks using – Great Heavens! Ciarán thought it looked awful, all scribbly and scrunched up, with ridiculously high ascenders. He was determined to stick to his familiar Irish hand, which was far more pleasing to the eye. He also didn't understand why sheepskin parchment was the norm here, while some of the older scribes were even writing on papyrus. And they looked at him like HE *was the unsophisticated one! Didn't they know that calfskin was far superior? Ciarán shook his head in bemusement at the strange standards in this monastery.*

He picked up his quill in his right hand and absentmindedly sharpened it with the knife in his other hand. At least some things were the same – the goose feathers that were kept in the writing cupboard, ready to be trimmed to their desired shape by the scribes, the rich tang of the gall ink and the musky smell of the parchment – as familiar to him as the sea salt air that blew through his home monastery. Again, Ciarán sighed deeply, trying to push down the feelings of homesickness. Aware that he was attracting attention from his brother scribes, he found his place again on the manuscript he was copying on the wooden lectern to his left. Focusing on the parchment on the wooden board in front of him, and using his pen knife as a placeholder, he dipped his quill in the viscous black liquid and began to write. Immediately he was home again, his body falling into the rhythm of his penstrokes and the methodical arc back and forth to the ink pot. His surroundings melted away as he became absorbed in his task, free from the troubles of his earthly existence.

In the sixth century two significant events occurred in Italy that paved the way for monastic manuscript production in Europe: Benedict of Nursia composed his rule for cloistered men and women, and Cassiodorus founded Vivarium, a monastery, library and biblical studies centre. Benedict (480–548) was a Christian

Roman who had lived for three years in a cave in Subiaco, Italy, as a hermit, but was persuaded (against his better judgement) to become abbot of a nearby monastery. It didn't exactly work out. Benedict was so strict that the monks got fed up and tried to poison his wine, and so he stomped off back to a life of solitude. Eventually though, he left his cave again to found twelve monasteries in Subiaco. He also founded the famous monastery at Monte Cassino around 529, situated on a hilltop between Rome and Naples, where they followed the *Rule of St Benedict*, his set of instructions for monastic life. These rules promoted communal living with obedience to the abbot or abbess, and focused on a daily routine of regular prayer, work and rest. There were also many references to the importance of reading and study in Benedict's *Rules* – including Rule 48: 'In the days of Lent every year they shall each receive a book from the library, which shall be read in its entirety according to the Rule, these books are to be given out at the beginning of Lent.' Although book production or scriptoria are not mentioned, the way that books are interwoven into monastic life firmly suggests that a supply of books was necessary. We saw in the previous chapter how rules for monastic life had been circulating in the East, with, for example, the *Rules* of Pachomius and Basil (and indeed these previous versions influenced Benedict's rule along with John Cassian's *Institutes of the Coenobia*) but it was the *Rule of St Benedict* that was adopted throughout the Western monastic world and became the dominant order through the medieval period.

Cassiodorus (*c.* 485–*c.* 585) was a Roman senator who retired from public life to found a monastic school on his family estate at Squillace in southern Italy. It was named Vivarium, which means 'place of life' in Latin and was a term used for the keeping or raising of animals. The estate at Squillace apparently had fish pools in its grounds teeming with life, which may explain why it became known as Vivarium – or, on a more metaphorical level, it may have represented the flourishing of intellectual life. It was intended as an idyllic retreat to focus on biblical studies, far away from the turmoil on the Roman borders. In his *Institutions of Divine and Secular Learning* (a study guide for his monks), Cassiodorus describes the 'irrigated gardens and fish-filled streams' of Vivarium.[1] The *Institutiones* are scattered with references to the natural world, perhaps mirroring the lush, fertile environment that surrounded Cassiodorus. He metaphysically portrays the psalter (a book of psalms) 'like a heavenly sphere thick with twinkling stars . . . like a beautiful peacock . . . a paradise for souls, containing numberless fruits on which the human soul is sweetly fed and fattened'. He referred to St Ambrose as 'a writer of milky smoothness' and Jerome's eloquence as 'like the sun'. He also described notes that he added to a text on the prophets thus: 'grape-cluster shapes of these glosses have been properly entered in this codex so that the vineyard of the Lord might seem filled with a heavenly richness and to have produced the sweetest fruits.'[2] Cassiodorus's writing teems with life and fecundity (a bit too much, some might say), but the metaphorical and metaphysical connections between the Christian word, nature and the kingdom of God indicate just how fundamental the written word was to Christian ideology.

At Vivarium, Cassiodorus furnished his library with classical works as well as Christian texts, wanting to preserve Roman culture at a time when the empire was rapidly declining. In his *Institutions*, as well as instructing readers on studying, he also gives guidelines to the scribes. We can perhaps imagine a place of intellectual freedom and liberal-mindedness, with Cassiodorus putting a scriptorium right at the heart of this enterprise. Rather than regarding book production as a task for those enslaved by the Romans or treating it as a conspicuous act of piety by certain individuals, we see Cassiodorus promoting the notion of the scriptorium as a necessary cog of a functioning monastery.

In Cassiodorus's writing, it is easy to imagine an idyllic scribal life set in the calm surroundings of Vivarium. Although in reality a scribe's life could be an arduous and uncomfortable one, Cassiodorus went to great lengths to accommodate his scribes, with 'self-fuelling mechanical lights' burning continuously with bright flame to aid them at night. He also provided a sundial and a water clock that 'continually indicates the number of the hours by day and night, allowing the scribes to keep track of time'. Although there are no other details about a physical scriptorium (and Cassiodorus does not use the specific term), it would seem there was an area set aside for copying, to house the lamps and water clock. Being a scribe at Cassiodorus's Vivarium seems like quite a life – the gorgeous Mediterranean sun beating down on lush gardens, listening to the birdsong and the burbling of the water clock while you write words of scripture on beautifully prepared parchment. Cassiodorus even paid attention to bookbinding, bringing men in to cover 'the loveliness of sacred letters with external beauty'. He tells us that he has collated 'many types and patterns of bindings for books in one volume so that the interested reader himself can choose the form of cover he prefers'.[3] This 'sample book' rather creates the image of a book production showroom, where one could flick through the various designs as one would today with a swatch book.

Cassiodorus instilled some important discipline for scribes in his *Institutes*. He highlights the importance of their task – 'to fight with pen and ink against the unlawful snares of the devil. For Satan receives as many wounds as the scribe writes words of the Lord.' He outlines the need to transcribe correctly, because although scribes remain in one place, their works travelled out into the far corners of the world, carrying on their message. He recommends checking with past orthographers to make sure they are using the correct spellings, which also indicates the vast library that was available on hand at Vivarium. Cassiodorus was also quite hot on grammar, with a whole chapter in his *Institutes* devoted to 'How Carefully the Text of Holy Scripture Ought to be Corrected'. This chapter explains the importance of cases of nouns and of verbs, but also lists the scripture phrases that should not be altered, because even though they are grammatically wrong, 'words evidentially spoken under the inspiration of the Lord cannot be corrupt.'[4] This again highlights the sanctity of the 'word of God'.

CASSIODORUS'S TEXTS became popular throughout the Christian world, as did the texts of Spanish scholar Isidore of Seville (*c.* 560–636). His most famous work, *The Etymologies*, is an encyclopaedia intended to encompass all human knowledge, including grammar and rhetoric, maths, music, science, law, religion, the natural world, buildings, ships, food, clothes and tools. It was divided into twenty books and drew on classical and Christian sources, preserving material that would otherwise have been lost. *The Etymologies* became so popular that it was possibly the most copied text after the Bible among medieval scholars and was a staple reference text for any monastic foundation. Fortunately for us, Isidore also includes information on book production in his sixth book, 'Books and Ecclesiastical Offices'. Here, he lists the canonical texts of the Old and New Testament, the history of libraries, materials used for book production and an explanation of ecclesiastic terms such as 'baptism', 'sacrament' and 'penitence', which indicates just how closely intertwined the relationship was between early Christianity and the book. Isidore gives us a section each on wax tablets, papyrus and parchment, but it is the section on 'copyists and their tools' that introduces a new writing tool – the quill. Isidore writes:

> The scribe's tools are the reed-pen and the quill, for by these the words are fixed onto the page. A reed-pen is from

> a tree; a quill is from a bird. The tip of a quill is split into two, while its unity is preserved in the integrity of its body, I believe for the sake of a mystery, in order that by the two tips may be signified the Old and New Testament, from which is pressed out the sacrament of the Word poured forth in the blood of the Passion. (Book 6, ch. 14)

So at least from the seventh century we see that the quill, from a swan or goose, was a common writing implement. For Christian scribes, the vertical slit at the tip of the nib (that acted as a reservoir to hold the ink) also held a symbolic biblical value, representing the two Testaments, and the ink flowing from the quill represented the blood shed by Jesus.

Isidore also gives the etymology of some book terms, which remind us just how closely the codex is linked to the natural world. The Latin word for feather/quill (*penna*) comes from *pendere*, 'to hang' – as in 'flying, for it comes . . . from birds'. (It is easy to see how our modern word 'pen' has come from the Latin word *penna*.) The leaves of books that we call folios 'are so called from their likeness to the leaves (*folium*) of trees'.[5] The terminology is a constant reminder of the fact that medieval manuscripts were wholly reliant on nature for their production, and that references to the natural world run right through the heart of manuscript production.

In all aspects of manuscript production, both men and women were involved. Despite there being a higher percentage of evidence and surviving manuscripts from male houses, this by no means indicates that it was just happening there – both men and women were instrumental in the development of book production. An early centre of female monasticism and book production was overseen by Caesaria of Arles. Her monastery was founded by her brother, the bishop Caesarius, in 512. He also wrote a rule for Caesaria (*Regula ad Virgines*), which was the first set of Western monastic guidelines written exclusively for women. The rule begins by recommending that any girl who desired 'to renounce the world and enter the holy fold . . . must never, up to the time of her death, go out of the monastery'.[6] Seen through a modern lens, it seems to deny cloistered women any kind of freedom – although it is not known how rigidly these rules were followed, if at all. Also, in some cases, a cloistered lifestyle may have been a preferable and safer option for the women.

According to *Regula ad Virgines*, every cloistered woman was expected to be able to read. In the *Life of Caesarius*, written by his close associates shortly after his death in 542, the work at Caesaria's monastery is described as 'so outstanding that in the midst of psalms and fasts, vigils and readings, the virgins of Christ beautifully copy out the holy books, with their mother herself as teacher'.[7] So here is evidence of a manuscript-making operation in this female monastery, producing high-quality manuscripts with Caesaria overseeing the production. It is a great pity that (to date) none of these manuscripts has been identified. It would be a truly wonderful thing to see the script and manuscript production techniques used by these women in the early sixth century. It's worth noting that many antique manuscripts do still survive in fragments today, but we do not know where they were copied and by whom – so it's possible that we may still be witnessing their craft without realizing.

The Insular Movement, 500–850

At the end of the sixth century, the monastic rule of Benedict was being adopted by Western religious houses and Cassiodorus's *Institutes* had promoted the production of manuscripts as an essential part of a monastery. However, the political landscape of Europe in late antiquity and the early medieval period was a rocky terrain, with many opportunists rushing in to fill the vacancy left by the Roman empire. It often resulted in Christianity flourishing or withering, depending on its regional warlords. However, a fundamental principle of Christianity was to spread the gospel (good news), so missionary work to non-Christian areas became an honourable undertaking. As part of the Roman empire, Christianity had a foothold in England in the early centuries, but had been pushed further west with the arrival of the Germanic pagan tribes such as the Angles, Saxons and Jutes in the fifth century.[8]

There is a popular myth about how Christianity came to be (re)introduced to England in the sixth century. Apparently, one day, Pope Gregory the Great (*c.* 540–604) was in the marketplace in Rome and saw some young enslaved English people with golden hair and blue eyes. When Gregory asked his companion who they were, his companion replied that they were Angles (English), to which Gregory replied 'Non Angli sed angeli, si forent Christiani' (Not Angles, but angels – if they were Christians), which then inspired Gregory to convert the English to Christianity. Whether this story is true or not, Gregory did send the monk Augustine to Canterbury in 597 to found what was to become St Augustine's Abbey. Augustine brought with him a collection of manuscripts, and it is highly likely that one of these was the St Augustine's Gospels (CCCC, MS 286) that still survives to this day. It is a copy of Jerome's Vulgate, immediately identifiable by the *per cola et commata* layout, and written in an uncial script. Even more excitingly, it contains images, which makes it the oldest illustrated Latin gospel in existence. Admittedly, it only has two pages of illustrations, but they are very impressive. There would originally have been more, but as with many precious manuscripts, pages have been damaged over time or stolen. The first full-page image (fol. 125r) is divided into twelve squares, each depicting a scene from the last days of Jesus (similar to the Stations of the Cross). In a time when literacy was a rarity, the use of images was a powerful tool to convert people to Christianity. Gregory the Great, in a letter to Serenus of Marseille, wrote, 'what Scripture is to the educated, images are to the ignorant . . . they read in them what they cannot read in books.'[9]

The second full-page image in St Augustine's Gospels is a portrait of Luke the Evangelist on fol. 129v. Many gospel manuscripts from the late antique/early medieval period would open each gospel with an illustration of the respective evangelist, often depicted with his evangelical symbol – Matthew is represented by a man, Mark a lion, Luke an ox or a calf and John an eagle. In St Augustine's Gospels, Luke is shown sitting on a chair between marble columns, with his symbol, the ox, above. As in many images of the evangelists, he has a book on his lap, representing the importance of the codex and the sacred word to Christianity. This manuscript was probably made in Rome. Analysis of the manuscript has revealed that pigments used in the images were red lead, yellow ochre, brown ochre, woad and an organic purple.[10] This surviving manuscript is a great example of the early medieval book network, and undoubtedly these illustrated books from the Continent would have influenced and inspired book production in Britain.

Augustine is often credited with bringing Christianity to the British Isles, but as mentioned, there were already Christians living there quite happily. In common with the development of Christianity elsewhere, the British and Irish Church was made up of different strands. There was not one homogeneous 'Celtic Church'. Irish monasticism had been thriving since the fourth century, when Christianity had been introduced by enslaved people, refugees and traders from Britain and Europe.[11] Although Ireland had never been part of the Roman empire (and so the Latin language was never imposed there), the new religious communities embraced literacy and book production

Portrait of Luke the Evangelist, St Augustine's Gospels, 6th century.

with enthusiasm and innovation. They developed their own script, known as Insular script, which can be seen in the iconic Lindisfarne Gospels (*c.* 700) and the Book of Kells (*c.* 800). The script has distinctive wedge-shaped tops to ascenders and red dots surrounding large initial letters. They also wrote their texts with spaces between each word, unlike many of the Roman-influenced manuscripts.

The Cathach of St Columba (RIA, MS 12 R 33) is an Irish manuscript dating from the late sixth century and is one of the earliest surviving psalters.[12] It is written in Latin in Jerome's style of *per cola et commata* and each psalm begins with a rubric (a title or heading in red). In these surviving 58 folios (the manuscript is thought originally to have been almost double the size, with 110 folios), we can see a style of decoration and writing developing in Ireland that was to become influential throughout Britain and Europe. The first letter of each section is significantly larger and fancier, decorated with spirals and red dots, sometimes incorporating an animal-head motif (see fol. 48r). These animal features later fused with the cultural influences from the Germanic settlers in England and developed into zoomorphic initials, where the initial partly or wholly depicts an animal form, which we see in abundance in the Lindisfarne Gospels and the Book of Kells. The gorgeous curves on the rounded m initials were made with a compass, and if you look closely, you can see the holes pricked by its central point (fol. 21r). The red pigment used for the dotted decoration and rubrics was red lead, and there are also traces of lead white in the manuscript, indicating the sophistication of pigment manufacture in Ireland (or at least their trade links). Here we see a distinction between the illustrated manuscripts of the Roman tradition, where the decoration was a separate image to the text – and the Insular manuscripts, where the decoration becomes part of the page layout, interwoven with the text.

The text was written in a style known as diminuendo – a large capital letter, with the subsequent letters getting gradually smaller until they merge into a regular-sized script (fol. 48r again). This main script, not quite a majuscule and not quite a minuscule script, is known as Insular half-uncial. It is immediately recognizable as Insular, since the ascenders, for example, on the letters *h* and *d*, have a thickened top, like a triangle or a wedge. This is not seen in Continental manuscripts with uncial or half-uncial script, so would appear to be a new development by the Irish monastic scribes. So, from the other side of the Christian Roman world, we have these new innovations that suddenly make the Roman uncial script look a bit old-fashioned and clunky. The sizes of the letters within the script are dynamically changing, and the initial letters are becoming ornate and playful. We do not know for sure where the Cathach manuscript was written, but we can ascertain certain things about its production. It is made of calfskin parchment – assuming the original manuscript was 110 folios, you would need approximately 18–27½ calves to provide enough parchment.[13] Therefore, you are already looking at quite a large number of livestock, indicating a well-stocked and/or wealthy monastery. The text was written by one competent scribe, demonstrating that Irish scribes were not just well educated and fluent in Latin, but willing to explore new ways of writing, for example, adding wedge endings to the ascenders. The decorated initials also show a new way of adding interest and character to the page format and in-text design. They were using tools such as compasses to create a perfect arc on initials. The use of red and white lead pigment indicates that the pigments were either made on site at the monastery, which would have required a certain level of manufacturing skill and equipment, or were available through trade networks. Either option demonstrates a conscious choice in the decoration of the manuscript: selecting red lead, for example, a pigment that needed to be made rather than one that was more readily available from the ground, such as red ochre, shows a deliberate level of consideration being given to the visual effect on the page.

We are not quite finished with this manuscript yet. It is not known where or by whom this manuscript was produced, but the elements of book production mentioned above suggest a certain professionalism. Apart from Cassiodorus's details on the writing facilities at Vivarium, we do not know what 'scriptoria' looked like in this period, if such a thing even existed. There is no surviving archaeological evidence of specific writing rooms, nor of images or descriptions of scriptoria in books. Therefore, it might be easier to think of a scriptorium as a 'centre of manuscript production' – part of a monastery but not necessarily contained to a single place or room. It is the sum of the accumulated effort of a certain group of scribes and the ethos of the monastic house, rather than condensed to just bricks and mortar (or wood, or stone).

Anyway, the Cathach of St Columba, according to tradition, belonged to Columba (also known as Colum Cille), a missionary monk who went on to found many monasteries. It is said that while studying at the abbey founded by Finnian in 540 in Movilla, County Down, Columba copied Finnian's psalter (the Cathach) without permission, which led to a dispute about who was the rightful owner of the copied book, indicating that copyright was a pertinent issue even in the sixth century. Possibly unrelated to this incident, soon after Columba sailed with twelve companions to Iona, a small island located off the west coast of Scotland, to found a new community in 563. This foundation on Iona went on to become one of the most respected in the early medieval period. It is doubtful that the surviving Cathach is the original copy made by Columba from Finnian's psalter, but as the *Codex Sinaiticus* was representative of early Christian book production, the Cathach is representative of the work capable

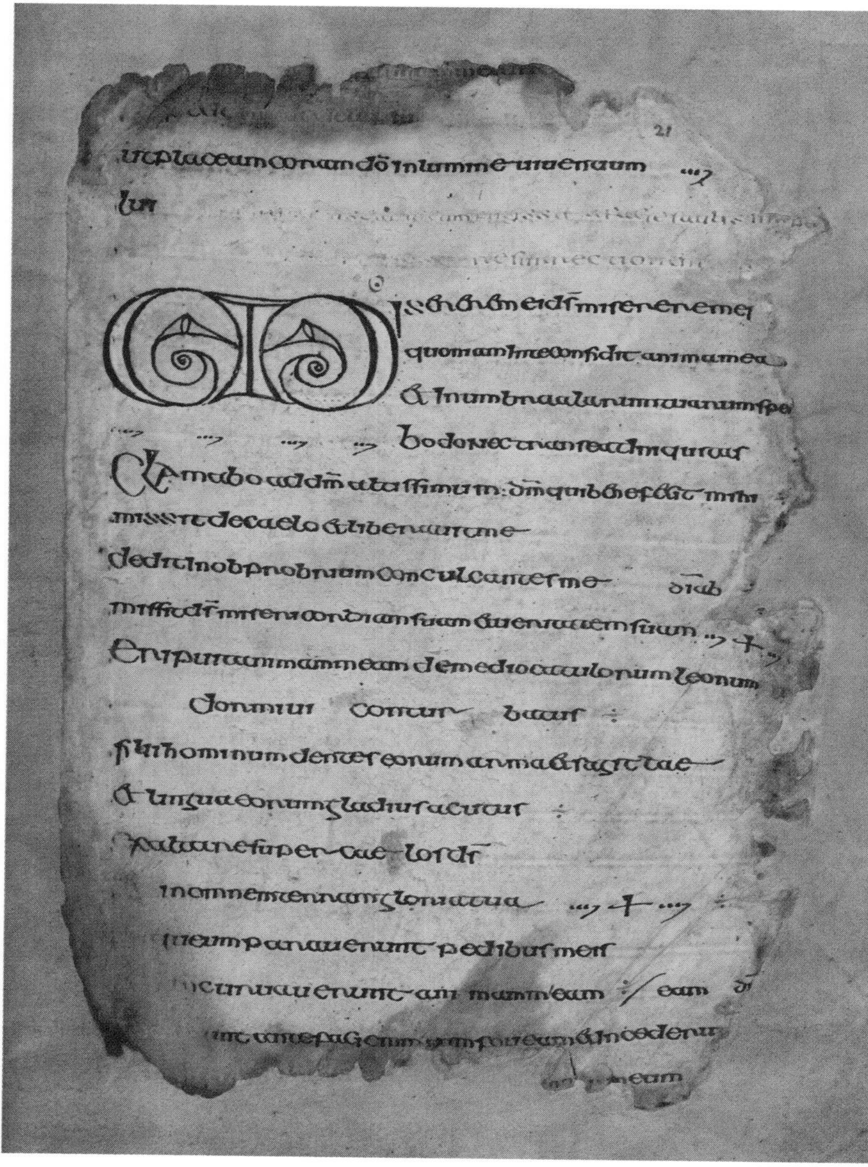

Folio from the Cathach of St Columba, 7th century.

of being produced by Irish monks in the late sixth/early seventh century.

We know that Columba worked in his own individual cell on Iona to produce manuscripts, as the *Life of Columba* makes several references to him writing in his sparsely furnished cell – one story relates how a clumsy visitor knocked over Columba's ink well in his haste to greet him![14] A cell atop a small knoll excavated at the monastic site is alleged to have been the very one Columba lived and worked in, although his fellow monks probably lived in communal quarters. The monastery on Iona became a hub for monastic study and book production, and in 634 a missionary from there named Aidan established a community at Lindisfarne, an island off the coast of Northumbria. The Irish style of manuscript production thus spread to Scotland and Northumbria, and we will see in due course how this allowed the creation of manuscript masterpieces such as the Lindisfarne Gospels and the Book of Kells. Even today, the islands of Iona and Lindisfarne have a unique spiritual atmosphere, occupying a liminal space between land and sea, which perhaps allowed the religious inhabitants to open up their minds and explore their creativity within manuscript decoration. Although these places were not isolated – the coastal waters of Britain and Ireland were busy transport routes – there would have been moments of complete stillness, allowing the inhabitants to easily tune into their natural surroundings and enter a spiritual realm.

Irish monks played an important role in the spread of Christianity and manuscript culture in the sixth and seventh centuries. Columbanus (Irish: Columbán – not to be confused with Columba) also had the missionary bug and longed to travel to the Continent to found monasteries and teach pagan tribes about Christianity. This missionary activity was known as *peregrinatio*, translated as 'travelling abroad'. Yet *peregrinatio* meant more to early medieval religious people than just a holiday

– it was a religious undertaking, putting their trust in God and leaving their homeland and kinspeople (possibly forever) to go on a pilgrimage into the unknown. When Columbanus was about forty, the abbot, Comgall, gave his permission for Columbanus to leave Bangor Abbey for pastures new. Columbanus supposedly took twelve companions with him (echoing Columba and reminiscent of the twelve disciples of Christ) and travelled to France, founding several monasteries. The most well known of these was Luxeuil Abbey, founded around 590, which went on to become a centre of Christian influence and importance, with the Irish scribes producing manuscripts there. Columbanus imposed his own (stricter) *Rule of St Columbanus* on his houses, but it increasingly clashed with the Benedictine Rule that was gaining popularity on the Continent. There was also an ongoing dispute about Easter, with Britain and Ireland celebrating Easter Sunday on a different date to the Roman Christians. After a while, Columbanus had irritated enough of the royal court and local clergy with his inflexibility, and they ordered him to leave.

Columbanus was supposed to return to Ireland, but he meandered through the Alps for a while and eventually settled in Bobbio in northern Italy. He founded a monastery there in 614, which, like Luxeuil, also went on to become a monastic powerhouse, known for its impressive library. There is a manuscript, the Bobbio Orosius (Milan, Biblioteca Ambrosiana, MS D. 23. Sup.), which was produced at Bobbio in the distinctive Insular style, with wedged ascenders and decorated initials with diminuendo, at the beginning of the seventh century. It also has the oldest surviving example of a 'carpet' page, another feature of Insular manuscripts. These pages were brightly coloured designs of interlaced patterns, staggering in their intricacy and usually placed at the beginning of a gospel, almost like an internal book cover to mark each section. Parallels have been drawn between these carpet pages and prayer mats used in the Eastern Mediterranean and Coptic Egypt as a way of mentally preparing the reader for a spiritual act. Further examples can be seen in the Book of Durrow, Lindisfarne Gospels and the Book of Kells, as well as Hebrew and Islamic manuscripts, indicating the cultural cross-sections of the early medieval world. So, by the end of the sixth century and the beginning of the seventh, the Irish Christians had brought their scriptoria to England and the Continent. The spread of Western Christianity had come full circle – originating in the Eastern Mediterranean and spreading out to its furthest reaches, and then being brought back by the Irish missionaries, founding their monasteries right in the heart of the Continent.

THESE MONASTERIES in France and Italy went on to develop their own scribal hands. The Merovingian script evolved from a later Roman cursive and was used by administrative scribes preparing charters at the Merovingian royal court. The script was adapted in the seventh and eight centuries by the monasteries at Luxeuil, Laon, Corbie and the female monastery of Chelles as a kind of standardization – although all four monasteries developed their own distinct features. Merovingian scripts are visually quite startling (see, for example, Bern, Burgerbibliothek, Cod. 611). The script is very scrawly, but as with the Insular script, communities were developing their own scriptorium styles, experimenting with letterforms and decoration to stamp their own identity on the manuscripts they were producing.

Other scripts were used in other parts of the Continent during the early medieval period – in the fifth century Visigothic script started to evolve in the Iberian peninsula (Spain and Portugal) from the Roman cursive script. The script continued to develop and was used in that area up until the thirteenth century.[15] (See BL, Egerton MS 1934 for an example of eighth-century

Visigothic script.) Uncial script was still seen as the gold standard of manuscripts, particularly in and around Rome, and as a result, script development stagnated somewhat in this part of the Christian world. However, by the end of the eighth century, a different script started to emerge in the Beneventan region of southern Italy. This script was developed enthusiastically by the scriptorium at Monte Cassino (the abbey founded by Benedict of Nursia about 250 years previously and still going strong) through the ninth and tenth centuries and was adopted by other monasteries in southern Italy and the Dalmatian coast (modern-day Croatia). Beneventan script continued to be used in certain areas up until the fifteenth century – see BL, Add MS 30337 for an eleventh-century scroll from Monte Cassino written in the Beneventan style.

BEFORE WE GO any further into developments on the Continent, let us first return to Britain and Ireland in the seventh century, to witness the exciting things going on there with book production. This really was an extraordinary period in manuscript decoration. The kingdom of Northumbria was particularly rich in cultural influences, with sea links to the Continent and Ireland, and in circa 634 an Irish monk called Aidan was sent from Iona (Columba's monastery) to found a monastery on the island of Lindisfarne. He and his monks would have brought their pre-owned manuscripts from Iona and even Ireland, but soon set up a manuscript production centre at Lindisfarne to furnish the new monastery with books.

There was also a strong Roman influence swirling around in Northumbria too, much of it introduced by Benedict Biscop (*c.* 628–690), a Northumbrian noble who enthusiastically converted to Christianity and travelled extensively to Rome. The main purpose of these visits was to buy books, as well as to immerse himself in the Christianity practised on the Continent. When the time came for him to establish the joint monasteries at Monkwearmouth–Jarrow, he was keen to promote the Roman version of Christianity as well as being able to provide a well-stocked library. On one trip to Rome, he took his close friend and abbot of the Jarrow monastery, Ceolfrith, and managed to pick up a manuscript now known as the *Codex Grandior*. Although Biscop and Ceolfrith were unaware of its origins, this manuscript was produced at Cassiodorus's Vivarium, maybe even by Cassiodorus himself. This *Codex Grandior* was a pandect: that is, it contained all the Christian books of the Bible in one volume and would have been quite a hefty tome (hence the name *Codex Grandior*). Excitingly for the Christians in far-removed England, this Bible was the fancy new Vulgate version by Jerome, and represented the very height of manuscript fashion. Although Jerome had written his Vulgate in the late fourth century, it was only now gaining popularity across Europe and would have been very much sought after by the discerning Christian scholar. Sadly, this copy no longer survives, but Biscop acquiring this volume and bringing it back to his monasteries would definitely have injected a new flavour into the manuscripts being produced in the Northumbrian monasteries at the time.

The twin monasteries of Monkwearmouth and Jarrow attracted many monks – it is estimated that at its peak there were six hundred inhabitants.[16] It became known for its well-stocked library (including the *Codex Grandior*) and manuscript production, most notably by the historian and scholar Bede (672/3–735). Bede had entered the monastery as a young boy and never really left, but largely thanks to Biscop's extensive library collection, he was able to produce his greatest work, the *Ecclesiastical History of the English People* (731 CE), alongside biblical commentaries, hagiographies and a martyrology, as well as grammar and science treatises. Bede's texts soon became desired items for monastic libraries, at home and abroad, and demand for his work fuelled manuscript production in the northeast.

By the end of the seventh century, Northumbrian book production was a hotbed of creative activity, with a range of cultural influences. We first saw the swirling circular patterns and animal motifs in the Cathach of St Columba, with the Insular script decorated with red dots and wedged ascenders. This style developed further on Iona and Lindisfarne, under the influence of the Irish missionaries who founded their monasteries – and started to fuse with the cultural influences from the Germanic tribes who had settled in England, bringing with them their own animal imagery and interlaced knotwork, as seen in the exquisite designs in the Staffordshire Hoard.

Elements of these fusions can be seen in fragments of a mid-seventh-century gospel manuscript kept at Durham Cathedral Library (DCL, MS A II 10). The design is similar to the Cathach – it has the wedged Insular half-uncial script, with large capital letters full of swirling patterns and red dots, followed by diminuendo. However, the most striking visual difference is the addition of colour. Pigments of orpiment (yellow), red lead (red), woad (indigo) and vergaut (green) have been added to the monogram '*INI*' on fol. 2r to create an arresting first impression.[17] Insular manuscripts often use monograms in their opening titles – in this case the first three letters of 'initium' have been blended together to form one symbol, complete with zoomorphic features. On fol. 3v, there are three large *D* shapes, each containing a (now faded) red text, that are surrounded by an interlaced pattern in yellow against a black background. Although most of the text is written in Insular half-uncial, on fol. 3v we see an early appearance of Insular minuscule under the main text on the left-hand side. This is a less formal, cursive script that was developed in Ireland and probably used to save space in this instance. This manuscript is very similar to two Bobbio manuscripts, Bobbio

Orosius and Bobbio Jerome (Milan, Biblioteca Ambrosiana MS S. 45. sup.), also from the early seventh century, but DCL, MS A II 10 is thought to have been made at Iona (or possibly Lindisfarne), written by an Irish scribe.[18] There are always uncertainties about the exact place of origin for all these Insular-style manuscripts, as they are all so alike and their networks were so far reaching. One thing we can say is that this scriptorium style began in Ireland and moved with the missionaries to Iona, Northumbria and the Continent, blending with other cultural influences along the way.

The Insular style peaked around the eighth century with the Lindisfarne Gospels and the Book of Kells, written in an Insular half-uncial script. They have carpet pages and initials so swirlingly intricate they make your eyes hurt. Strange creatures looking like birds and dragons morph into letterforms, like optical illusions. This disorientating effect may have been deliberate to create a religious experience in itself, pulling you into the image to go on a journey within the swirls and patterns, taking you into another world. The concentric circles, interlaced knotwork and zoomorphic designs were a perfect fusion of Irish and Germanic styles. There are also plenty of monograms (where two or more letters overlap to form one symbol). These can often be quite difficult for the untrained eye to read, such as the monogram for Matthew on fol. 18v in the Lindisfarne Gospels. The famous Chi Rho page on fol. 29r is particularly spectacular. Christ written in Greek is Christos or ΧΡΙΣΤΟΣ, and this image shows the first three letters (ΧΡΙ) displayed together in an elaborate display of knots, spirals and beasts. There are also four full-page portraits of the evangelists in this manuscript. They are depicted with their symbols, and all are shown as seated scribes, ready to write, with parchment or papyrus in front of them and quills in hand. The portrait of Matthew is very similar to an image of the Hebrew priest and scribe Ezra, from a manuscript

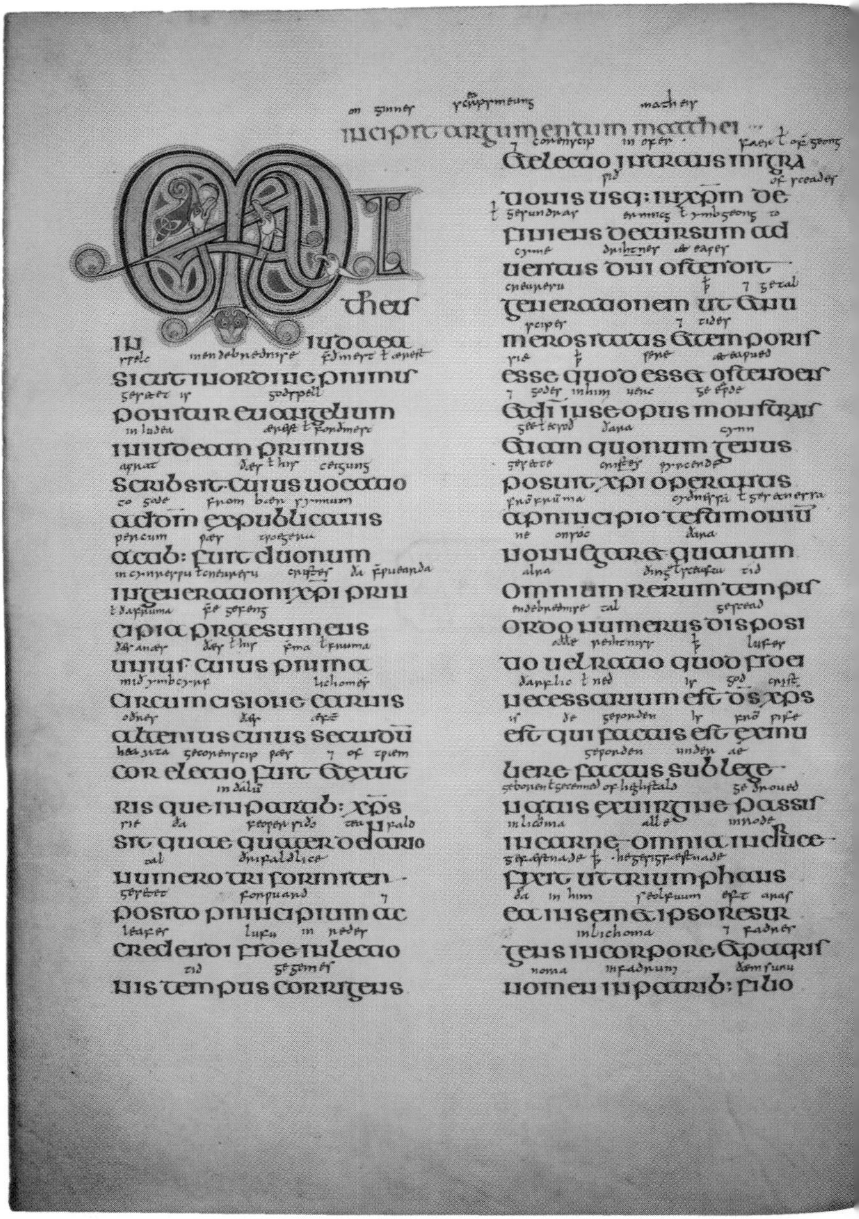

Monogram of Matthew (Mattheus), Lindisfarne Gospels, *c.* 8th century.

that was produced at nearby Monkwearmouth–Jarrow – the *Codex Amiatinus* – reflecting the Mediterranean influences that were also feeding into the Lindisfarne Gospels via Biscop's library. Images of codices also feature heavily in these evangelist portraits in the Lindisfarne Gospels, underlining the message that these words are sacred, coming from God through the evangelists' hands – and therefore the symbolic value of these written words forming a direct line with God would have been implicit to any medieval Christian. This manuscript was intended for ceremonial use, to be looked at with awe and wonder. It would probably have been brought out and paraded in front of the congregation before the reading of the gospels at mass, the same way this ritual is performed today in many Catholic churches.

Even more incredible is that the Lindisfarne Gospels were written and decorated by one single scribe. A colophon was added to fol. 259v in the mid-tenth century by a monk called Aldred, who wrote that 'Eadfrith, bishop of the Church of Lindisfarne . . . wrote this book . . . And Æthilwald, bishop of the Lindisfarne-islanders, bound and covered it without, as he well knew how to do. And Billfrith the anchorite, he forged the ornaments which are on the outside and bedecked it with gold and with gems and also with gilded silver.'[19] If this is to be believed, and it is generally accepted that it is, then Eadfrith, Bishop of Lindisfarne (698–*c.* 722), was almost solely responsible for creating and decorating one of the most famous medieval manuscripts. The text is written in a beautiful accomplished Insular half-uncial, reflecting a scribe at the top of their game – and the images suggest an artist of the highest skill. The colophon further demonstrates that scribes and producers of books were regarded with high esteem.

The Book of Kells, written circa 800, surpassed even the complex artistry of the Lindisfarne Gospels. It is not known exactly where the manuscript was produced, but it may have been partially made at the monastery of Iona, before being finished at the new monastery at Kells in 806. Unlike the Lindisfarne Gospels, the Book of Kells was a team effort, with four scribes writing in half-uncial and three artists creating the decoration (scribes and artists may have been interchangeable). The similarity in script and style indicate that this was produced by an accomplished scriptorium, with scribes and artists working symbiotically to create an Insular masterpiece. The Chi Rho page (fol. 34r) is a mesmerizing display of interlace and swirls, with zoomorphic and anthropomorphic figures suddenly forming shapes before your eyes. The image is packed with religious symbolism such as cross shapes and moths representing the Crucifixion and Resurrection, and cats representing the Devil, indicating the many different levels of meaning these manuscripts encompassed.[20]

It is hard to imagine the amount of time and expertise it would have taken to produce manuscripts of such staggering proficiency. Apart from anything else, think of all the practical considerations, such as getting hold of a large amount of decent parchment. The calfskins would have been inspected and selected, with only the skins with no scars or imperfections chosen (these may have been caused naturally from insect bites or injury while the animal was alive, or made by clumsy strokes inflicted on the skin while being removed from the carcass). It is estimated that at least 129 calfskins would have been used to make the original 258 folios in the Lindisfarne Gospels (one calfskin will produce only one bifolium for a large book), so a large number of monastic livestock would have been needed, or at least the finances to purchase them from elsewhere. Then the skins would have been stretched and scraped with the utmost skill, to create smooth, creamy parchment fit for writing on. The ink used was iron gall ink, made from growths found on oak trees that had been used by the Christians since at least the fourth century. The oak galls were either foraged locally or imported from the Mediterranean.

Then there were the colours to consider. The artist would have selected their basic palette and then blended the pigments together. The main pigments in the Lindisfarne Gospels have been identified by Raman spectroscopy as red lead, woad (indigo), orpiment (yellow), verdigris (green) and lead white. Also identified were an organic purple (probably orchil), chalk, organic red or pink, iron gall black and carbon black, and ground gold.[21] Already from that list you can tell something about manufacturing and trade at the Lindisfarne scriptorium. Red lead, white lead and verdigris could all have been made on site with the right equipment and skillset. You would need raw ingredients of lead for the red and white, and copper for the green verdigris, plus vinegar and heat. These were all methods used since at least classical times, so were tried and tested. Lead and copper were available in abundance from the North Pennines, so they would have been easily sourced. To make lead white, seal some lead sheets in a container with vinegar and leave somewhere warm. After a month or so, scrape off the top layer that has accumulated on the lead and heat it. Stir continuously until the pigment goes white. To make red lead, just keep stirring the pigment on the heat and it will change from white to yellow to orange to red. (Nowadays these pigments are for restricted use only, because of their toxicity – so just imagine how nasty it would have been extracting this pigment in the medieval period, with minimal safety precautions.) To make verdigris, it's the same initial process – suspend copper sheets over vinegar in a sealed container and leave somewhere warm. After a while, a layer of verdigris will have formed on the copper, so just scrape it off and grind it up. Therefore, the green, red and white pigments in the Lindisfarne Gospels would have been relatively easy to produce, with the right infrastructure.

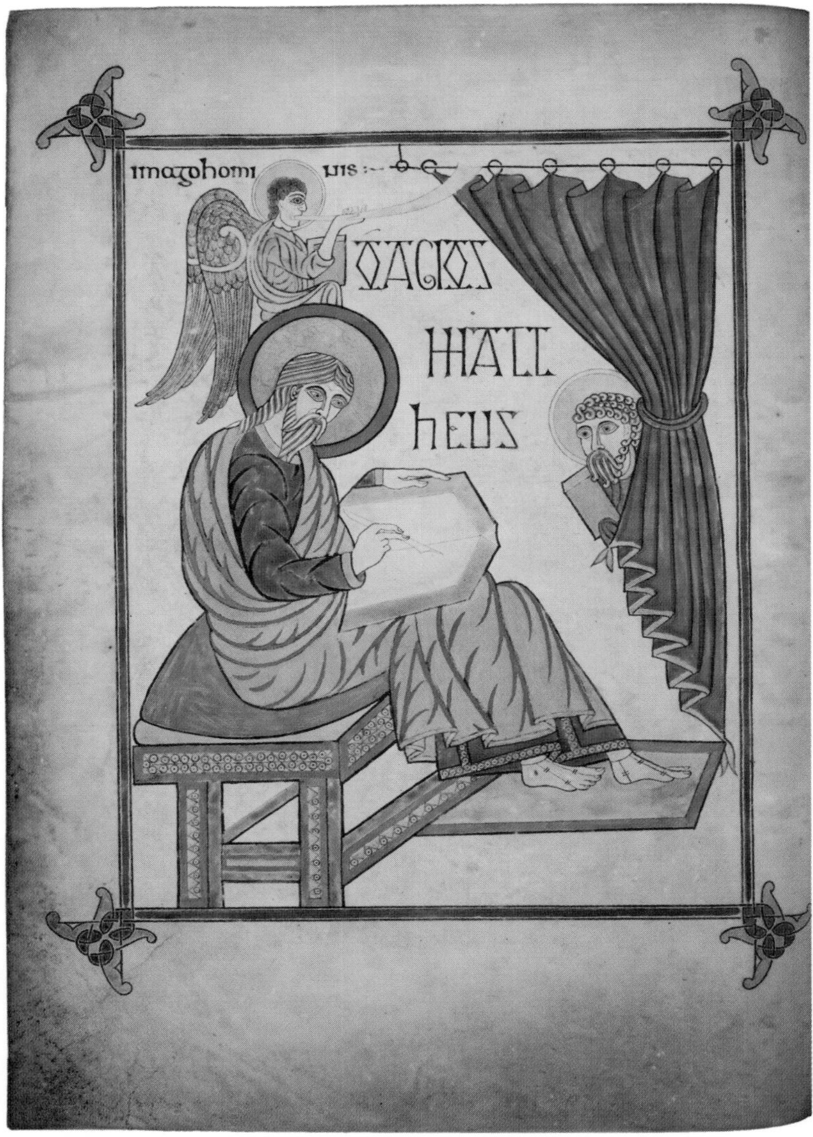

Portrait of Matthew (Mattheus), Lindisfarne Gospels, *c*. 8th century.

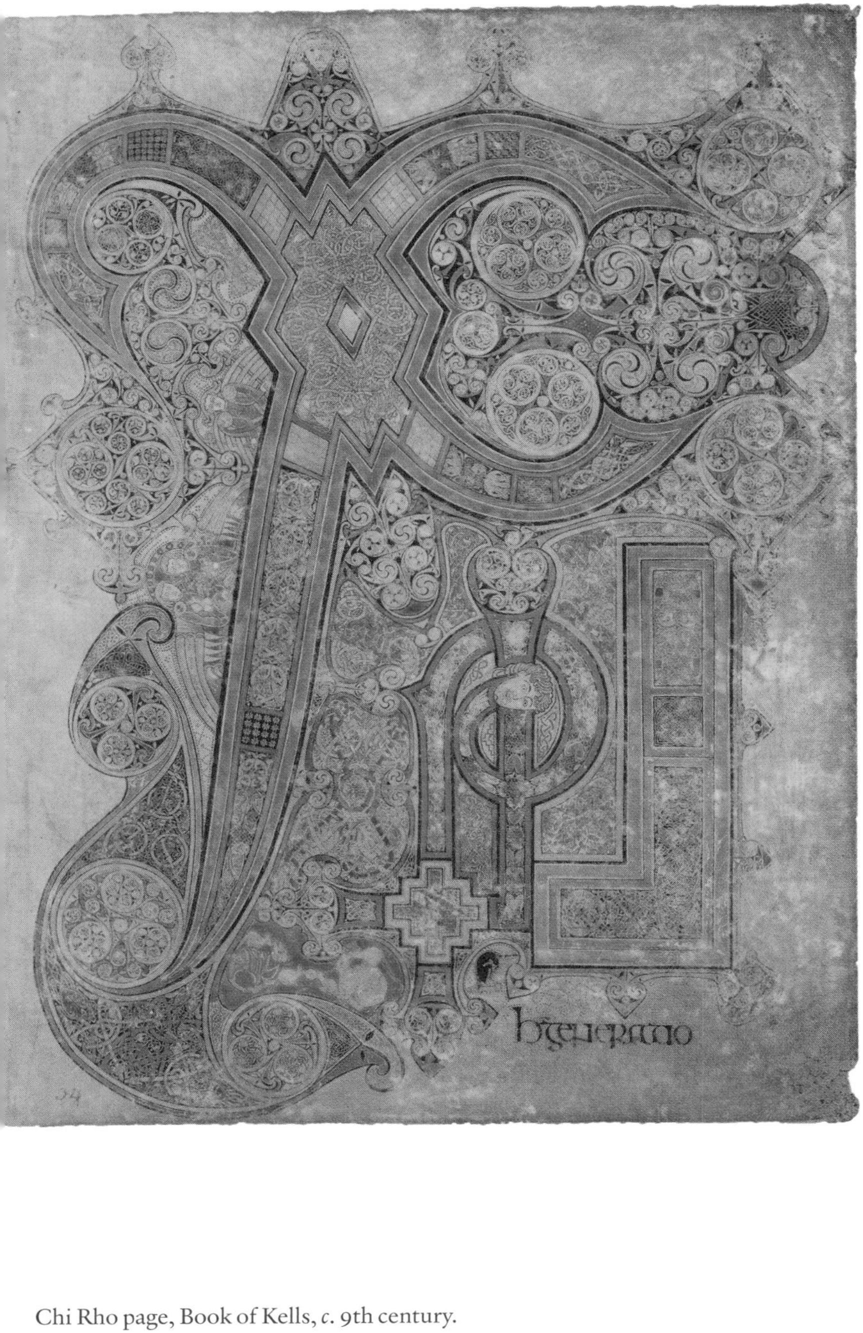

Chi Rho page, Book of Kells, *c*. 9th century.

The blue pigment was made from woad – a plant grown naturally in England and Europe, so again, locally sourcing that shouldn't have been too much of a problem. Except for woad to yield a good enough blue you would need to sow the seeds the year before, to harvest the following year. And of course, your crop is dependent on the environment, so you have to hope there are no floods, severe frosts, plant diseases and so on. Also, you will need an awful lot of woad leaves to extract the pigments. So, there's a certain amount of long-term planning that needs to go into making sure you have an adequate palette for your manuscript decoration.

And then we have the yellow pigment, orpiment, which gives us an idea of the trade links available to the northeast of England in the medieval period. Orpiment was not available naturally in England, so it must have been sourced from the Continent, or even further afield. It was a popular colour in manuscripts from this period, which indicates there was a flourishing trade supply. The Latin word for orpiment is *auripigmentum* (gold pigment) because it gives out a brilliance similar to gold, and if you look at any of the manuscripts from this period, you would be forgiven for mistaking the orpiment for gold. Technically, a manuscript can only be classed as illuminated if it is decorated with gold or silver, and the Lindisfarne Gospels would scrape into that category by the thinnest of margins. There are four small additions of gold on the incipit (opening) pages of the gospels (fols 27r, 95r, 139r and 211r), a few words in ground gold recording their evangelical symbols: *☧ ihs xps matheus homo*, *marcus leo*, *☧ lucas vitulus* and *+ iohannis aquila*. There are also tiny embellishments of gold at the end of the letter *l* on Matthew's incipit and in the centre of the letter *q* on Luke's incipit. Elsewhere, orpiment is used as a convincing substitute for gold, such as around the halos of the evangelists. Another colour used in the Lindisfarne Gospels is vergaut, a forest green, created from blue and yellow – most commonly orpiment and woad. (You can also see this pigment in DCL, MS A II 10.)

So, taking the Lindisfarne Gospels as a case study of early medieval manuscript production, you can see the level of sophistication and complexity it displays, not just in its amazing artwork, but the vibrant palette. Prick marks in the parchment also indicate the use of compasses and dividers to plan out the intricate patterns on the decorated pages, and grid lines can be seen on the reverse side of one of the carpet pages on fol. 94r–v. This gives an important insight into the planning and execution of these elaborate drawings. These grid lines have been drawn in 'leadpoint', which was basically a stick of lead used like a pencil to leave a grey outline, and this is one of the earliest examples of leadpoint in a European manuscript.[22] Compare this manuscript to the early Christian texts on papyrus, in a basic script and with no decoration, and we can see how far we've come. Of course, the Lindisfarne Gospels is a very high-end example of early medieval manuscript production, but comparison with other examples from the same place and time reveals similar use of pigments, script and decoration.

Let us move now, not in time but in place, about three days' walk south from Lindisfarne down to Monkwearmouth–Jarrow. Sometime around the end of the seventh century, the abbot Ceolfrith commissioned three large pandects (single-volume Bibles) to be produced by his scriptorium, using the Vulgate text from the *Codex Grandior* that Biscop acquired on one of his visits to Rome. Only one of these pandects remains intact today, the *Codex Amiatinus*, originally intended as a gift to Pope Gregory II in Rome – and for several reasons, it is truly magnificent. First, it is absolutely huge. Enormous. It measures 49 centimetres high, 34 centimetres wide and 18 centimetres thick, weighs 34 kilograms and consists of 1,030 folios. Second, it is of such high quality and so closely resembles the Roman style of book

Portrait of Ezra, *Codex Amiatinus*, early 8th century.

production that up until 1888 it was believed to have originated there. Third, it is the earliest surviving complete version of the Latin Vulgate.

While the manuscripts made for the Northumbrian monasteries were written on calfskin parchment (as would be expected for a high-quality item in England), the *Codex Amiatinus* was written mostly on goatskin, with some sheepskin. This is highly unusual for an English manuscript, but not so unusual for a Continental manuscript, suggesting that the parchment was prepared in southern France or Italy and ordered in by Ceolfrith specially.[23] It is also written in an uncial script, further cementing the monastery's allegiance to Rome, in Jerome's trademark style of *per cola et commata*. Seven different scribes worked on the pandect, and while some differences between hands are visible, the uniformity of script indicates they were all trained in the same scriptorium. It is even possible that Bede was involved in the production of this manuscript – certainly he was there while it was being made. Despite the clear favouring of Roman book production methods, we can also see local influences creeping in. The scribes use the Irish practice of word separation rather than the *scriptura continua* that would have been common in the Continental books at the library of Monkwearmouth–Jarrow.[24] Although in-text decoration is kept to a minimum compared to the intricacy of the Lindisfarne Gospels, there is an interlaced initial L at the beginning of the gospel of Matthew that seems very much related to the Insular style (fol. 805r).

The frontispiece to the *Codex Amiatinus* is an image of the Hebrew scribe Ezra, which has already been mentioned as being very similar to the portrait of Matthew in the Lindisfarne Gospels, and perhaps indicates that both manuscripts consulted the same resource, such as the *Codex Grandior*. It's possible that the image of Ezra was actually a self-portrait of Cassiodorus, which does create a lovely symbiosis with scriptorium development

– Cassiodorus wrote about his scriptorium at Vivarium, Biscop picked up the *Codex Grandior* which supposedly was made at Vivarium (perhaps even by Cassiodorus himself), and then Cassiodorus was represented through the image of Ezra in the *Codex Amiatinus*. Although the *Codex Grandior* has not survived, perhaps it lives on in the Lindisfarne Gospels and *Codex Amiatinus*.

The figure of Ezra/Cassiodorus in the *Codex Amiatinus* is sitting in front of a book cupboard, called an *armarium*, with nine volumes of the Bible laid on the shelves. Ezra himself is seated on a wooden stool, with his feet slightly raised on a wooden footrest and a codex open on his lap. The stool is decorated with a vine scroll, a motif borrowed from classical decoration. This vine scroll motif becomes more visible in manuscripts as the medieval period progresses and is used liberally in manuscripts from the twelfth and thirteenth centuries. Ezra holds a quill in his right hand poised to write on the parchment, and a wooden table holds a vessel with separate compartments for red and black pigment. Other scribal equipment surrounds Ezra, including a brush, inkpot, dividers and a stylus, providing visual information on the typical tools of a scribe. This image also gives a great insight into how books were bound in this period – if you look closely, you can see the patterned design on the book covers, the titles in rustic capitals and the straps used to keep the manuscript closed. We can also see that books were stored in cupboards flat on their sides (lessening the drag on the spine), while today they are stored upright with spines vertical.

The palette used in the *Codex Amiatinus* was slightly more ambitious than the Lindisfarne Gospels, and not all the pigments have been identified. Red lead was used for reds and oranges, along with red ochre. Verdigris and vergaut was used for greens, but the pigment used for blues has not so far been identified. Orpiment was used for yellow. An ochre was used for brown and an organic substance, probably orchil or folium, was used for purple. White was chalk or lead white.[25] Gold and silver were also liberally applied to the images in the manuscript. The portrait contains gold on the back wall behind the book cupboard and on Ezra's halo, breastplate and cuffs. Although much of this has worn away, the effect would have been dazzling at the time. There is also the addition of a purple folio with yellow letters written in orpiment, harking back to those purple and gold manuscripts that were popular in late antiquity (and thoroughly disapproved of by Jerome). Here orpiment has been substituted for gold, and only close scrutiny of the manuscript would give away the fact that it is not gold. The capitals of the columns on this folio, although now discoloured black, were silver, which must have created quite a brilliant effect against the purple background and bright yellow text. Brushstrokes are visible on this folio, indicating that the purple pigment was painted on rather than the parchment dyed in a purple dye bath.[26] It is highly unlikely that this purple was the prohibitively expensive Tyrian purple; it was more likely a local substitute like orchil, obtained from lichens. Like the Lindisfarne Gospels, all the materials used in the *Codex Amiatinus* also point to a well-stocked and professional scriptorium. Apart from anything else, a huge amount of parchment would have been needed for all three pandects – the imported goatskin for the *Codex Amiatinus* and local calfskins for the Monkwearmouth–Jarrow manuscripts – so we can only assume that the scriptorium was a well-supplied and efficient operation.

The *Codex Amiatinus* also has a title page that originally would have displayed a dedication from 'Ceolfrith of the Angles' to the church in Rome (St Peter's). However, we have here a shameless case of medieval monastic fraud. The codex did leave Monkwearmouth–Jarrow for Rome with Ceolfrith, but unfortunately Ceolfrith died on the way in 716. The manuscript was still presented to the pope in Rome by Ceolfrith's companions, but after that, no more is heard about it. Then, lo and behold, it turns up at the Abbey of the Saviour, Mount Amiata, in the tenth century – with a mysteriously altered dedication page! Where it once read *Ceolfriðus Anglorum* (Ceolfrith of the Angles), it now says *Petrus Langobardorum* (Peter of the Lombards) – and where it was originally dedicated to *Corpus Petri* (the body of Peter), it is now dedicated to *Cenobium Saluatoris* (the monastery of the Saviour). How on earth could that have happened?! The thing is, parchment has a very special quality, in that the top layer can be scraped away with a knife to erase the text, and then written over, often with no noticeable difference to the untrained eye. When you reuse a piece of parchment in this way, it becomes known as a palimpsest – although in this case it's probably better to call it attempted fraud by the monks at the abbey to disguise its origins. If you look at the dedication page, you can clearly see the changes in the colour of ink on the first, second and fifth lines. In the fifth line in particular you can see the brown ink with the words Petrus Langobardorum and where the original darker ink has been scraped off removing the words Ceolfrithus Anglorum. We can suppose that, at the time, the colour of the two inks was the same and it's only over time that one has significantly faded to produce such a contrast – particularly when such care has been taken to match the original lettering. In particular, the first two letters of *corpus* have been adapted to *cenobium*, and the original *C* that formed the first letter of Ceolfrith has been recycled and turned into the *E* in the second letter of Petrus. One can't help but grudgingly admire the innovation of the scribe here.

This monastic subterfuge, along with the extremely high standard of production, meant that for hundreds of years the *Codex Amiatinus* was assumed to be of Italian or Byzantine origin, certainly not from a rainy old backwater on the western fringes of the Christian world. However, now that its true origin is known, this manuscript is acknowledged as a truly amazing feat of book production. The skill and craftsmanship that went into producing a volume of this size, not to mention the logistics (it is estimated that it took several years to complete), are staggering and can only have come from an extremely skilled scriptorium. At the same time, the monastery at Lindisfarne produced the Lindisfarne Gospels, different in script and decoration, but equally as impressive. Imagine how these codices would have looked to local pagan populations, most of whom would have been illiterate. The sheer size of the *Codex Amiatinus*, with the gold glinting off its pages, and the animalistic forms, mind-bending patterns and jewelled exterior of the Lindisfarne Gospels, must have looked like they came from another world. Truly the book then, especially in the early medieval period, would have been a powerful weapon with which to convert people to Christianity. Unfortunately, the Viking attacks (particularly on Lindisfarne in 793) took the impetus out of the Insular movement. It's fair to say in this period the Vikings did not have much appreciation for the written word, but they were quite partial to the bejewelled bindings that decorated them and enjoyed raiding monasteries in north Britain and Ireland for their riches. However, we will leave things here and check on how things were developing in the south of England, before circling back to the Continent for a new wave of innovation in book production.

Christianity spread in a two-pronged movement from both the northwest and southeast of Britain and Ireland. The monastery of St Peter and St Paul, Canterbury, founded by Augustine at the end of the sixth century, became a wealthy and successful house. Shortly after 670, a school was established in Canterbury by Theodore of Tarsus (Archbishop of Canterbury) and Hadrian (Abbot of St Peter and St Paul), who had been sent to England by Pope Vitalian. We know of Hadrian through the writings of Bede, who praises him as a man from the nation of Africa and 'well versed in holy Scriptures, trained both in monastic and ecclesiastical ways and equally skilled in the Greek and Latin tongues'. The school Hadrian and Theodore established became known not just for teaching scripture, but also 'the art of metre, astronomy, and ecclesiastical computation', attracting students from far and wide.[27] Theodore and Hadrian's vast accumulated knowledge was a result of their learning from North Africa and Asia Minor, which fed into their teaching – for example, Hadrian used riddles as teaching aids. Riddles were a North African tradition, and early English scholars, such as Hadrian's student Aldhelm, became particularly fond of them, demonstrating the intercontinental flow of cultural influences.[28] Owing to the scarcity of books in the south of England in the seventh century, Hadrian and Theodore would also have brought their own libraries with them, and some fragments remain from what could have been Hadrian's personal collection. A late fourth-century manuscript, now only surviving as five folios in BL, Add MS 40165, contains a collection of letters from Cyprian, Bishop of Carthage (*c.* 210–258). The fragments were written in North Africa, possibly Carthage, in uncials of black and red ink. Although we cannot say for definite that this belonged to Hadrian, it is symbolic of the movement of books throughout the early Christian world, with codices from North Africa being used in southeast England, while codices from Ireland circulated in mainland Europe.

Archaeological evidence from tooth enamel has shown that North Africans were present in Britain and Ireland from the Bronze Age,[29] and more would have lived there as soldiers during the Roman period. Fragments of North African slipware dating from the post-Roman era have been found all across Britain, some with inscriptions, indicating that North African culture continued to be familiar in Britain – so this codex would not have been an unusual item.[30] The codex fragments also provide us with an example of book production in North Africa from the late 300s – it is written on parchment (not papyrus) in four columns, with biblical quotations in red and *nomina sacra* in the text. It also has additions to the text in an Insular hand, which indicates it was still being used in England in the eighth century. Again, this demonstrates that the medieval world and book history grew out of the fusion of many cultures.[31]

Manuscript Production in Europe, 800–1050

Towards the end of the eighth century, innovations in manuscript production shifted focus to mainland Europe. Charlemagne (Charles the Great, 747–814) was an adept ruler who in his lifetime was king of the Franks, king of the Lombards and Holy Roman Emperor. He expanded the Carolingian empire, which united western and central Europe after centuries of instability. Not only was he a warrior king and politically astute, he was keen to develop a culture of learning and scholarship. This period is often called the Carolingian Renaissance. He assembled great scholars around him at court, including Alcuin of York (735–804). Steeped in the Northumbrian culture of learning and taught at the liberal, cultural cathedral school of York, Alcuin was regarded as one of the great intellects of his day and went on to become the headteacher of the cathedral. While there, he further expanded the already impressive library that contained many classical works, and developed a reputation for being a great teacher of Latin grammar and rhetoric. Charlemagne was 'collecting' scholars from his kingdom and beyond in the 770s and 780s and persuaded Alcuin to join his royal court on the Continent as master of the palace school. Charlemagne's court must have been a great melting pot of cultural and artistic influences (largely owing to the vast territory he had conquered), and he wanted to bring together all these strands to promote a new unity in the liberal arts and Christianity. He hankered after the great days of the Roman empire, wanting to recreate their grand achievements, and was particularly concerned about the decline of the Latin language in his kingdom. In 789, he issued the *Admonitio generalis* to reform Carolingian society. It included a rule that every monastery and cathedral must provide a school for teaching children, and that any copying of manuscripts must be done only by men 'of appropriate age' (ch. 72). Charlemagne also wanted a scribal uniformity across his empire, with manuscripts written in a clear hand that could be easily read by all – this script came to be known as Caroline minuscule. Alcuin is largely credited with putting the structures in place for this to happen. The irony is that Charlemagne never fully mastered the art of writing, and Alcuin continued to write in his own Insular hand, despite the new Caroline minuscule script being adopted throughout Europe.

Up until then, manuscript production in monasteries in western and central Europe had been trundling along quite happily in its own individual way. BL, Add MS 31031 is a typical example of a Merovingian manuscript from the second half of the seventh century, possibly from Laon. The decoration within the manuscript features zoomorphic initials, with the popular motifs of birds and fish. The initial *B* on fol. 55v shows an upright fish as the straight stroke of the *B*, with two curved birds forming the rounded bowls of the letter. It is coloured in brown, green and yellow, as are the enlarged letters that separate the sections.

Insular influences were still seen in manuscripts from France and Italy. The English missionary Boniface (675–754) had established a monastery in Echternach (modern-day Luxembourg) and been instrumental in founding the monastery at Fulda (modern-day Germany); and with his friend and kinswoman Leoba, founded a female monastery at Tauberbischofsheim. This led to further fusion between Insular and Continental styles, with manuscripts written in Insular script well into the ninth century. A copy of Charlemagne's *Admonitio generalis* from around 800 was written at Fulda in an Insular minuscule (HAB, Cod. Guelf. 496a Helmst.)

The mid-eighth to the mid-ninth century saw a rapid growth in new monastic communities, resulting in an increased demand for texts. Alcuin wrote that 'our greatest need these days is copying sacred books.'[32] Charlemagne and Alcuin pushed the adoption of this uniform script, Caroline minuscule, that would be used throughout his empire. This script was not 'invented' at the court of Charlemagne, it was probably already developing in Frankish monasteries during the eighth century, but Alcuin brought this script into the palace school and scriptorium, and then out to monastic and cathedral schools. Charlemagne also initiated a programme of copying ancient Latin texts, including Cicero, Seneca, Horace and Ovid (probably from Alcuin's library) – and without his passion for reviving the Roman empire, many of these would have become obsolete. So, with this huge back catalogue of texts to copy, as well as the rise in new monasteries to equip – not just with liturgical texts but with the latest bestsellers like Bede's commentaries – there was an impressive output of manuscripts in the Carolingian period. Once Alcuin had established Caroline minuscule at Charlemagne's court, he ensured the new monastic and cathedral establishments set up schools providing education to children, thus moulding the next generation of scribes. The court also developed its own art movement known as the Ada School, after a gospel produced for Charlemagne's half-sister, Ada. There are ten gospels known to have been produced by scriptoria with links to the court from between around 780 and 820, including the Lorsch gospels (Biblioteca Apostolica Vaticana, Pal. lat. 50/Alba Iulia, Biblioteca Documenta Batthyaneum, s.n.) and the Harley Golden Gospels (British Library, Harley MS 2788). These illuminated manuscripts display classical influences fused with Insular and Merovingian styles. Considering the sumptuousness

Portrait of Mark the Evangelist, Harley Golden Gospels, produced by the Ada School at the court of Charlemagne, 9th century.

of the surviving manuscripts, it can be supposed that these were luxury items for only the wealthiest of monasteries, such as at St Riquier and Soissons. Humbler establishments would have far less glamorous manuscripts furnishing their book cupboards.

Alcuin retired from court around 796 and accepted the abbacy at St Martins in Tours, where he devoted the rest of his life to improving the scriptorium there and working on texts on grammar and punctuation. At Charlemagne's request Alcuin also corrected and revised Jerome's Vulgate, and the scriptorium produced large, illuminated pandects for dissemination throughout the empire, as well as liturgical and classical texts. Many English clergy came to Tours to visit Alcuin (which irritated the monks already there trying to concentrate on their work but must have furthered the cultural exchange between England and the Continent). Alcuin wrote a verse 'On Scribes', proclaiming:

> It is an excellent task to copy holy books
> and scribes do enjoy their own rewards.
> It is better to write books than to dig vines:
> one serves the belly but the other serves the soul.[33]

Caroline minuscule script spread widely through the Carolingian empire, first to the main writing centres of Aachen, Tours, Corbie, Fleury, Laon, Reichenau, Lorsch, Saint Gallen, Bobbio, Murbach, Saint Riquier, Reims and then further afield to Germany and northern Italy. The script flourished in Europe between the ninth and twelfth centuries, thus achieving Charlemagne's goal of having a standardized script. Caroline minuscule is a very rounded script and is quite easy on the eye: all characters stand alone and are clearly distinguished. It uses an ampersand, and particularly distinctive letterforms are *g* and the long *s* (a good tip to distinguish any script is to look at the *g* – it can vary wildly between scripts and individual scribes).

An excellent early example of Caroline minuscule is BL, Add MS 11848 from the abbey at St Martins, Tours. This illuminated manuscript was probably produced about 820–30, under the tutelage of Abbot Fridugisus (807–34), successor to Alcuin. It's also the earliest known gospel book from Tours to have evangelist portraits. The script is neat and even, with uncial and rustic capitals at the beginning and end of some sections. There is a decorated initial *B* on fol. 1v with knotwork that is quite Insular in style, but this is unsurprising when you consider Fridugisus was English. Another decorated initial *Q* on fol. 110v is also typically Insular, accompanied by text in a classical uncial script. This fusion of Insular and Continental styles is known as Franco-Saxon and flourished in Francia in the later ninth century and in England in the later tenth century.[34] The palette includes carbon black, indigo, lead white, orpiment, red lead and vermilion – which is similar to the Lindisfarne Gospels, except there is no verdigris here and a different red pigment, vermilion, is present.[35]

The Tours gospels are written in *per cola et commata* style, with each new section indicated by a large red capital letter. There are also visual aids to navigating the Bible text, with the name of the evangelist at the top centre of the right folio, and the book number on the top centre of the left folio. Unusually, the original medieval treasure bindings for this manuscript are still intact, made of oak with a silver plate covering. The foliage metalwork and central panels are thought to be original, although the corner enamels are later additions. The jewels that now adorn the covers probably replaced coloured stones. Just to add a little bit of extra holiness, there are also fragments of bones embedded in the front board, presumably the relics of a saint – which might seem gruesome to us but was perfectly acceptable in the early medieval world. It also underlines that the message of the medieval book was so much more

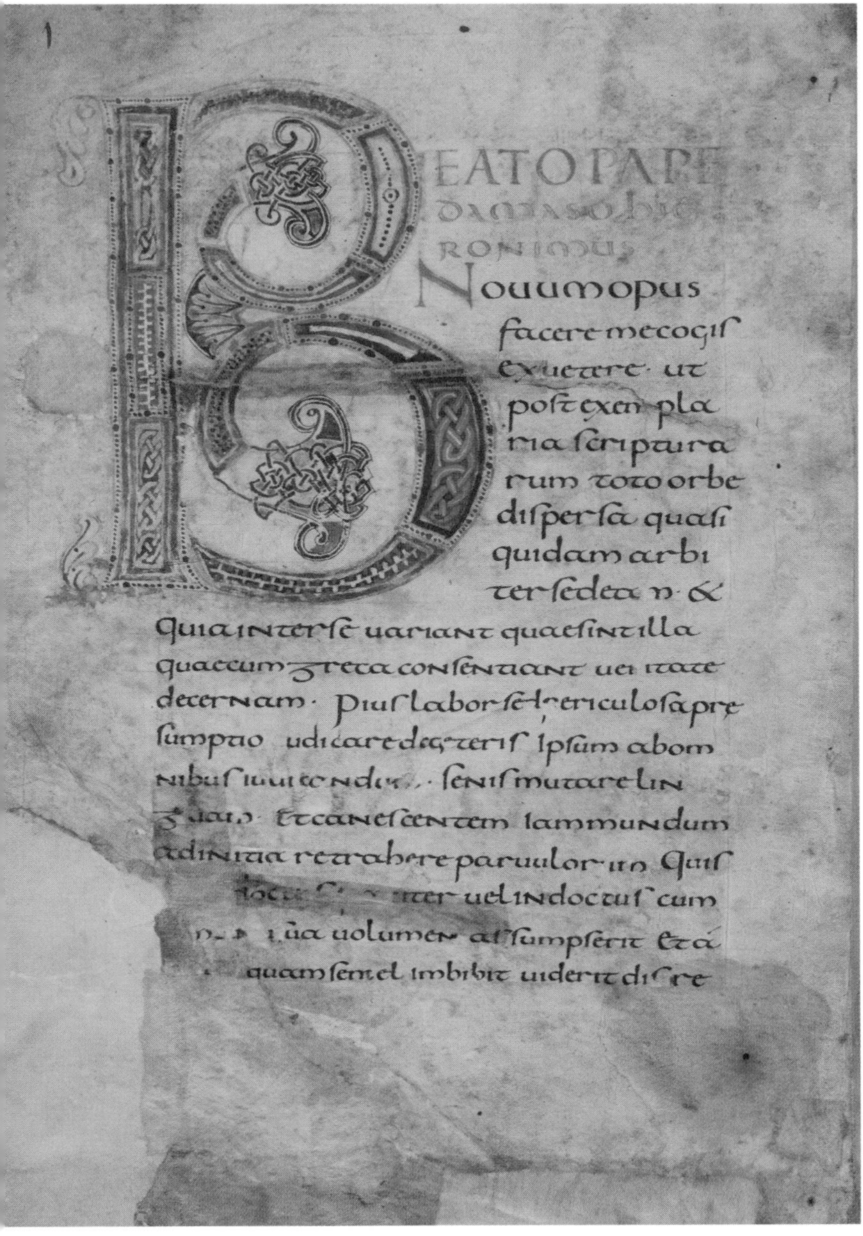

Franco-Saxon artwork with Caroline minuscule script, from a gospel book, 9th century.

than simply text – it embodies the whole ethos of Christianity through the physical object.

DESPITE MUCH of Carolingian artwork emulating the late antique style of the *Vergilius Vaticanus*, there was also a lot of experimentation with layout and design during this period. The Utrecht Psalter (Utrecht, Universiteitsbibliotheek, MS Bibl. Rhenotraiectinae I Nr 32) is a large manuscript written in rustic capitals, interspersed with engaging ink drawings in brown to illustrate the psalms. This format with captivating images within the text gave added depth to the reading experience and demonstrates the innovation and creativity going on at the scriptorium at Reims, France. The penwork gives an impression of action and liveliness. Another manuscript from the same area, the Ebbo Gospels (Épernay, Bibliothèque Municipale, MS I), also demonstrates this style, with figures painted with swift lines in an agitated style, indicating that this movement was part of the artistic heritage at Reims.

Hrabanus Maurus (*c*. 780–856) was an accomplished scholar and pupil of Alcuin's who became abbot of Fulda. Under his direction, the abbey became a cultural hub and a prolific producer of manuscripts. While there, Maurus wrote the poem *In Praise of the Holy Cross*, which was then illustrated in an extraordinary manuscript which embeds the verses in grid systems of letters and looks rather like a wordsearch. Although 'pattern poetry' was not a new thing (this style of wordplay was very popular in late antiquity), the sheer logistics of formatting these word images must have been an absolute headache. The original from Fulda no longer exists, but copies were made of it, including Biblioteca Apostolica Vaticana, Reg. lat. 124, dating from about 840.

BL, Harley MS 647, probably created in Reims circa 820, also combines words and images in an artistic way. It is a copy of

Constellation Centaurus in Hyginus's *Astronomica*, 9th century.

Cicero's translation of the *Aratea* (a poem on the constellations) and each page has the poem written underneath a representation of the constellation in red dots. Even more skilfully, the text from Hyginus's *Astronomica* is combined with the constellations and written in a pattern that forms the shape of the constellation, with some additional paintwork. So, for example, on fol. 12r, the stars of the constellation Centaurus are marked in red dots, and the head, hair, hands and hooves of the centaur are painted, while the shape of his body is filled in with the words of the text. The text is written in red and brown rustic capitals, and the poem underneath is in Caroline minuscule. These examples are to emphasize that working in a scriptorium need not have been a dreary, daily grind. Just think of the imagination and planning that would have gone into producing these word-and-image combinations – and how wonderful it would have been to see your creation come to life.

IN GERMANY, Switzerland and northern and central Italy, Carolingian art (though not its script) was gradually replaced by Ottonian art, named after the rulers of that period. The Ottonian dynasty (919–1024) wanted to emulate the Carolingian support of the arts and were keen patrons of monastic centres of book production. Similar to the Carolingians, the Ottonian movement was based on the Roman style of painting but preferred dramatic posturing and strong bands of colour – particularly purple, which they obtained from the folium plant. The Ottonians also fostered close links with the Byzantines, and in 972 Otto II married the Byzantine princess Theophanu, which led to the influence of Byzantine art on their developing style. The 'Reichenau school' manuscripts – possibly produced at the island monastery of Richenau, or other regions such as Lorsch and Trier – represent the height of this manuscript art. An early example is the Reichenau Epistolary (Fitzwilliam Museum, MS McClean 30) from 960 to 980, with richly decorated pages in purple and turquoise, and gold and silver letters. One of the most sumptuous manuscripts produced in this era was the Pericopes of Henry II (Munich, Bavarian State Library, Clm 4452), a gospel lectionary commissioned by the king for Bamberg Cathedral (1007–12). This beast of a manuscript is heavily adorned with a gold cover inlaid with jewels and Byzantine enamels, with an ivory centrepiece. It measures 42.5 by 32 centimetres and consists of 206 folios. Inside, it is written in a neat Caroline minuscule, spaciously laid out with wide margins. The beautiful, illuminated miniatures take up a whole page each, often unfussily decorated with figures against a generous gold backdrop and plain bands of colour, creating a striking effect. The illuminated initials are filled with swirling foliage and decorated with red, purple and turquoise.

CAROLINE MINUSCULE was the dominant script in Europe well up to the eleventh century, but it took some time to be embraced by English scribes, not really taking hold until the tenth century (whereas Irish scribes largely ignored it and stuck to their Insular script). In England, two different scripts came to be used – Caroline minuscule for Latin and Insular minuscule for Old English.[36] Insular minuscule developed in various ways in England between the ninth and eleventh centuries – first into pointed minuscule, then square minuscule, then round minuscule (and of course there are enormous inconsistencies with the development of each script, it did not go in a straight chronological trajectory). One shining example of Old English script is in the Exeter Book (Exeter Cathedral Library, MS 3501), an anthology of Old English poetry written around 970 by a single scribe. It is possibly the oldest collection of English literature, containing around forty poems and a hundred riddles. Some of the riddles – no. 44 in particular – are dripping with innuendo:

A curious thing hangs by a man's thigh,
under the lap of its lord. In its front it is pierced,
it is stiff and hard, it has a good position.
When the man lifts his own garment
above his knee, he intends to greet
with the head of his hanging object that familiar hole
which is the same length, and which he has often filled
before.[37]

The Exeter Book is immediately identifiable as being in a different language from Latin, even if you are not particularly familiar with either. Crucially, the letters look different. The Old English alphabet contains letters that are different to the Latin alphabet – such as ash (æ), eth (ð), thorn (þ), wynn (ƿ) and yogh (ȝ). The Exeter Book is written in square minuscule (the dominant script in the tenth century) – a boxy script that can be identified by looking closely at the letter *a*. If it looks like a *u* with a horizontal line across the top, then it is probably square minuscule (but as always with sweeping statements about script features, caveats apply).

By the early eleventh century there was a separation of scripts, with an English vernacular minuscule script used for Old English texts and Caroline minuscule for Latin texts. There was an unprecedented amount of literature written in Old English in eleventh-century vernacular minuscule – law texts, homilies, charters, penitentials, poetry, wills – to the extent that it is likely that most scribes were trained in the vernacular script, with only elite scribes also writing in Caroline minuscule. It is difficult to identify any monastic scriptoria writing in a prescribed style of English vernacular minuscule, but centres of manuscript production at Canterbury, Exeter and Worcester bear some features of uniformity.[38] This distinction between Old English and Latin scripts continued after the Norman conquest for a generation or so, but gradually made way for the Romanesque script. We

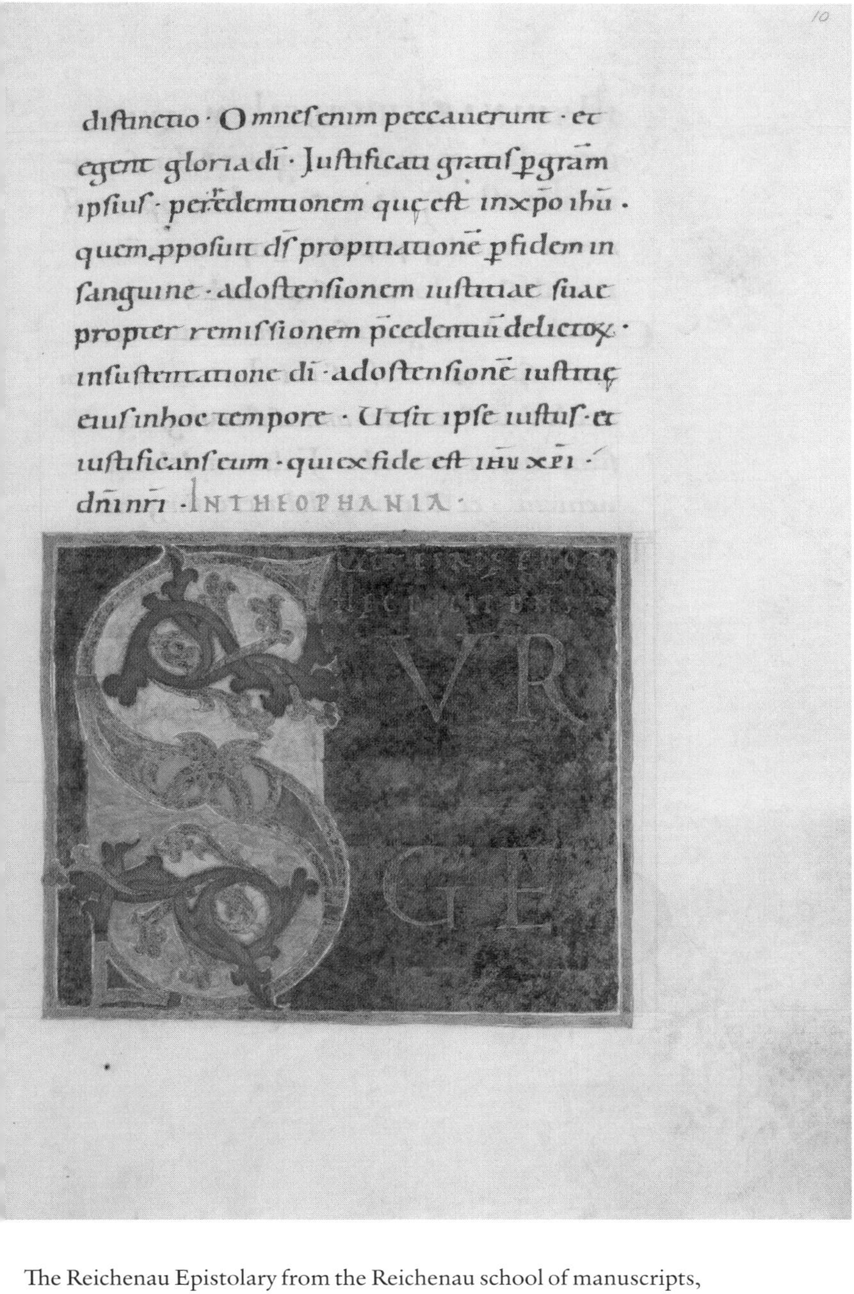

The Reichenau Epistolary from the Reichenau school of manuscripts, 10th century.

can see from this how a script only ever lasts as long as its users – once it stops being taught to training scribes, it dies out after about thirty years. After the conquest, Anglo-Norman became the secondary language to Latin, and vernacular English, while still found in manuscripts, kept a low profile until about the fourteenth century.

Although Caroline minuscule was supposed to be a uniform script across the Christian West, regions such as Ireland and England still managed to keep their own scribal identities. An English Caroline minuscule started to develop in the mid-tenth century, long after it had been enthusiastically adopted on the Continent. Christ Church, Canterbury, operated a particularly slick scriptorium in the tenth and eleventh centuries, producing high-quality manuscripts written in a distinctive round English Caroline minuscule. Notable achievements include the Harley Psalter (BL, Harley MS 603), partly written by the scribe Eadwig Basan, who was probably a monk there circa 1012–23. He can be identified as the sole scribe in several other prestigious manuscripts, such as the Hanover Gospels (Hanover, Kestner-Museum, WM XXIa 36), the Grimbald Gospels (BL, Add MS 34890) and the Eadwig Psalter (BL, Arundel MS 155), as well as contributing to other manuscripts and charters produced at Canterbury. He left a colophon in the Hanover Gospels, 'The monk Eadwig, with the surname Basan, wrote this book,' and it is probable that he was also an illuminator. Clearly, from his involvement in such deluxe illuminated manuscripts, he was a person held in high regard at the Christ Church scriptorium. From about 1050 onwards, this large, rounded English Caroline minuscule was found not just at Canterbury, but at the scriptoria of Exeter, Winchester and Worcester, indicating its reach across England.[39]

ANOTHER PLACE on the periphery of Christian Europe was the Iberian Peninsula, most of which had been under Islamic rule through the early medieval period. However, Christians and Jews had lived relatively peacefully in Al-Andulus (the Muslim-controlled part of the Iberian peninsula) since the eighth century and were able to practise their own religions privately. A fusion of cultures developed – many Iberian Christians adopted the Arabic language and customs, with church architecture incorporating decorative patterns and the horseshoe arch so distinctive of Al-Andulus design (that had actually been adapted from the original Visigothic arch). In manuscripts as well, the horseshoe (or keyhole) arch was depicted in the canon tables, noticeably different to the Roman arches normally seen in canon tables in other Latin manuscripts – compare the tenth-century Biblia Hispalense (Biblioteca Nacional de Madrid, VITR/13/1, fol. 278r) to the tenth-century Ottonian gospel book (BnF, MS Latin 8851, fol. 9r). Manuscripts produced by the Iberian Christians had a distinctive style of their own, developing from their Visigothic roots, and continuing to use the Visigothic script while absorbing the Islamic influences that surrounded them.

THIS CHAPTER has looked at the spread of monasticism and manuscript culture in the early medieval period. It spread from the East to the West, from the desert fathers in Egypt and Judea, via Rome, to the far corners of Ireland – with the Irish missionaries then bringing it back again to the heart of Europe. Cassiodorus's Vivarium painted an attractive image of a scriptorium against the lush backdrop of the Italian mountains, which although unlikely to have been replicated throughout the Western monasteries, did at least represent the importance of the scriptorium to the monastic ideal. By the seventh century there were houses following the Benedictine rule, reciting the psalms at regular intervals and producing manuscripts that still survive today. Monastic centres such as Monte Cassino and Bobbio flourished, and became intellectual and cultural hubs, attracting the sons and daughters of royals and nobles (and as a result increasing their social standing and financial streams). After the work of the Irish missionaries in the sixth and seventh centuries, new monasteries were founded in Britain and Francia, with the Irish scribes leading the development of manuscript innovation. They created a unique script and decoration that still amazes today in its intricacy and symbolic layers. Regional scripts were developing, showing real creativity and experimentation with letterforms and decoration (some more successfully than others). Following the boom of book development in Britain and Ireland, the Carolingian empire then rose up to take the mantle, developing a script that would be adopted widely throughout Europe (although Monte Cassino, Ireland and Iberia held onto their own cultural influences). In the later centuries of the first millennium, scriptoria settled into a routine, firmly established within the monastic domain and confident in using script and decoration. Well-funded monasteries, such as Canterbury in England and Tours in France, produced ever more sumptuous volumes, expanding their palettes and artistic skills to create illuminated manuscripts of staggering beauty. There was a constant ebb and flow of cultural influences on manuscript development, blending Germanic, Irish, English and Frankish styles together. We will now depart from the development of the monastery and scriptorium in tandem and narrow our focus to just the scriptorium. We will look at what evidence we do have for scriptoria, including archaeological remains, images in manuscripts and written testaments.

Three

Locus Scribendi – The Place of Writing

A French convent in the tenth century

The Librarian slips away unnoticed from the choir as her fellow sisters sing Benedictus Dominus. With the harmony of their voices in her ears, she steps silently from the abbey into the cool stone of the north cloister. Plunged into stillness, she observes the motes of dust caught by the early morning sun and feels the energy of a new day. She strides purposefully towards the wooden cupboards lined up against the cloister wall, her hand automatically reaching for the keys hanging from her belt. Approaching the smallest cupboard, she noiselessly unlocks the door and it swings open, revealing the treasures within. Stacks of cut parchment fill the top shelf, with quills, ink, knives, dividers, rulers, pumice stones and gum sandarac on the middle shelf. The lower shelf is for the painters and illuminators, with paintbrushes, earthenware jars of coloured pigments and shells of powdered gold.

She breathes in deeply, inhaling the heady combination of parchment and ink that has accumulated overnight within the stock cupboard. She makes a mental note to request more calfskin from the local parchment maker, and to check it carefully this time. The last batch had too many holes, either from insect bites inflicted on the live animal, or from careless treatment of the skin while it was being prepared. The sisters had to be skilful in selecting the right parchment to ensure they could hide the holes in the book gutter or write around it without too much distortion of the text. The sound of the sisters moving through to the chapter house filters through, and she rouses herself to start setting the room up for the morning's work. She has special permission from the abbess to miss the morning prayers and chapter, so she must not use this time idly. For many years, since she started as a young novice, she had longed to hold the position of Librarius and be responsible for looking after the books belonging to the house. Last year, by the graciousness of God and the mother abbess, she had been given the keys to the book cupboards after the untimely death of Sister Agnes. Now every day she makes sure that all the books are issued and returned safely, and kept in good condition. She also looks after the materials for the scribes, ensuring that there is a regular supply of parchment and ink, and that the sisters only take the tools they need for the day. A large commission has come in from the bishop, who has asked the abbess to supply five new copies of the gospels to be gifted to his new patrons. Although her sisters at the abbey are highly skilled, this is an onerous task, and her days are now filled checking the work of the scribes.

A young lay sister hurries breathlessly from the kitchen, ready to assist with putting out the scribal materials. The Librarian smiles kindly at her, and between them they silently lay out the instruments on the wooden desks that run along the garden side of the cloister wall. Once the lay sister has placed the inkwells on each desk, the Librarian takes a large flask from the cupboard, removes the wooden stopper and carefully fills each well with ink. A small pile of ruled parchment is placed on each desk. When they have finished, she checks each desk again to make sure everything is ready for the scribes and painters. The scribes have parchment, quills, a knife for sharpening and erasing mistakes, pumice to smooth the surface, a pot of ink, sand to absorb the wet ink and a cloth for wiping those inky fingers. The painters have their dried pigments ready in oyster shells to be rewetted, with brushes and water on a shelf underneath, away from the parchment. The illuminator, in a sheltered area at the end of the cloister, has her shells full of ground gold, her dogtooth burnisher and some sticky egg glair. The weather is starting to turn and there is a chill in the air, so the Librarian lights several braziers that line the stone wall. This would normally be a luxury only allowed on very cold days, but as the bishop is furnishing them with extra materials and firewood for the quick completion of the gospels, she does not skimp on providing the hardworking scribes with comfort. She knows only too well the aches and pains that scribes suffer, hunched over a desk all day until your hand cramps and your muscles are calling out for relief. Her years as a scribe at the abbey eventually earned her the position as Librarian, but she does not let herself forget the tedium of copying out texts all day. She makes sure the scribes have regular breaks and sustenance, and in return, the sisters work diligently and graciously.

The Librarian and the lay sister suddenly hear the women filing out of the chapter house. In a moment the ones destined for the scriptorium will filter through and sit at their desks to start the morning's work, grumbling quietly that their quills are too soft, or that mice have been nibbling at the parchment overnight, before settling down to create beautiful letters and images as their prayer to God. The lay sister is dismissed with a nod of the head from the Librarian and slips away, unnoticed by the sisters already lost in an air of concentration. The Librarian takes up her seat at the end of the cloister near the book cupboards, ready to assist any scribe in difficulty, or to reprimand anyone else entering the area while the sisters are working. Taking up the top batch from the neat pile of quires written by the sisters the day before, she opens a copy of the gospels, finds the right page, and starts meticulously checking the texts.

So far on our journey we have established that writing down and disseminating religious texts was a vital part of the early Christian movement. The codex was regarded as a physical

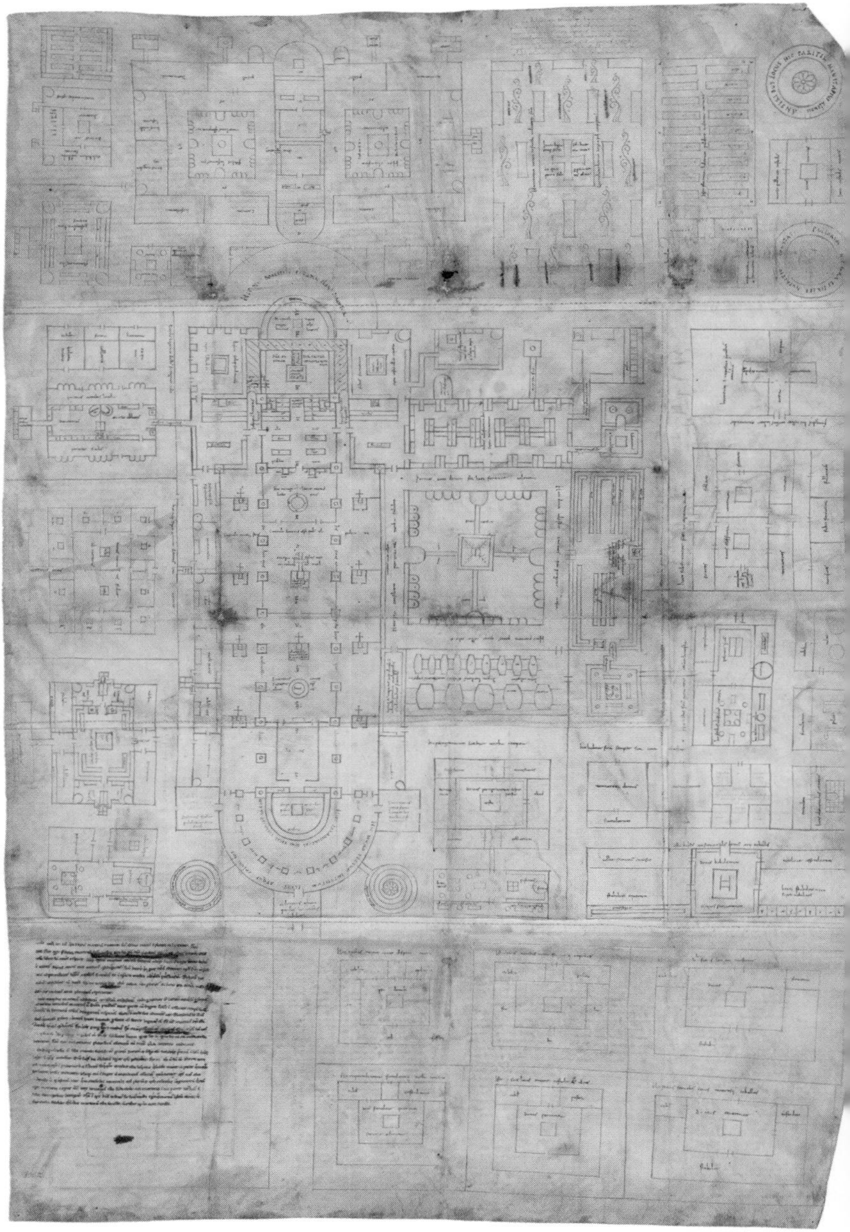

Monastery plan from St Gall, 9th century.

manifestation of the word of God and decorated accordingly with bright colours, precious metals and jewels. We know that the *Rule of St Benedict*, which became the standard monastic order in the early medieval period, encouraged reading and studying as a daily activity. Cassiodorus wrote about his physical scriptorium at Vivarium, his idyllic retreat in the Italian mountains, where the scribes were equipped with a water clock and excellent lighting. We have, most importantly, the physical evidence of scriptorium output – with thousands of surviving medieval manuscripts bearing testament to the extraordinary skill and dedication of monastic scribes.

Yet we still lack the archaeological and pictorial evidence of a monastic scriptorium – the actual room and its contents. In this chapter, we will look at how scriptoria were depicted and described by the medieval people themselves. The best source we have, and the one probably most responsible for our modern-day interpretation of a scriptorium, is a monastery plan held at the library of St Gall Abbey in Switzerland with a labelled room for the scribes (St Gallen, Stiftsbibliothek, Cod. Sang. 1092). The abbey was named after Gallus, one of Columbanus's twelve companions who left Bangor in the sixth century to follow him to the Continent on *peregrinatio*, according to his hagiography. On the journey, Gallus fell behind with illness, and subsequently settled as a hermit in Alemannia where he died circa 646. Shortly after, he became venerated as a saint, with a church established on the site of his hermit cell. This church became the abbey of St Gall in the eighth century and was an important centre of art, science and culture, with a renowned library and scriptorium (and much of its manuscript collection survives intact today). The abbey retained strong links with Ireland, and there are many examples of Insular script from the library of St Gall, indicating the flow of monks and manuscripts from Ireland to the Continent.

This surviving library collection also includes a unique floorplan of an unspecified Benedictine monastery compound, including the church, cloister, workshops, livestock pens, infirmary, guest accommodation and kitchens. It was made around 820–30 on five pieces of parchment stitched together, measuring 112 by 77.5 centimetres. The orderly grid lines are drawn in red ink and labelled (in Caroline minuscule, as we would expect for the time) in brown ink. It is unclear whether it was intended as an actual architectural blueprint for a monastery intended to be built, or whether this just represented an ideal vision of the perfect monastic compound, but it is an extraordinary view of monastic life and very much in keeping with the Carolingian vision of order and uniformity.

As tempting as it is to go down a rabbit hole and explore all the different areas, for our purposes we are looking at a rectangular building attached to the top left of the church on the plan. It is labelled *Infra sedes scribentium, supra bibliotheca* (Below, the seats for the scribes, above, the library). Looks like we've found an official scriptorium! In the plan, there are seven desks shown, running along the north and east walls, with a window in between each desk to maximize the light. The position of these windows would diffuse the glare from the sun as it travelled from east to west throughout the day and they were probably glazed – a luxury but a necessity.[1] There is a large square desk in the centre of the room, and long benches along the south and western walls. The central desk has been supposed to be the store cupboard for books and possibly materials, with the benches for the supervisor and resting scribes. The presence of desks implies that the scribes were working at writing tables, rather than using wooden lap boards, although it's possible that the scribes would be writing on lap boards on the benches and the artists would be painting at the desks. One might argue that light would be even more important to the artists than to the scribes. On this plan, only 'seats for the scribes' are labelled, so we have no idea whether painting and illumination was expected to be done in this area.

Although this plan is not of a monastery that we can identify today, it does give a good idea of the self-contained and self-sufficient community within the monastic walls. It demonstrates the separation of the monks from the outside world, but also how much support was needed to maintain their lifestyle. Apart from the odd overseas pigment import, this map shows that everything needed to create an illuminated manuscript was there on site. There are livestock – so a scribe would have a choice of sheep, goat or calf parchment, and geese to provide the quills. Pigments such as weld, madder and indigo could be grown in the gardens, kermes (a red pigment) harvested from crushed insects, eggshells ground to make chalk, and lead white, red lead, verdigris and vermilion manufactured in the workshops. Bookbinding materials such as book boards, leather straps and covers could be obtained from the wood turners and leather workers. What an amazing thing to be able to produce something that came almost wholly from your community, through so much combined skill and effort. It is almost incomprehensible to us today that something made up of so many diverse materials could be transformed into something so captivating as an illuminated manuscript, with many of those materials potentially coming from within a few minutes' walk of the scriptorium. The animals that made the parchment and the plants that made the pigments were part of their daily landscape, creating a deep-rooted connection to the natural world. They may have seen the animals raised from birth, or planted the seeds and watched them grow. If the completed manuscript stayed in the monastery, turning those folios must have been an incredibly intimate experience, evoking their communal memories of past scribes and firmly centring them to their community. While the plan of St Gall is an ideal, it is not so far removed from the on-site facilities that we can still see traces of today in monastic remains. For example, Bury St Edmunds had cowsheds, a brewery and a granary, Waltham Abbey had a forge, and Rievaulx Abbey had a tannery and a fulling mill. Practical duties were probably carried out by lay brothers and sisters – members of the monastic community from the lower social classes who performed the manual tasks. Although most lay workers were illiterate, they could be highly skilled artisans, which freed up the monastics to spend more time at prayer or study. Yet it must be noted that the only definite location we have of a scriptorium on a monastic plan is the one from St Gall – which seems to be an ideal. The room is not even referred to as a 'scriptorium', but the seating area for the scribes.

However, a tenth-century monk at St Gall called Ekkehard IV wrote a chronicle of the monastery called *Casus S. Galli*, noting that it was the custom for three of the senior monks 'with the permission of the Prior, to meet in the scriptorium during the interval of Lauds at night' (*permissu quidem prioris, in intervallo laudum nocturno convenire in scriptorio*) – here specifically referring to a 'scriptorium'. So, this tells us there was a designated area in the abbey grounds to produce manuscripts. Another stray comment later suggests that the scriptorium was near the warming room (*et proximum pyrani scriptorium*).[2] It's just a pity that no archaeological evidence remains for its exact location, and these crumbs don't give us much to go on, considering the large amount of monasteries in existence in the medieval period.

SO, WHAT ABOUT IMAGES of scribes in the manuscripts? Unfortunately, we don't see many scribes writing together – they tend to be shown as solitary figures.[3] In Bible manuscripts, the four evangelists are quite understandably shown individually, preceding their gospel book. The Hamburg Bible (Copenhagen, Royal Library, MS GKS 4 folio (I–III) features

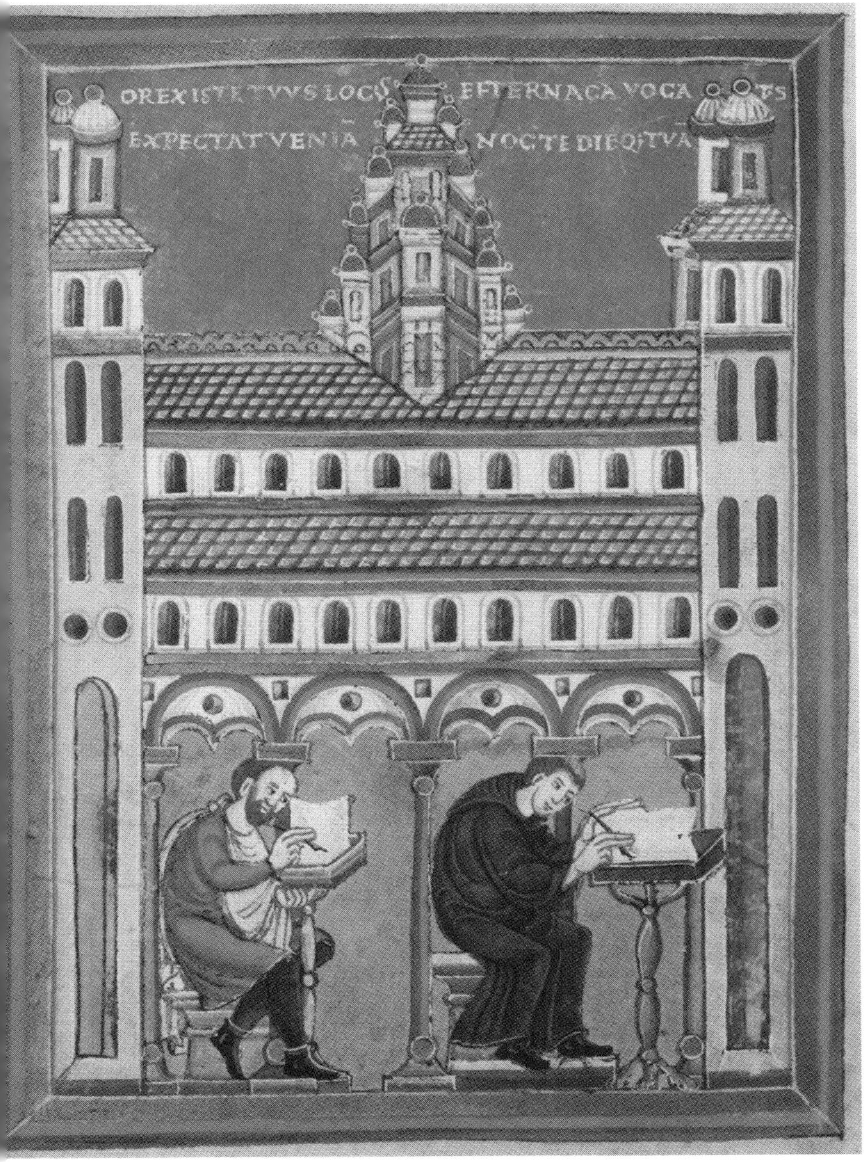

A secular and a monastic scribe working together at Echternach, *Pericopes of Emperor Henry III*, 11th century.

images of saints Jerome and Paul engaging in various aspects of book production, including purchasing parchment from a layperson, but all the scribal activity is shown in solitary surroundings. 'Ordinary' religious scribes (who weren't saints or evangelists) are also shown alone, for example, the monk-scribe copying from an exemplar (Saint-Omer, Bibliothèque municipale, MS 287, fol. 1r), or the serene image of Sister Elsbeth Stagel about to write on ruled parchment from a fifteenth-century manuscript (Nürnberg, Stadtbibliothek, Cent v. 10a, fol. 3ra). Some are even more relaxed, as one thirteenth-century manuscript shows the monk Guillaume from Saint-Martin de Tournai sitting up in bed making notes on a tablet, surrounded by open books and looking very cosy in his single cell (Bibliothèque Mazarine, MS 753, fol. 9r).

Cambridge, Trinity College, MS R.17.1 is a twelfth-century manuscript known as the Eadwine Psalter, after the chief scribe involved in its production. Fol. 283v shows a full-page portrait of a monk-scribe working alone on a manuscript, his tonsured head leaning over the open book with quill and knife in each hand. The portrait of the scribe Eadwine is framed with the following inscription: 'I am the chief of scribes . . . whose genius the beauty of this book demonstrates' – although this manuscript was created through the collaboration of many scribes and artists. It seems rather unfair to have just Eadwine visualized and celebrated for this remarkable codex – but it's unlikely this is a self-portrait and colophon by Eadwine himself, rather a later commemoration to Eadwine as the organizer of this manuscript project. This manuscript also contains a fascinating plan of the plumbing system at Christ Church, Canterbury. Although it does not include the main cathedral, the detail of the cloisters and monastic buildings gives no indication of a separate scriptorium, which again suggests that writing was not done in a specific room. Unlike the plan from St Gall's, this plan is a real-life working model of a monastery, and the lack of a labelled scriptorium is significant.

There are a handful of images showing scribes in close proximity to each other in manuscripts, but we do not know how accurate they are in depicting a 'typical' scriptorium. They often show monks and laypeople working together, perhaps to emphasize that this was an important manuscript that involved the collaboration of scribes and skilled artists.[4] Yet the monastic compound was traditionally forbidden to laypeople, even when working on the same project, so perhaps we should regard these images as representation rather than real life. You can usually tell a monk from a layperson by their dress: monks wore robes and had tonsured heads, while laypeople normally wore tunics with either bare heads or a close-fitting coif (see Bremen, Universitätsbibliothek, MS 217). Another image from a tenth-century manuscript shows the Spanish monastery of San Salvador de Tábara with a small area for the senior scribe and his assistant, with another assistant cutting parchment in a separate room (Madrid, Nat. Hist. Archaeological Museum, Cod. 1097 B).[5] It all looks a bit rickety and makeshift, not the spacious and well-set-out image that the plan of St Gall conjures up. A charming image from Copenhagen, Royal Library, GKS 4 folio III, fol. 142v shows haloed saints Paul and Timothy sitting together and working collaboratively, with Paul in the process of sharpening his quill while Timothy rubs pumice over some parchment, though their surroundings are undefined.

The best image we have of a (possible) scriptorium is a fourteenth-century Spanish manuscript that shows a seated monk facing two other figures, all at angled desks with parchment and scribal tools in hand (Madrid, Biblioteca de San Lorenzo de El Escorial, fol. IV). However, the person seated at the back is not religious, judging by his clothes and hair, and the middle person, while dressed plainly and possibly with a tonsure, is not in full

Three figures seated in an apparent scriptorium, from Alfonso x's *Book of Games*, late 13th century.

monastic garb. Perhaps this is a depiction of a classroom rather than a scriptorium – but it seems like the closest image we have to a group of scribes in a communal setting. It is interesting to note that the use of pillars here to separate the figures does very much resemble a medieval cloister, and analysis of other images of scribes often reveals them framed within an arch with two pillars either side – again suggesting a cloister. A particularly good image is Cambridge, St John's College, MS A.8, fol.103v, with a monk-scribe called Samuel copying from an exemplar held by Josephus, the Jewish historian. In the background there is a row of columns that immediately calls to mind a cloister. This is not a ground-breaking discovery – the cloister area was used for teaching novices, so it is just as likely to have been used for reading and writing, and there are numerous medieval written records that support this. The monastic cloister was a continuous covered walkway in a square that had evolved from the peristyles and atriums of classical architecture. It was often attached to the south wall of the abbey or cathedral, with columns surrounding a garden in the centre. The cloister was a space permitted only for monastic inhabitants, and it acted as a physical and metaphorical gateway to the outside world, as the religious members had to pass through the cloister to go to church, and again to return to their spiritual life.

THE MYTHOLOGY OF the 'scriptorium' persists, perhaps because so many people buy into it. Idealized plans and stray comments about 'warming rooms' for scribes become received wisdom and form the basis of the mythology of the monastic scriptorium. We have noted the lack of archaeological evidence and the dearth of images of a scriptorium/writing room, but what did the medieval religious people say about where they produced their books? Let us first turn to an early Irish account of writing. This manuscript (St Gall, Cod. Sang. 904) is a copy of a Latin grammar text, written in Ireland circa 845. The manuscript text is peppered with Irish glosses – notes in the margins that expand or explain the main Latin text. The scribe has added a note over the bottom of two pages that reads (translated from Irish):

> all around me greenwood trees
> I hear blackbird verse on high
> quavering lines on vellum leaves
> birdsong pours down from the sky over and above
> the wood
> the blue cuckoo chants to me
> dear Lord thank you for your word
> I write well beneath the trees.[6]

What a wonderfully atmospheric description. It paints a picture of an idyllic setting with the scribe writing outdoors, communing with nature and God, slightly reminiscent of the bucolic scenes at Cassiodorus's Vivarium. However, there are practical factors to be considered. Ireland, unlike southern Italy, is not known for its balmy climate. Writing outdoors would only be possible in the warmer months, and even then the frequent rain and wind would still cause problems. Also, anyone that has ever worked under a tree would tell you that all sorts of things fall out of trees when you're sitting underneath them – leaves, insects, bird poo and so on. Although we shouldn't entirely doubt this scribe's idyllic description of a particular day's work, it seems unlikely that working outdoors under trees was the normal everyday practice for scribes – certainly in the northwestern part of the Christian world.

Later medieval accounts broadly refer to working in the cloister. *Narratio Herimanni*, an account of Odo, the early eleventh-century abbot of Tournai, includes this description: 'he [Odo] greatly encouraged the writing of books and used to rejoice that the Lord had provided him with so many scribes. If you had gone into the cloister, you might in general have seen a dozen young monks sitting on chairs in perfect silence, writing at tables, carefully and skilfully constructed.'[7] It sounds lovely! Furthermore, a stray remark from the historian Eadmer of Canterbury (*c.* 1060–*c.* 1126) records how he was 'sitting in the cloister one day, as usual, busy with the book I was writing'.[8]

Another French source, *Liber ordinis Sancti Victoris Parisiensis* was written in the early twelfth century under the guidance of the abbot Gilduin. St Victor's was a house of regular canons, meaning that the house followed the *Rule of St Augustine*, a looser rule which combined the regular monastic lifestyle with the duties of priests. Houses of this kind were often city- or town-based and integrated much more with the local community. This flexibility grew in popularity after the eleventh century and many Augustine houses were founded, with book production still an essential part of their lifestyle. The *Liber* outlines the customs followed at the Abbey of St Victor, Paris, adhering to the *Rule of St Augustine* but tailored to their own community.

The *Liber* provides some great details about scribal practice. Chapter 19, describing the duties for the office of the librarian (*librarius/armarius*), says:

> Fixed places for this work [writing] are to be arranged apart from the community, but within the cloister, where the writers can concentrate more quietly on their work without disturbance or noise. Those sitting and working there should carefully stay silent and not wander about idly. No one should go to them except the Abbot, Prior, Sub-Prior and Librarian etc.[9]

It goes on to say:

> To all writers in the cloister, whether those who are ordered or those who are permitted to write, let the librarian furnish everything necessary, so that no one chose at his pleasure this or that, neither writing location, nor quill knife, nor scalpel, nor parchment, nor anything else, but let all take without refusal or objection what he shall give as proper for the work.[10]

It's worth mentioning that the monastic 'library' often did not actually mean a room full of books, as we would think today, but referred to the book chest (or *armarium*) that contained the books (as we saw in the Ezra image of the *Codex Amiatinus*). Sometimes the book chest may have simply been a recess carved into a wall in the cloister. Another medieval source, a customary from Barnwell Abbey, tells us the book cupboard:

> ought to be lined inside with wood, that the damp of the walls may not moisten or stain the books. The cupboard should be divided vertically as well as horizontally by sundry

> shelves on which the books may be ranged so as to be separated from one another; for fear they be packed so close as to injure each other or delay those who want them.[11]

The lining of the interior with wood suggests the book cupboard here is indeed cut into the stone wall. So, the hunt for a 'library' and a 'scriptorium' as separate physical places may be fruitless, as they could easily have been incorporated into the general daily activity in the cloister. In the St Victor and Barnwell accounts, the librarian's responsibility for the books is heavily emphasized – the *armarius* (or *librarius/precentor*) oversees loaning out books and making sure they are returned in a suitable condition. The librarian is also responsible for the maintenance of the books, regularly inspecting them to make sure they are free from bookworm and other damage. The Barnwell customary also highlights that the librarian is responsible for mending and binding books (*per librarian libri debent emendari . . . honeste ligari*).[12]

Some important evidence comes from two English Benedictine customaries describing the 'carrels in the cloister' (a carrel is an individual study room or cell, which some libraries still have today). The thirteenth- and fourteenth-century customaries from Westminster and Canterbury make it clear that the scribes, illuminators and those adding musical notations have priority in using the carrels – they are 'not for the use of any brother, except for the ones writing, illuminating or adding musical notes'.[13] What a wonderful snippet of information – not only is the cloister described as having individual study rooms called carrels, but they were used specifically for writing and illuminating. These isolated booths would be especially useful for the illuminators, who would want complete stillness while working with gold leaf.

The *Rites of Durham* expand on the cloister set-up. This late sixteenth-century anonymous account is a somewhat wistful recollection of the monastic customs that were in place at

Durham before the Reformation erased them. It describes the north wall of the cloister (most abbeys had the cloister attached to the south wall, so the northern walkway would have been the most sheltered side) with wooden carrels by every window, where the monks sat to study, with a desk to put their books on. The north cloister windows were 'finely glazed' and had a wooden ceiling, which allows a visual image to start forming of religious members working in enclosed wooden cells in cloisters, with the light coming in through the window onto their wooden desks. Although this only refers to study rather than writing, it's reasonable to assume that the library and scriptorium (as entities) worked closely together. The writer of this text also refers to the wooden cupboards that stood against the north wall 'all full of bookes'.[14] A transcription from a lost manuscript belonging to Abingdon monastery mentions that the carrels in the cloister and the book cupboard had their locks broken when the abbey was

Stone carrels carved into the cloister of Gloucester Cathedral, late 14th/early 15th century.

attacked in 1327, so as well as further evidence for the location of carrels, we also learn that they and the book cupboards were locked when not in use.[15]

There is physical evidence to back up the existence of carrels – the cloisters at Gloucester cathedral have a magnificent row of twenty stone-carved study carrels along the south walkway (because here the cloisters were unusually built on the north side of the abbey to make the most of the water supply). Each carrel measures approximately 120 centimetres wide and 50 centimetres deep, with two small windows. It is easy to imagine the monks seated at wooden desks, here facing towards the eastern cloister, clean parchment in front of them and a freshly sharpened quill in hand, ready to dip into their inkwell. It would make sense to be facing east in this particular cloister, to allow the right-handed scribes more movement on their writing side. The light gently diffuses through the windows, and the stone creates a cocooning effect when sitting inside the carrel. They are open on the right side and there are no markings on the stonework to indicate where a door once hung, but perhaps there would have been heavy drapes to divide the booth from the cloister walkway. Like the glazed windows at Durham, these cloisters are enclosed, which must have been a blessed relief to the poor scribes writing here during cold spells – although some red staining on the stonework suggests that the Gloucester monks might also have had braziers to provide some extra heating.

Other scribes weren't so lucky as to be kept warm in a cosy carrel, as a monk from Ramsey Abbey in Huntingdon scribbles down in the margin: 'As we sit here in tempest, in rain, snow and sun, No writing or reading in cloister is done.'[16] This paints a much more realistic image of real life in a draughty monastery than the Irish monk sitting beneath his tree in the sunshine! An account from Anglo-Norman chronicler Orderic Vitalis (1075–*c.* 1142) suggests that he also worked in a cloister that was subject to the elements. When he comes to the end of his fourth volume of his *Ecclesiastical History*, he tells us that he is so cold he is stopping for the winter and will resume in the spring:

> now, numbed by the winter cold, I turn to other pursuits; and, weary with toil, resolve to end my present book here. When the warmth of sweet spring returns I will relate in the following books everything that I have only briefly touched upon, or omitted altogether.[17]

There seems to be enough evidence gathered here from visual and written sources in manuscripts, and surviving monastic architecture, to name the cloister as the location for the production of manuscripts. Here was a place where scribes and illuminators could be supervised, but still separated into isolated booths to allow for concentration. Yes, it would have been cold, particularly in the winter months in the monasteries of northwest Europe, but as cloisters developed, so they became more enclosed, as at Gloucester and Durham. There would have been the opposite problem in southern Europe where the blistering summer sun beat down unrelentingly, and the cloisters would no doubt have offered some welcome shade. These accounts also give us an important insight into the logistics of the scriptorium. The librarian oversaw scribal equipment and keeping the cupboard stocked with the necessary equipment – which presumably would have been a cupboard similar to the *armarium* (book cupboard) and located nearby. Although the ones at Gloucester are stone, carrels would probably have been wooden and furnished with wooden desks and stools, which is probably why there is so little remaining evidence for them. Scribes and illuminators seem to have had priority use of the carrels, as they made such ideal spaces for working without disturbance. Silence was expected in this area, with no one wandering idly around. This patchwork of accounts, customaries and stray bits of information pieces together a solid case for medieval monastic inhabitants using the cloisters for their scriptorium.

So, time to put the traditional image of a scriptorium – based on the idealized plan from St Gall – to one side and create a new one, set in the cloisters. Imagine a monk or nun on a wooden stool, bent over a wooden desk. They have a window to their left-hand side, looking out onto the cloister garden. They are in a wooden study room, with an ink pot, parchment, quill and knife to hand. The muffled and echoey sounds and smells of monastic life drift through to the scribes – the clatter of food being prepared in the kitchen and the distant chanting of students reciting the psalms, the delicate aroma of rosemary, thyme and lavender from the cloister garden. They write methodically, with concentration and diligence, with the soft light of the day filtering through their window. Every now and again, they lift their heads and refocus their strained eyes on the soothing colours in the cloister garden. It is probably quite cold, but perhaps there are extra clothing allowances, or braziers glowing. In another carrel, an illuminator also works silently, expertly removing a sheet of gold from a leather pouch attached to their belt. Carefully poised over the already-scribed manuscript, the illuminator quickly prepares the adhesive surface before skilfully laying down the gold leaf – gently, smoothly, deftly. In the end carrel, a painter carefully adds colour to a large decorated initial B. The acanthus leaves form concentric rings in the bowls of the letter, with delicate interlace decorating the finials. With a skilful hand, the painter finishes with lead white highlights that bring the art to life.

THE CLOISTER WOULD seem a fitting location for those orders that lived communally – but what about the orders who lived in a single cell, emulating the hermit lifestyle of the early Christians in the desert? Some early Irish monks had their own beehive cells to live and work in, and Columba had his own cell on Iona. The later medieval Carthusian order also preferred to live in small individual rooms leading off from a central cloister, in a community of shared solitude. These individual monastic cells often consisted of two or three separate living areas for working, praying, eating and sleeping. Here, the monks would have produced manuscripts in their own cells. From the twelfth-century *Consuetudines of Guigo I*, written as a guide to the new order, we know that Carthusian monks were permitted writing materials in their cells, including inkwells, knives, tablets and styli. On Sundays, when they gathered together in the cloister, they could stock up on ink, quills and parchment from the sacristan, along with new books to transcribe.[18]

Even scribes in communal houses could have had private offices if they were important enough. Nicholas of Clairvaux was secretary to Bernard of Clairvaux (1090–1153), the key figure in the founding of the Cistercian order. Nicholas writes of his *scriptoriolium*, his little writing cell. Describing his private office with the cloisters to the right, where the learned monks study, and the infirmary to the left, his small room

> is pleasant to the feelings and delightful to the eyes and soothing to withdraw to. It is full of the choicest godly books, in the sweet contemplation of which I learn to despise the vanity of the world . . . This cell has been given to me for reading, for writing, for composing, for contemplation, for praying and adoring the God of majesty.[19]

He also refers to this writing cell as *domunculam* (little house). Of course, the abbot or abbess of a house would have had their own office to write in and conduct their daily affairs, and one imagines that respected scholars such as Matthew Paris at St Albans or Abelard of France would have had the kudos to command their own private working space. As with all things to do with monasteries, there is no hard and fast rule, and arrangements would have depended on the size, wealth and status of the house, as well as the religious order and even the individual preferences of the abbot or abbess and patrons of the house. Demand for manuscripts ebbed and flowed, so it was perhaps not worth dedicating a whole room in the compound to a fluctuating market.

However, St Albans does indeed seem to have had a dedicated room, mentioned in the *Deeds of the Abbots of the Monastery of St Albans*, a manuscript compiled by Matthew Paris (*c.* 1200–1259), the famous chronicler and scribe of the abbey. In 1077, shortly after the Norman conquest, Paul of Caen was appointed abbot of St Albans. In the *Deeds*, Abbot Paul is described as a lover of the written word (*scripturarum amatore*) and it's noted that he built a scriptorium at the abbey for the writing of books (*construxit scriptorio libros praelectos scribi fecit*). The scribes were chosen from afar (presumably from Paul's homeland of Normandy) and were to receive a daily ration of food.[20] This would imply that these were hired scribes, not monks trained on site at St Albans. This was not unusual – often secular scribes and artists were hired to assist with manuscript production. The customary from Barnwell also stated that one of the librarian's jobs was to 'personally hire those who write for money'.[21] Nobles and royalty would always need clerks for administrative purposes, so there would have been clerical scribes around for hire. Perhaps Paul had a scriptorium built to accommodate his secular manuscript makers away from the cloistered area.

There are further references to the scriptorium (and it should be noted that this text actually uses the word 'scriptorium'), as it apparently had fallen into disrepair by the time Simon became abbot in 1167, so he had it repaired and enlarged: *scriptorium quoque, tunc temporis fere dissipatum et contemptum, reparavit* (He also repaired the writing room, which at that time was run-down and disregarded).[22] He also insisted that the scriptorium should have one 'special writer' (*scriptorem specialem*) permanently installed at the expense of the abbot, which could again suggest a hired scribe rather than a monastic inhabitant. Thomas Walsingham, who compiled the later section of the *Deeds*, described himself as precentor and *scriptorarius* (head of the writing room), who supervised the building of a new writing house (*domus scriptoriae*), funded by the abbot Thomas de la Mare (1349–1396).[23] Walsingham also bought, wrote and repaired books to furnish the library of the monastery and the library of the scriptorium. However, as there are no archaeological remains to indicate where this scriptorium was, it is probably unwise to start dreaming again about the 'traditional' scriptorium. While St Albans does apparently refer to a designated building for the production of manuscripts, there is precious little evidence from other European medieval monasteries. Demand for manuscripts was not consistent throughout the medieval period, centres of book production rose to prominence and faded again as the supply was met, so why build a permanent room to cater to such a fickle market? And long-standing monasteries would have been renovated and updated when funds permitted, with older foundations destroyed and new layouts constructed. Although we are wedded to the word 'scriptorium' for writing room, various monastic accounts show that other terms were interchangeable, such as *domus scriptoriae* (writing house), *domunculam* (little house), *locus scribendi* (the place of writing) and *scriptorium* (writing desk). But what we can be sure of from these accounts is that the monasteries took book production seriously and considered the copying of texts a monastic responsibility.

SO, WHAT HAVE WE LEARNT about the 'scriptorium'? Did it exist? Well, sort of. There were definitely 'writing areas' – probably in the cloister, sometimes in separated booths. The term 'scriptorium' is a loose definition, which probably meant different things to different monasteries. Perhaps we are looking at it the wrong way and should approach it from a more metaphysical angle. In a sermon recorded in a twelfth-century manuscript from Durham, the close spiritual connection between manuscript production and God is carefully detailed (DCL, MS B.IV.12, fol. 38r). It had long been accepted that writing was a form of prayer for a monastic scribe, but this sermon portrays the many different aspects of manuscript production as an allegorical relationship with God. The text begins by considering how we may become scribes of the Lord, describing the creamy parchment as representative of our pure conscience, written on by the quill of memory. Furthermore:

> the knife that shaves the parchment removes the sin and vice from our conscience, the pumice that smooths the parchment also takes away our vain and idle thoughts, and the fine chalk that whitens the parchment makes our conscience bright. The ruler for drawing lines represents the will of God, and the lead stick guided by the ruler represents our devotion to the holy work. The quill, split in two for writing, stands for the love of God and our neighbours, and the ink is humility itself, which is at the centre of every holy work. The array of colours used to illuminate the manuscript depicts the grace and light of heavenly wisdom, and the writing desk (*scriptorium*) represents the tranquillity of the heart, where we record all our good deeds. The exemplar we must copy is the life of our redeemer. The place where we write (*locus scribendi*) is beyond the worldly realm (*contemptus mundi*), our

aspirations are elevated from the low ground to the summit of a mountain.[24]

This is an important text in several ways. Practically, it walks us through the steps of making a manuscript – the parchment is shaved by the knife, then it is smoothed with pumice and chalk is applied to whiten the parchment. A ruler and 'tool' (stylus or lead stick) is used to mark the lines, the quill and ink to write on the parchment, followed by the decoration – all done at a writing desk. But through the allegorical language, we can understand how the whole process was intrinsically part of a medieval religious scribe's relationship with God. It opens up a new idea of the scriptorium as well – not a physical place, or a monastic style of manuscript production – but a spiritual place. *Locus scribendi, contemptus mundi* means literally 'the place of writing is the contempt of the world'. *Contemptus mundi* was an idea of spirituality, where you were focused on a higher level and unconcerned with the materiality of the earthly realm, because a greater life was waiting for you in heaven. Basically, you had your mind's eye on the celestial prize. So, this concept of the writing place, or scriptorium, transcending all earthly boundaries and operating on a higher plane is an important key for unlocking the mind of a monastic manuscript maker. For them, there was probably little difference between the practical and metaphysical aspects of manuscript production – a monastic scribe occupied both worlds. Some of this sermon is reminiscent of Cassiodorus's and Origen's writings mentioned earlier, where the psalter is likened to a heavenly sphere thick with stars and the split nib of the pen represents the Old and New Testament.

We do not know the author of this sermon, but it is a Durham manuscript written in the early twelfth century, when it was a flourishing centre of manuscript production. It is tempting to think that the composer of this sermon was also a manuscript maker, but it is also likely that any inhabitant of a monastic compound would have been familiar with the steps of production. The scribe of the sermon certainly would be familiar with the process, and writing out this sermon would have added an extra layer of symbolism. Seeing how deeply this sermon goes into the relationship between manuscript production and its spiritual meaning demonstrates just how much of a monastic vocation this was. This adds another layer to the concept of the scriptorium, as something metaphysical, beyond the ephemerality of this physical world. Writing is generally a private affair, and the quiet of the monastic cloister is definitely conducive to entering a deeper state of consciousness – so why should we not regard the scriptorium as a spiritual realm, rather than a physical one?

LET US NOW CONSIDER the specific centres of book production. They can be hard to trace, and some sleuthing is needed. Those with longstanding collections, such as St Gall and Durham, are relatively easy to define – we can assume some were produced there since we know they were centres of manuscript production and the library has remained intact to this day. However, with the dispersal of manuscripts over time throughout the world, tracing the origin of a manuscript can be hard. Sometimes, a manuscript may helpfully include a written *ex libris* (from the library of) or have a shelfmark to indicate where it was housed in the library, although that doesn't necessarily mean it was produced there. Occasionally, a scribe added a colophon and provided some details about when and where the manuscript was written, although this is the exception rather than the rule. Often, we need to apply a bit of detective work, bringing together certain traits that can identify a particular scriptorium – such as distinctive scribes/scripts, decoration and/or the way the manuscript was assembled. However, these traits often only last a generation or so, as centres of book production wax and wane according to demand, finances, patronage, war, famine, plague and so on.

The monastery at Chelles (which was one of the early producers of manuscripts in Merovingian script) was presided over by Charlemagne's sister, Gisela, at the start of the ninth century. It was known as a centre of excellence, educating many aristocratic women and producing many high-quality manuscripts. There is a collection of surviving manuscripts on Augustine's Commentary on the Psalms where nine female scribes from Chelles have added their names to the end of their sections: *Girbalda scripsit* (Girbalda wrote this); *Gislildis scriptsit*; *Agleberta scripsit*; *Adruhic scripsit*; *Altildis scripsit*; *Gisledrudis scripsit*; *Eusebia scripsit*; *Vera scripsit*; and *Agnes scripsit* (there is a tenth scribe, but the folio where her section ended has been lost).[25] All the scribes write in a uniform Caroline minuscule (as you would expect from a monastery closely associated with Charlemagne), but with subtle differences between the hands, so it can be assumed that these were individual scribes all trained at the same scriptorium.[26] Additionally, the last folio of each quire is numbered with roman numerals, to help keep the written text in the right order when assembling the manuscript – so this was a really well-organized operation, with ten different scribes writing their allotted amount, numbering each quire as they went and then naming their finished text.

Another case in point is the scriptorium at Frankenthal, Germany, that had a period of productivity in the late twelfth century. From one fifteenth-century *ex libris* identified in a twelfth-century manuscript, 26 other manuscripts with the same *ex libris* were examined and, as a result, 64 scribes were recognized as working at the scriptorium of St Mary Magdalene in Frankenthal around 1145 to 1200.[27] One of the best examples from this scriptorium is the Worms Bible (BL, Harley MS 2803), written around 1148 by four scribes who had different roles. The first scribe did most of the writing, rubrication and decoration, while the second scribe was a pupil, whom we can see 'learning on the job' as the manuscript progresses. The third scribe corrected the text and a fourth wrote the running titles and generally tidied the whole thing up. The scribal hands identified in this manuscript produced at Frankenthal were then matched to other manuscripts. Further hands working together were then identified, creating a whole chain of scribes in Frankenthal up to around the year 1200. The different roles that the scribes played in assembling the Worms Bible indicate that Frankenthal was a highly organized scriptorium in the second half of the twelfth century.[28]

Sometimes, a single scribe is immediately recognizable from a certain distinguishing feature in their script. For some, this might be an over-flourished tail on a descender, or a quirkily shaped *g*, but others might have more unusual characteristics. There was a scribe in the thirteenth century who has come to be known as the 'tremulous hand', on account of his shaky, left-leaning script. His writing has been identified in about twenty manuscripts all associated with Worcester, so it is likely he was a monk there. He added annotations to Old English manuscripts – translating individual words into Middle English or Latin above the Old English words, to 'update' the text for readers. It is thought that his shaky writing was down to a condition called essential tremor, a neurological disorder that causes involuntary and rhythmic shaking, particularly in the hands. There is a curious occurrence in one manuscript (Oxford, Bodleian Library, MS Junius 121, fol. vi r), where his writing suddenly improves dramatically from the line above, perhaps because he had just had a rest, or even had an alcoholic drink, which can temporarily calm tremors.[29] (Mild ale was a common beverage for all medieval people.)

Who Were the Scribes?

Now we have explored the writing place, let's meet the scribes. Although scribes and artists were not always from monastic orders, for the moment we will focus on the ones that were. When a man or woman entered a religious house as a novice, they underwent a period of training to prepare themselves for a life of religious devotion. In the earlier medieval period, there was a tradition of child oblation, where a child was 'donated' to an institution at around ten years old to be brought up by the religious men or women. However, this practice of offering such young children went out of fashion as the medieval period went on, with many orders rejecting the practice altogether and not permitting entrance to anyone under the age of fifteen and then eighteen.[30]

When a novice entered a Benedictine house, they had to surrender all their worldly possessions and were provided with 'cowl, tunic, stockings, shoes, belt, knife, stylus, needle, handkerchief and writing tablets' (*RSB*, ch 55). This immediately outlines how important writing and studying were to the Benedictines – the very meagre list still includes a stylus and writing tablets. Novices were taught in the cloister (presumably away from the scribes who would need silence to concentrate), where they would learn Latin as well as the customs of the house and their daily duties.[31] It seems likely that those novices who showed a particular flair for writing would have been encouraged to take up scribal duties within the monastery. Generally, the most productive scribes would have been the younger, fitter ones, with the benefit of better eyesight and bodies that didn't stiffen when bent over all day.[32] Students probably learnt by copying lines written out by the master. This can be seen in the manuscripts from the scriptorium at Frankenthal, where the senior scribe provided some sample lines of script, and then the pupil took over.[33] A scribe, provided they remained in good health, could perhaps have a writing life of forty or fifty years (or even more).[34]

It is always tempting to fall back into the romanticized idea of the scribe, serenely working away in a little bubble of contented concentration – but even monastic scribes liked to moan every now and then. We have a realistic account of what it was like to be a scribe from an addition to an early ninth-century French manuscript on the law codes of the Burgundians. The scribe writes in Caroline minuscule:

> O most blessed reader, wash your hands and thus take hold of the book, turn the pages carefully, keep your hand far from the page. Those who don't know how to write think it is easy. O how hard it is to write! It strains the eyes, breaks the kidneys, tires all of your limbs at the same time. Three fingers do the writing, but the whole body labours. Just as a sailor wishes to arrive at his home port, so does a scribe long for the last verse.[35]

This scribe is telling it how it really is – and there are many similar additions found in other medieval manuscripts, proving that this was a shared feeling. We can feel the pain of this scribe, speaking to us across hundreds of years to communicate just how thoroughly fed up they are. It would have been back-breaking work, bending over a desk for hours on end, with the constant repetitive action of dipping your quill in the ink. Imagine the overwhelming feeling when faced with a new text to copy, perhaps several hundred folios long – having to painstakingly form every single letter, while sitting on a hard wooden stool in a cold cloister. Like all of us, scribes would have had good days and bad days, and the little comments they have left in the margins of manuscripts speak to us on a very human level.

The manuscript Laon, Bibliothèque municipale, MS 26 is a copy of a commentary on the psalms by Cassiodorus dating from the ninth century. It was written in Latin by an Irish scribe, who has added glosses and various comments in their native language. Like many of the manuscripts written in an Irish hand, it is not known for certain whether this was written in Ireland or by an Irish scribe who had moved to the Continent. There is a suggestion that this was written on the Continent and that the head of the scriptorium checking the copied text would not have understood the Irish glosses – allowing the mischievous scribe to get away with jotting down their gripes.[36] They wrote these little comments at the top of the page, giving a fascinating snapshot into the musings of an ordinary scribe:

> The day is cold. This is natural, it is winter (fol. 6r)
> This wind is poisonous (fol. 6v)
> It is time for us to begin to do some work (fol. 17r)
> God bless my hands today (fol. 18v)
> This parchment is hairy (fol. 21r)
> This parchment feels thin to me (fol. 23r)
> I feel quite dull to-day. I do not know what is wrong with me (fol. 24r).

Another manuscript we have already looked at (St Gall, Cod. Sang. 904, with the description of the scribe writing underneath the tree) also has many other scribal asides. One entry: 'this page has not been written very slowly' is presumably a response to a rebuke for not being fast enough.[37] Other comments include:

> The bitter wind is high tonight, it lifts the white locks of the sea; in such wild winter storm no fright of savage vikings troubles me (p. 112)
> The vellum is defective, and the writing (p. 195)

New parchment, bad ink, O I say nothing more (p. 214).

Even more interesting is that there are some comments in Ogham, an early medieval script used in Ireland, with each letter consisting of a series of strokes on a central line. The top of p. 195 has an Ogham inscription that translates as 'killed by ale' (that is, a terrible hangover) – so you see, these scribes were just as fallible as we are today. Another scribe in a different manuscript finishes their writing with: 'This work is written, master, give me a drink; let the right hand of the scribe be freed from pain' (Leiden, Universiteitsbibliotheek, VLF 5, fol. 172v).

While many of these comments would have been written by religious inhabitants of a monastery, there were also freelance scribes who travelled around for hire, and certainly after the twelfth century, manuscript production became more commercial. Universities (or proto-universities) started appearing in Europe, first in Bologna at the end of the eleventh century, followed by Paris and Oxford in the mid-twelfth century. These new university towns were transformed, creating a commercial demand for books for students and teachers, and scribes and artists embraced the opportunity to set up workshops and centres of manuscript production. This meant the manuscript industry was no longer confined to the monasteries, but branched out into the commercial world, which in turn led to greater innovation and experimentation with book techniques and decoration. However, far from the slightly cheeky comments left by monastic scribes, the additions made by a certain freelance scribe, Raulinus of Framlingham, were of a different nature altogether. Raulinus was an English scribe who worked in Paris in the mid-thirteenth century, and was hired to produce a Bible in Bologna along with two artists. This gives an idea of the mobility of scribes and artists in the thirteenth century – they went where the work was. Yet it is Raulinus's unsavoury comments that really stand out in this manuscript – written directly underneath the Bible passages, or sometimes even on the same line, he speaks disparagingly of two women he has had relations with in Bologna, informing the reader that they are harlots and whores. His major gripes seem to be against a certain Meldina, who was only interested in his money, and Vilana, who apparently stole his cloak. Whether these interpolations are from Raulinus's personal experience or just something he made up for a bit of fun, the spiteful, coarse language he uses in a Bible text seems a far cry from the innocent grumblings of the early medieval monastic scribes. Although Raulinus's uncouth tone is quite shocking, this may be representative of the new class of freelance scribes for hire.[38]

The new scribes could certainly still be just as grumpy as the monastic scribes, as we can see in a comment left by Henry of Damme in 1444. After copying out a chronicle, he listed his expenses:

> 11 golden letters, 8 shilling each,
> 700 (initial) letters with double shafts, 7 shilling for each hundred,
> 35 quires of text, each 16 leaves, at 3 shilling each

After which he writes, 'For such a (small) amount I won't write again.'[39] As well as giving an insight into the kinds of prices that scribes were paid, it also tells us that Henry of Damme was doing his own illuminating and coloured initials within the manuscript, so this was a sole endeavour, rather than the collaboration often seen in the monastic houses. Henry's financial grievance is a far cry from the monastic ideal of writing books as a spiritual practice for personal edification though – for him it seems to be purely focused on the end result and the money.

Let us not forget the artists. We know from treasures such as the Lindisfarne Gospels and the Book of Kells that monastic

Working artists, Dover Bible, vol. II, 12th century.

art could achieve dizzying heights. However, there were many instances where freelance artists were employed by monasteries to produce a particularly sumptuous book. The exact status of the Alexis Master, an accomplished painter identified in the St Albans Psalter produced in the first half of the twelfth century, is unknown. The psalter is associated with Christina of Markyate, a local anchoress, and the manuscript contains many beautiful, illuminated images of biblical scenes painted in Romanesque fashion (an artistic style that flourished in the eleventh and twelfth centuries). The Alexis Master (named after a section of the psalter that is illustrated with delicately coloured washes to portray the life of the saint Alexis) was possibly an artist from the Continent, or could even have been English, but was certainly highly skilled and in tune with the latest artistic developments in Europe. It is not known for sure whether the Alexis Master was a monk at St Albans, a monk who had moved to St Albans from elsewhere, or a hired lay artist – but he often depicts monks' clothing incorrectly, which suggests that he was not a member of the monastic order.[40]

Master Hugo was a later Romanesque artist, who contributed to the Bury St Edmunds Bible, *c.* 1135 (CCCC, MS 2, in three volumes). We can be fairly certain that Hugo was a professional artist rather than a monk, as he is addressed by the secular term *magister* (master) rather than brother in the *Memorials of Bury St Edmunds Abbey*. Master Hugo's painting style has Byzantine influences, suggesting that he had travelled to the east Mediterranean, or was at least familiar with the wall paintings and manuscript images from that area. There is a depiction of working artists in the Dover Bible, made in Canterbury circa 1150 (CCCC MS 3 and 4). On fol. 242v of the second manuscript, there is a small image of two artists working – one has a brush in one hand and is holding a shell or some other container with pigment. The other artist is grinding some pigment on a slab with a stone, with a spatula-type tool in his other hand. Both are clearly laypeople, attested by their headwear and clothes. So, while scribes were largely of the monastic variety, there does seem to have been more collaboration with lay artists – presumably because finding skilful artists within a community was harder than finding those who could write with a neat hand.

MANY SCRIBES FINISH their text with a colophon (from the Greek word for finishing touch), sometimes even supplying their name – although this was not so common with monastic scribes. A religious scribe writing in Old English wearily signs off 'this ends here. God help my hands' (*þus her ge endod. God helpe minum handum*, BL, Cotton MS Tiberius B V, fol. 28v). Another scribe seems to have been in a melancholic mood, writing in an Irish medical text:

This is sad, o fair little book!
A day will come in truth,
when someone over your page will say,
the hand that wrote this is no more.[41]

These words were a common addition in manuscripts, a reminder that while the scribes may have passed away, their words live on. A twelfth-century manuscript from Winchester (Oxford, Bodleian Library, MS Bodley 451) has the following addition on fol. 119v: 'may the scriptrix remain safe and unharmed forever' (*salva et incolomis maneat per secula scriptrix*). *Scriptrix* is the female version of *scriptor*, so we know this was written by a woman religious, probably from the house of Nunnaminster.[42]

There is a scribal sign-off of a more cryptic nature in München, Bayerische Staatsbibliothek, Clm 1086, fol. 71v. The 'nun from Heidenheim' was an eighth-century English woman at the monastery of Heidenheim, Germany, which was founded in 752 by Wynnebald, an English missionary. While there, she wrote a hagiographic account of the *Life of Wynnebald* and the *Life of Willibald* – a travel account of her kinsman Willibald's pilgrimage to Jerusalem, which he related to her personally. In between the two texts in the earliest surviving manuscript, she wrote a cryptic message that reads:

Secundumgquartum quintumnprimum
sprimumxquartumntertiumcprimum
nquartummtertiumnsecundum
hquintumgsecundumbquintumrc quartumrdinando
hsecundumc scrtertiumbsecundumbprimumm.[43]

While this looks incomprehensible to our eyes, if you understand that this is a code, it can be deciphered. The Latin numbers written here represent each vowel in order, so *primum* translates as *a*, *secundum* is *e*, *tertium* is *i*, *quartum* is *o* and *quintum* is *u*. By replacing the Latin numbers with vowels, we get the following message: *Ego una Saxonica nomine Hugeburc ordinando hec scribebam* (I, a Saxon nun named Hygeburg, wrote this). So, there we go, a woman from England named Hygeburg, writing in a monastery in Germany in the late eighth century, and having a bit of fun with a linguistic puzzle.

The Dutch manuscript Leiden, Universiteitsbibliotheek, BPL MS 2541 ends on a rather sad note, and is a particularly rich source of information about a difficult time for the scribe. The last page finishes: 'Pray for the person who made this book, which was completed in 1484 in the city of Maaseik, where we were taking refuge after our convent had burned down.' The scribe came from St Agnes, a monastery for regular canonesses. The fire occurred in 1482, when the monastery was caught up in a battle between two rival families and was burnt to the ground, forcing the canonesses to flee to the nearby town of Susteren.[44] Despite their displacement, the canonesses seem to have carried on producing manuscripts, which today form the largest surviving collection of texts from a Dutch female house.

Although monastic scribes were generally not supposed to slap their credentials all over a freshly scribed manuscript (it was all about the humility), we do have examples of scribes immortalizing themselves in images. An English manuscript, partly written by monastic reformer Dunstan in the mid-tenth century, shows an ink drawing of Christ, accompanied by a smaller kneeling figure of a monk (Oxford, Bodleian Library, MS Auct. F. 4. 32, fol. 1r). The inscription above the figure reads 'I ask, merciful Christ, that you may protect me, Dunstan,' so although we don't know for definite that Dunstan drew this, it does seem pretty likely. And we have already seen the full-page image of Eadwine, the scribe depicted in the Eadwine

Psalter from Canterbury and described as the 'chief of scribes' – although probably not produced by Eadwine himself.

Far less shy and retiring was Matthew Paris, who quite happily drew a self-portrait in one of the manuscripts he was writing. The image shows a monk drawn in ink kneeling below a miniature of the Virgin Mary and child – he has helpfully added 'Brother Matthew Paris' next to the figure so we know exactly who it is (BL, Royal MS 14 C VII, f. 6r). From a late twelfth-century book of sermons, we have another image and an inscription from Guda, who belonged to a religious community in Westphalia, Germany (Frankfurt am Main, Universitätsbibliothek, MS Barth. 42, fol. 110v). Inside a coloured and decorated initial *D*, there is a female figure in a religious habit surrounded by an inscription reading 'The sinful woman Guda wrote and painted this book' (*Guda peccatrix mulier scripsit et pinxit hunc librum*). Despite showing humility by referring to herself as a sinner, she looks out from the page directly at us and firmly grasps the string of words that declares her authorship, looking at ease with her accomplishment.[45]

Also from the late twelfth century, we have some labelled self-portraits of the monk Rufillus of Weissenau, who depicted himself as a scribe (Amiens, BM, Lescalopier 30, fol. 29v) and as an artist (Cologny, Fondation Martin Bodmer, Cod. Bodmer 127, fol. 244r). The image of him as an artist is particularly useful, as it gives an idea of the medieval artist's tools and working conditions. So, while scribes writing in monasteries were generally supposed to be anonymous, we do have these occasional surviving examples of scribes and artists reminding the reader 'I did this.' A visual depiction of a scribe or artist, particularly a self-portrait, creates a real link with the reader, even (or perhaps especially) after hundreds of years.

SCRIBES TOOK A LOT of pride in their manuscripts, and often passed on warnings to readers to treat their work with care. A French manuscript from the Cluniac priory of La Charité-sur-Loire was written by the prior Renaudus circa 1161, and he finishes with a colourful colophon in green and red that reads: 'May this book be far from the hands of those who do not know how to treat precious books with care' (BL, Yates Thompson 17, fol. 142r). An eleventh-century manuscript from Monte Cassino written by the scribe Stephanus requests that whoever touches his manuscript 'should have clean hands' (Biblioteca del Monumento nazionale di Montecassino, MS 80, p. 330).

Scribes also didn't mince their words when it came to giving instructions to other scribes. We saw Alcuin's verse 'On Scribes' in Chapter Two, where he tells scribes that writing books is better than planting vines. Yet he also issues a stern warning:

> Here let them take care not to insert their silly remarks;
> may their hands not make mistakes through foolishness.
> Let them zealously strive to produce emended texts
> and may their pens fly along and follow the correct path.
> May they distinguish the proper meaning by colons and
> commas, and put each point in the place where it belongs.[46]

One can probably assume that Alcuin and the Irish scribes (with their 'silly remarks') were definitely not on the same page when it came to scribal discipline. Ælfric of Eynsham (*c.* 955–*c.* 1010) was another prolific English writer, whose collection of homilies has this warning at the beginning:

> Now I desire and beseech, in God's name, if anyone will transcribe this book, that he carefully correct it by the copy, lest we be blamed through careless writers. He does great evil who writes false, unless he correct it; it is as though he

> turn true doctrine to false error; therefore should everyone make that straight which he before bent crooked, if he will be guiltless at God's doom.[47]

It is understandable that an author such as Ælfric, who had painstakingly composed his homilies, would want to make sure that his words did not lose their meaning over the course of time. We see many examples of human error – lines being repeated or skipped, or words being incorrectly transcribed by someone perhaps not fluent in Latin – and then that mistake gets repeated by the next scribe, and the next scribe, and so on. A scribe's work was often checked by a senior member of the scriptorium, and we can see examples of their corrections in the margins. A manuscript produced for a small female priory in Wintney, Hampshire (BL, Cotton MS Claudius D III) by the Cistercian abbey in Waverley shows corrections by a different scribe on fols 28r, 52v, 53r and 56v, where words have been missed out or misspelt by the original scribe. These corrections would have been done by the *librarius* or even the abbot at Waverley. We also see other scribes commenting on the work of previous scribes (or at least the exemplar they copied it from). A scribe criticizing the translation of a Bible text from Latin to Dutch provided an updated version in the margin, along with the words 'This is how I would have translated it.'[48]

Stealing books was taken very seriously. Many manuscripts had a book curse (anathema) added to the flyleaf, giving a warning of what would happen to any sticky-fingered individual removing said book without permission. Bearing in mind the huge amount of resources that went into making just one manuscript, it is understandable that books were valued as precious commodities that communities would want to keep hold of. A typical example of a book curse is found in Stonyhurst College, MS 9, fol. 1r. This manuscript contains several folios from a thirteenth-century manuscript belonging to Tarrant Keyneston, Dorset, a female Cistercian house. The inscription reads: 'This is the psalter of the Blessed Mary at Tarrant, given by mistress Leticia Keynes. Whoever shall remove it or defraud in any way, a curse be upon them.'

Slightly more menacing is the text that Leofric, Bishop of Exeter, writes in the missal that he donated to Exeter Cathedral library: 'Bishop Leofric gives this missal to the Church of Saint Peter the Apostle in Exeter for the use of his successors. If anyone should remove it from there, let them be subject to eternal malediction' (Oxford, Bodleian Library, MS Bodl. 579, fol. 1r). Leofric writes this message in Latin, then repeats in Old English underneath, just to make sure his warning is clear. It would be a brave thief indeed who dared to steal this book with such an ominous warning from the highly revered bishop. However, rather than veiled threats of eternal damnation, some scribes went full throttle on meting out punishments. A German Bible from the monastery of Arnstein declares: 'A book of the Abbey of SS Mary and Nicholas of Arnstein. If anyone steals it: may they die the death, may they be roasted in a frying pan, may the falling sickness and fever attack them, and may they be rotated on the breaking wheel and hanged. Amen' (BL, Harley MS 2798, fol. 235v).[49]

ON A SLIGHTLY less violent level, animals (particularly cats) were another source of frustration for scribes, although the relationships were generally built on mutual understanding, with cats chasing away rodents. The Irish poem Pangur Bán is found in the ninth-century Reichenau Primer (St Paul im Lavanttal, Stiftsbibliothek, MS 86a/1). It is written from the point of view of a learned monk who observes his white cat and compares their skills when alone together – the cat's dexterity in catching a mouse, against his own skill at chasing meanings within scholarly texts:

I and Pangur Bán my cat,
'Tis a like task we are at:
Hunting mice is his delight,
Hunting words I sit all night.

Better far than praise of men
'Tis to sit with book and pen;
Pangur bears me no ill-will,
He too plies his simple skill.

'Tis a merry task to see
At our tasks how glad are we,
When at home we sit and find
Entertainment to our mind.

Oftentimes a mouse will stray
In the hero Pangur's way;
Oftentimes my keen thought set
Takes a meaning in its net.

'Gainst the wall he sets his eye
Full and fierce and sharp and sly;
'Gainst the wall of knowledge I
All my little wisdom try.

When a mouse darts from its den,
O how glad is Pangur then!
O what gladness do I prove
When I solve the doubts I love!

So in peace our task we ply,
Pangur Ban, my cat, and I;
In our arts we find our bliss,
I have mine and he has his.

Practice every day has made
Pangur perfect in his trade;
I get wisdom day and night
Turning darkness into light.[50]

Another Irish scribe provides a running commentary on a missing cat. Murchadh Riabach Ó Cuindlis was a professional scribe and in the early fifteenth century compiled *An Leabhar Breac*, a collection of historical, literary and religious texts (RIA, MS 23 P 16). He includes several comments on the weather: 'The wind from the lake is cramping me' (p. 235); 'Twenty nights from today until Easter Monday and I am cold and tired without fire or covering' (p. 33). He also writes a little message on p. 164:

> A kitten, which you rear so that it may be pleasant: when it has been made much of, it goes away from you to hunt. A bad person is like that: you bring him up according to his wishes, and when you make a man of him, your bad person deserts you.

This is followed by a sad little sentence written in a red box: 'The white cat is straying away from me.' The scribe follows up on p. 248, commenting, 'It is a wonder: the robin staying with us, and the cat fleeing from us.' It leaves us to wonder whether the scribe was ever reunited with the cat he was so clearly missing.

Much worse, though, was an incident that occurred when a scribe in the Netherlands left his unfinished work out for the night and a passing cat thought the newly scribed parchment would be a nice surface to wee on. The fifteenth-century scribe leaves the area blank, writing in the empty column:

> Here is nothing missing, but a cat urinated on this during a certain night. Cursed be the pesty cat that urinated over this book during the night in Deventer and because of it many others [cats] too. And beware well not to leave open books at night where cats can come.[51]

He also draws manicules on the page pointing to the soiled area, and a sketch of the offending cat. His irritation is clear even after all these years. Perhaps not as repellent – but certainly just as irksome – was the fifteenth-century manuscript from Dubrovnik that has distinctive cat paw prints in ink walking across the page.[52] Anyone with cats will find it quite easy to imagine this scenario, with a cat first jumping up and walking through the ink, then proceeding to walk nonchalantly across the open manuscript, perhaps even looking directly at the scribe while doing it, with absolutely no remorse.

But it wasn't just cats that vexed the scribes – mice could be just as irritating, taking a crafty nibble out of any parchment left out overnight. Hildebert, a lay scribe and artist from the twelfth century, drew a portrait of himself and his co-worker Everwin in their workshop at the back of a copy of Augustine's *City of God* (Prague, Bibliothek des Metropolitankapitels, MS A. XXI/1, fol. 153r). Hildebert sits in front of a wooden board with an open book and scribal equipment. He holds an object looking like a pumice stone in his raised clenched fist, ready to throw at a mouse stealing food from a nearby table. The words in his open book read: 'Damn you, wretched mouse, exasperating me so often!' Hildebert's frustration at his working conditions is clearly expressed in this image, so perhaps in this case a cat would have been a welcome companion to keep the mice at bay.

WE ALSO SEE pen trials and doodles from scribes in the margins. Pen trials (*probatio pennae*) were just scribblings or jottings to ensure that the nib was cut right, and the ink was flowing – similarly to the way we might scribble with a ball-point pen today to check it is working. The *Lebor na hUidre* (Book of the Dun Cow, RIA, MS 23 E 25) is a twelfth-century manuscript, and the oldest example of Irish vernacular writing. The book is named after its parchment, which supposedly came from the dun-coloured cow of St Ciarán of Clonmacnoise (*c.* 516–*c.* 549), giving a reminder of the corporeal nature of manuscript production, and how medieval people were not detached from the process. *Lebor na hUidre* is a collection of Irish historical, religious and mythical texts. A scribal addition at the top of p. 55 of the manuscript reads: *probatio pennae Mail Muri meic meic Cuind* (a pen trial here by Maelmuiri, son of the son of Cuinn na mbocht) with another similar jotting at the top of p. 70. Máel Muire mac Céilechair (meic Cuinn na mBocht) was a monk at the monastery of Clonmacnois and we even know a little bit about his life and death. In the Annals of the Four Masters (a chronicle of Irish medieval history), a sad entry for the year of 1106 reads: 'Maelmuire, son of Mac Cuinn-na-mBocht, was killed in the middle of the Daimhliag of Cluain-mic-Nois by plunderers' – which may well refer to a viking raid. Most medieval scribes were anonymous, so it creates a real connection here to know not only the name of the scribe, but the date and cause of his death, traced from a little jotting in the margin to test his quill.

There is also a lovely example of pen trials from a manuscript owned by Cuthswith, abbess of Inkberrow, Worcester (*c.* 700), who inscribed her ownership in an Italian copy of Jerome's Commentary on Ecclesiastes (Universitätsbibliothek Würzburg, M.p.th.q.2). On the first folio, she wrote in Insular script *Cuthsuuithae boec thaerae abbatissan* (the book of Cuthswith, abbess) and underneath repeats 'abbatissan' but with uncial 's' and 'a', perhaps denoting the fluidity between Insular and Roman scripts. As well as her stamp of ownership, there are also groups of repeated letters and odd words jotted down, probably to encourage the flow of ink from a quill, or perhaps just practising the right style of script. This manuscript was written in Italy in the fifth century, came to England for a while where it was owned by Cuthswith, and then moved to Würzburg, Germany, sometime in the eighth century, probably with the early English missionaries like Boniface and Leoba. Some missing leaves were replaced while in England, copying the uncial script, probably by one of the women at Cuthswith's house.[53] The pen trials were probably added when it moved back to the Continent, making this manuscript an example of the flow of books around Europe in the early medieval period, and also the shared authorship and collaborative nature of manuscripts and scribes. Many hands may contribute to the life of a single codex, from many different places and often hundreds of years apart.

Another unfortunate result of wielding a quill was inky fingers, and sometimes we have fingerprints left on the parchment to attest to this (Biblioteca Apostolica Vaticana, Reg.lat.1244, fol. 9r). A fingerprint – such a unique human identifier – has extra depth when you think that it is stamped on parchment, creating that skin-to-skin contact between human and animal. This fingerprint was probably left by a later reader rather than the scribe themselves, but nonetheless it serves as a visual reminder of all the hands that touched the manuscript in its lifetime, creating a tangible, tactile link with other readers across the centuries.

Doodles (as opposed to the elaborate artistic marginalia that we will look at later) were simple sketches penned by scribes in an amateur fashion, again similar to how we might doodle abstractedly when bored in a meeting or classroom. A large letter *O* particularly lends itself to being made into a smiley face or even a grumpy one, like the face seen in BL, Egerton MS

609, fol. 1r. The opening word *Beato* has the letter *o* filled in with a frowny face with staring eyes and a downturned mouth – quite intimidating, really. Other popular subject-matter is conveyed in skeleton and animal (or animalesque) drawings. A manicule (a drawn hand in the margin with finger extended, pointing at a particular section of text to highlight its importance) is a feature in many manuscripts, often added later by other scribes or readers. They enabled scribes to have a bit of fun and creativity: for example in a French manuscript on canon law, there is a doodle of a figure in the margin pushing a plough with a manicule drawn where the blade would be, and another manuscript has a delicately drawn bird, incorporating its beak as a pointer.[54] They can vary from very basic to very elaborate, from very abstract to very, very rude – for example, BL, Add MS 29301, fols 19v, 36r, 40r has erect penises in the margins acting as manicules (penicules?).

Even holes in the parchment could provide some artistic entertainment, transforming them into comical animals or winsome faces rather than trying to ignore them. BL, Add MS 47967 has a parchment hole that has been decorated on both sides of the folio, surrounding the hole with a pen-drawn fluffy layer and adding a mole-like head on fol. 62r and a sheep-like head on 62v. Other scribes (or perhaps later book owners) chose to sew parchment holes together, sometimes with elaborate patterns using brightly coloured silk thread (Aarau, Aargauer Kantonsbibliothek, WettF 9, fol. 31r).

LASTLY, what did the scribes copy? Obviously, religious texts were the main output for monastic scribes. The main staples for any monastic scriptorium would have included Bibles; liturgical texts (such as missals, martyrologies, choir books and so on); homilies (sermons); hagiographies (lives of saints); works by the patristic fathers such as John Chrysostom and Jerome; and works by Augustine. However, the medieval monastic mind was a curious mind, and a well-stocked library would have included chronicles, as well as medical, astrological, legal and classical texts (although probably not all written in-house). Rochester Cathedral Priory was a very well-organized library, as seen from its 1202 catalogue record (BL, Royal MS 5 B XII), listing over two hundred books. Besides a profusion of religious texts, including works by Augustine, Gregory, Ambrose, Jerome and Bede, they had texts on canon law (Gratian's *Decretum*), rhetoric, arithmetic, music, texts by classical authors such as Virgil, Lucan and Ovid, history texts, a mappa mundi (map of the world) and a lapidary (a text on the properties of stones). Although Rochester Abbey had a thriving scriptorium in this period, it is unlikely that all these texts were produced here. However, it does give a vital snapshot of the texts that were in circulation in this period and shows that medieval scribes were not limited to copying religious texts – and that medieval monastics in Europe did not have closed minds.

Many of the non-religious texts came from Islamic sources. There were many points of contact between the medieval Christian and Islamic world, such as Sicily, Spain and Jerusalem, and Europe benefited greatly from the impressive Islamic advances in medicine, maths and alchemy. Some classical texts had been lost with the growth of Christianity, but had been copied and preserved by Islamic scribes, and were then recopied into Latin. This raises an important point about textual transmission – once a text stops being copied, it ceases to exist. Eventually all the extant copies of that text will degrade and disappear. We may have references to it in other surviving works, but texts from the classical and medieval period only live on if they are constantly in circulation and being copied by scribes. Many texts have been lost over time, which is why it is so exciting when a next text is discovered – either in a neglected book collection, or the underlying text on a palimpsest, or even using X-ray technology to read the carbonized papyrus scrolls excavated from Herculaneum.

It is an often-repeated stereotype that people in medieval Europe thought the earth was flat – but (for example) Bede knew full well that the planets were round and moved through the solar system (although it was a common belief that the Sun revolved around the Earth, rather than the other way). Medieval polymaths such as Bede authored treatises on maths, science, astronomy and medicine. However, after the eleventh century there was an influx of Islamic texts into European scholarly circles, creating a new wave of intellectual stimulus. Scholars such as Gerard of Cremona travelled to Toledo in Islamic Spain to immerse themselves in the advanced Muslim learning and to translate texts into Latin for a European readership. Through the twelfth and thirteenth centuries, there was an increased demand for books, both by students studying law, medicine and theology, and the newly wealthy merchant class, who acquired personal prayer books. Courtly literature became a new genre, embodying nobility and chivalry in poetry and prose. Epic poems such as the *Song of Roland* and chivalric romances such as *Gawain and the Green Knight* fall into this category, as does Geoffrey Chaucer's *Canterbury Tales* and the allegorical *Le Roman de la Rose*. *Pearl*, a fourteenth-century allegorical poem, is a profoundly moving story of love and grief. So, contrary to modern popular opinion, people in the medieval period had a strong understanding of how the world worked, scientifically and emotionally.

THIS CHAPTER has hopefully shown that the idea of the scriptorium as envisaged in the plan of St Gall, lovely though it is, is probably nothing more than an imagined ideal. As evidenced from medieval images and accounts, it is more likely that the cloister served as the working place for scribes. In these sources, there is an emphasis on the isolation of the scribe, ensuring the cloister is kept quiet and free from idle wanderers who could distract the scribes. The carrels described in the sources, and still visible at Gloucester, seem to be for single occupants only, again highlighting the solitary nature of the work. The isolation of the scriptorium can also be considered on a metaphysical level – on a spiritual plane rather than an earthly one. We have had a glimpse into the lives of the scribes through the comments they have left on the page and shared in their contentment (while working under a tree), their irritation (with bad materials or cold weather), their playfulness (when writing a cryptic colophon) and their sadness (from losing a cat to losing a home). All these examples make the life of a scribe far more relatable, even across hundreds of years. It is so intrinsically human to express ourselves through writing, whether venting frustration or jotting down a silly doodle – and it is an incredible connection to the past. That scribe, hundreds and hundreds of years ago, touched that parchment with their hands, worked over it, breathed over it, felt happy/sad/cross/content/hungry/silly/bored or inspired – all the normal emotions we might feel during our working day – and sometimes they let us into their world by expressing that on the parchment. That tangible connection with the past, touching a manuscript that the scribe has touched – and goodness knows how many people in between – leaving invisible (and sometimes visible) fingerprints that link us inextricably with our past selves, is a uniquely human experience.

Four

Material World: Parchment and Ink

A parchment maker's yard, Canterbury, twelfth century

William heaves the bloated calfskin out of the water barrel and drapes it over a wooden beam to drain off. Slimy and gelatinous, the skin drips onto the straw and dirt covering the yard floor. William takes a cursory glance at the skin, immediately sizing it up and mentally calculating how many pegs will be needed to stretch it across the wooden frame. He examines the skin for any tears or marks, either from injuries caused while the animal was still alive, or flaying marks from the butcher's knife. His kinsman, Henry, is a skilled flayer, so William knows it is unlikely that he would have caused any damage, but his young apprentice is still learning his trade and often his knife carelessly slices through the skin. These holes need to be sewn together before the skin stretches, to prevent them getting any larger. Fortunately, there are only a few minor scar marks visible from insect bites.

The last droplets of water fall to the ground, glistening in the late spring sunshine. William goes inside the barn, selects a suitable wooden frame from the stacked pile and leans it up against the outside wall. He lightly hammers in wooden pegs to the holes around the edge of the frame. He also takes a bucket of water full of parchment scraps and a bundle of cords. Holding the skin out in front of him, he quickly locates the shadowy central line of the spine, and from there identifies the neck and the tail end. Taking a few parchment scraps from the bucket, he squashes them into a ball and pushes it through the skin on the neck end, forming a button. From the lengths of cord held in his mouth, he takes one and expertly slips the looped end over the button and pulls it tight. He winds the other end of the cord around the peg at the top of the frame. He repeats this process twice more, creating two buttons at the top and one at the bottom. The skin is now loosely attached to the frame, allowing William to work his way around it, forming buttons and attaching them to the pegs at an equal distance to allow for maximum stretch.

Although William has hands like shovels, his fingers are nimble – working quickly and deftly to wrap the cords round the buttons and attach them to the pegs. He is working in the shade, but he knows that the skins will dry out soon enough, making them harder to work with. Once all the cords have been tied, he steps back to make sure they are all evenly placed, and then turns the pegs to tighten the skin. It yields easily when wet, full of stretch and pliability. Taking up his lunellum, William swings his wide shoulders up and brings the lunellum down expertly on the skin at exactly the right angle, the sharp blade skilfully paring off micro-layers of membrane. As he settles into a rhythm, the noise of the yard fades into the background, and it is just William and the swooshing of his blade connecting with the skin, working top to bottom. This is when William is happiest – working as one with the skin, beginning to understand and know it. The thickness of the neck, the thinness of the belly, the scars, the discolourations – all completely individual features and testament to the life of that animal. This one came from one of the abbey farms, Henry told him, so it will have been well looked after in its short life. It will go back to the abbey too in a new form, as creamy parchment for the monks to write their holy words on.

William could not read, but often looked with wonder on the beautiful works that the monks created – the strange black symbols all in neat lines, the shine of the gold and the brightness of the paints. It made him proud to know that he was part of that process – he had been apprenticed to his parchment-maker cousin at the age of eight and had learnt the craft over many years. At first, he was sickened by the sights and the smells – the skins arriving (often still warm), all bloody with the head and hooves still attached, the smell of rotting flesh in the hot weather, the conversations of the older men, telling crude jokes and laughing loudly. But William had come to find a peace in the parchment process, feeling the skin change beneath his hands from a slimy thick mass into a beautifully smooth and fine sheet of parchment. There was something about the skin-to-skin contact, the constant touch, that William found calming to his soul. He understood the undulations and contours of the skin, and instinctively knew just how much pressure to exert to make the thinnest parchment. When he went home in the evening and lay in bed, he could still feel the parchment on the pads of his fingers – the suede texture of the skin side and the glossy coolness of the hair side. He once heard a wise man say that when a man dies, his flesh, skin and bones decompose to nothing – yet an animal can live on for hundreds of years, with its skin as a carrier of knowledge.

As William reaches the bottom of the skin, he scrapes off all the extraneous matter and wipes his blade on the straw. He straightens up, arms and back aching, and critiques his handiwork with a smile of satisfaction. The sun is now at its highest point, and he is hungry and thirsty. He tightens the pegs again and re-wets the skin, ready to work on the other side after lunch. Stretching out his tired muscles, he goes to join the other parchment makers in the barn.

We've looked at the early development of the scriptorium, but what about the practical side of making manuscripts? The materials and methods used for manuscript making in the medieval period were largely an extension of practices already developed in the ancient world. The wax tablet continued to be a staple tool for scribes, used for jotting down notes or writing drafts before being copied onto parchment. Pigments that had been used for thousands of years, such as orpiment and red ochre, continued to be used by artists, as well as manufactured pigments like red lead and lead white. Classical author Theophrastus wrote about the properties of various pigments in *De lapidibus* (On Stones), as did Vitruvius in *De architectura*. Pliny then used these sources and added his own in his first-century CE *Natural History*, writing about methods for making pigments as well as making papyrus and carbon ink. Some papyrus texts found in Egypt, the *Stockholm Papyrus* and *Leyden Papyrus V* and X, were written in Greek by the same scribe at the end of the third century. These texts contain (among other things) craft recipes on how to make ink, coloured metals, pigments and dyes – the bile of a tortoise and the urine of an uncorrupted youth come up worryingly frequently as ingredients.[1] These recipes then fed into a sixth-century text known as the *Mappae clavicula*, which also contained instructions on how to make metals, glass, mosaics, and dyes and tints for materials. Another anonymous medieval collection of recipes, *De coloribus et mixtionibus*, was also in circulation in the medieval period, with the earliest fragments identified in religious houses in eleventh-century England.[2] These two recipe texts are often found together in medieval manuscripts, along with other anonymous recipes. Other significant medieval handbooks are Theophilus' *On Diverse Arts*; a twelfth-century treatise including the use of painting and drawing materials, probably written by a German Benedictine monk called Roger; *The Art of Illumination*, an anonymous fourteenth-century Italian text focused specifically on decorating manuscripts; and Cennino Cennini's *The Craftman's Handbook*, written by an Italian painter around the beginning of the fifteenth century, containing information on a wide range of drawing and painting techniques.[3] These last three texts are invaluable as they are written from the personal view of an artist, so they are sharing their knowledge and experience as craftspeople. Many of these recipes for ink and pigments can still be followed today to achieve the desired result, so they are relatively functional.

Yet many of these recipes are brief. The materials used in manuscript making were so familiar to the people engaged in it that there was no need for them to document the processes. It is unclear who these early instructional texts were produced for – why bother writing down the recipes for producing pigments and inks when most of the people doing this work would have been skilled craftspeople but most probably illiterate? You very much get the feeling with many descriptions of these processes – from Pliny even up to the present day – that they are written by people standing behind the craftsperson, observing what they do from a position of academic or social superiority. They are collecting knowledge, to be written down and stored in a library. Yet the real knowledge of these processes would have been passed on orally and the skill would have been built up over years, with the body understanding the process, through muscle memory and the senses. There is a huge gap between the words written on the page and the immersive, physical process of making – the feel of the shaved parchment as you run your hand over it, the sweet woodland smell of simmering galls, the subtle sound of lapis lazuli pigment becoming finer as you grind it. These things are hard to capture in text yet would have been the everyday experiences of manuscript makers. There is also the possibility that they did not envision a future where these things were not commonplace – where there wasn't a butcher, parchment maker and tanner in every village, where ink wasn't made over the fire, where these sights and smells weren't the normal backdrop to daily life.

Common words for materials have changed over the years, as has the way we measure things, which can make medieval recipes hard to decipher. For example, a recipe might require an obol or a dram (weight measurements) of vitriol (iron sulphate) to be heated in a porringer (a shallow bowl). Rest assured you would also be given extremely vague instructions on how long to heat it, if at all – time was often measured in the length it took to recite the paternoster (Our Father). It may not come as a surprise by now to learn that urine or dung was a key ingredient in many recipes – the ammonia in urine is a good mordant, allowing colour to bind to a material, and burying things in animal dung is a good way of generating a constant heat. These waste products were free and readily available; it would make perfect sense to utilize them for their many useful qualities, even if the chemical understanding wasn't there. Who cares if they didn't know the science behind it? They knew that it did what they needed it to. The vagueness in recipes might also have been a certain amount of holding back – if you've learnt your craft over years, you are not going to want to share trade secrets with a wide audience. Many surviving recipes in manuscripts have often been cherry-picked from a range of texts to suit the needs of the individual – the same way we might write down our favourite food recipes in a book. These craft recipes are often found with medicinal recipes, as there was a lot of crossover in the ingredients.

Parchment

By late antiquity, parchment from a goat, sheep or calf was the preferred medium for European codices. While other cultures across the world used more humane writing surfaces such as bamboo, clay, tree bark, palm leaves, papyrus and paper, it cannot be denied that parchment is an extremely practical material, being hard-wearing and reusable. Although animals were generally bred for the main purpose of providing meat, there were countless other medieval uses for animal carcasses – their skin and bones were boiled down for glue, their bladders used for water containers, horns used as drinking vessels, and their intestinal fibres used to make strings for musical instruments. Nothing was wasted. Many religious inhabitants inclined towards a vegetarian diet, but would have had a demand for parchment, so meat was perhaps not always the prime purpose of livestock slaughter.

How do we get from a freshly flayed animal skin to parchment? There are a handful of medieval images showing parchment (see Copenhagen, Royal Library, GKS 4 folio II, fol. 183v and Stadtbibliothek Nürnberg, Amb. 317.2°, fol. 34v). There are also surviving 'textbooks' from the medieval period that give recipes or instructions on how to make parchment. One of the earliest parchment-making recipes is in a late eighth-/early ninth-century Italian manuscript (Lucca, Biblioteca Capitolare, MS 490). The recipe on fol. 219v gives an extremely brief description: 'Place the skin in limewater and leave it there for three days. Then extend it on a frame and scrape it on both sides with a razor. Leave it to dry, then smooth over.'[4] A twelfth-century German manuscript (BL, Harley MS 3915, fol. 148r) that contains Theophilus' text *On Diverse Arts* also has this parchment recipe at the end of the manuscript, detailing how to make parchment in the Bolognese fashion:

> Take goatskins and soak them in water for a day and a night.
> Take an entirely new bath of lime and water, place the skins in this, folding them on the flesh side.
> Move them with a pole two or three times each day, leaving them for eight days.
> Next you must withdraw the skins and unhair them.
> Rinse and soak in water and leave them for two days.
> Then take them out, attach the cords and tie them to the circular frame.
> Dry, then shave them with a sharp knife after which leave for two days out of the sun.

Moisten with water and rub the flesh side with powdered pumice.
After two days wet it again by sprinkling with a little water and fully clean the flesh side with pumice so as to make it quite wet again.
Then tighten up the cords, equalize the tension so that the sheet will become permanent.
Once the sheets are dry, nothing further remains to be done.[5]

If you had no idea about the parchment process, reading these instructions would still leave a lot of questions, so let's go through it in detail. First, you need a decent animal skin – goat, sheep or calf. On the Continent, all three were used, whereas in England, sheep and calf were the main types of parchment.[6] Calfskin was generally regarded as the highest quality (as it produces the creamiest parchment), whereas sheepskin was the lowest quality. This can be seen from the account book of Beaulieu Abbey in 1269/70, where the grades of calfskin cost 2*s* 6*d* for the highest and 16*d* for the lowest; and the grades of sheepskin cost just 12*d* for the highest and 3*d* for the lowest.[7] Calfskin is often referred to as vellum, but as it is difficult for the untrained eye (or even the trained eye) to determine exactly which animal parchment is from, we will use the catch-all term 'parchment' for calf-, sheep- and goatskin.

A 1762 source recommends using calves between eight days and six weeks old, otherwise their skin becomes too thick for parchment.[8] Previously it was thought that the parchment from aborted calves was used, as during the twelfth century some parchment was so thin it was rendered almost translucent. However, the delicate parchment was probably the result of advanced preparation techniques, and while foetuses were no doubt used when available, this was not a sustainable resource.[9]

One thing to note about calfskin is that there would not have been much meat on a six-week-old carcass, so rather than being bred for meat, it is possible that they were being bred mainly for parchment, with the meat merely a by-product. Of course, medieval practicality still played its part, as rennet, from the calf's stomach lining, was extracted to use in cheese production, and also, by slaughtering a calf so young, the mother cow would stay in milk – so there were still benefits.

The supply of sheepskin was almost unlimited in England in the later medieval period due to the success of the wool industry, making sheep parchment a cheap and readily available material. Sheepskin has a much higher content of lipids, making it

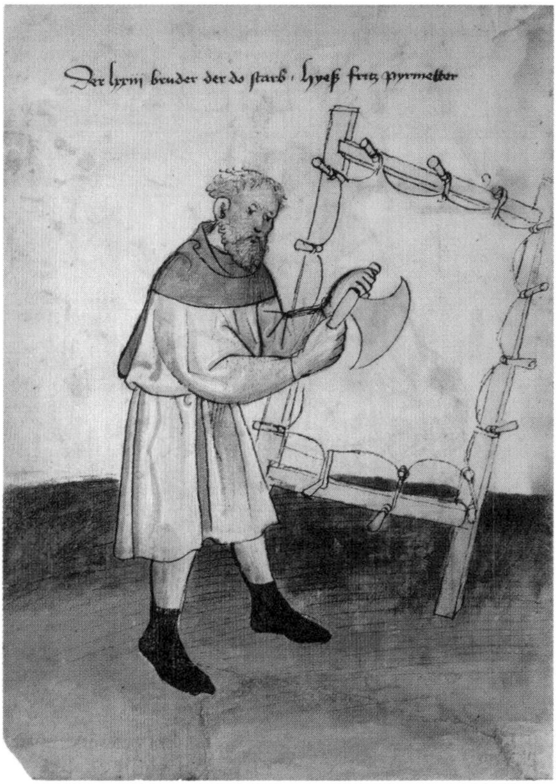

Medieval parchment maker, Mendel Housebook, 14th century.

significantly greasier than calf- or goatskin. However, this does give sheepskin an unexpected and unique advantage over the other two – the high lipid content makes the layers of parchment more susceptible to delaminating (where the layers split apart). This makes it hard to alter any text, as scraping the top surface off makes a dreadful mess. While this would not be a great advantage to a careless scribe trying to correct a mistake, it does ensure that official documents could not be altered after their creation – so sheepskin has a unique built-in anti-tampering device, making it an ideal material for land deeds and other legal documents.[10] Goatskin as a material is a happy medium, because you are not limited to young animals and it gives a good writing surface – although it is often yellower and more textured. Also, goats were not really desired for their meat in England, which probably explains why it was not used as much as parchment. It was imported in certain instances, as it was used in the *Codex Amiatinus*.

Removing the skin from the dead animal was a skilful process, and the medieval butcher needed to take care not to nick or cut through the skin with his blade. Sometimes marks from the butcher's knife, known as striations, can be seen on the parchment, for example, on folios 8r and 131v of the *Codex Sinaiticus*. Once the skin was removed (hopefully in one piece), it would be given to the parchment maker, probably with the head and feet still attached. At this stage, the skin would not be a very pleasant thing – it would be covered in blood, mud and faeces, with animal tissue still clinging to the flesh side. Once the head and lower legs were removed, it would get a rinse in water before being immersed in a bath of lime dissolved in water to remove the hair. The alkali in the lime solution breaks down the hair and fat, and prevents the skin being attacked by bacteria. The lime solution comes with its own dangers though – it dries and cracks your skin after prolonged contact and can even cause a nasty burn – so the animal skins would have been agitated with wooden poles. The length of this process to remove the hair was dependent on the strength of the lime solution and even the time of year – it took longer in winter or in colder climates. Once the hair started coming away from the skin easily, it was soaked to remove the lime and put, rubbery and bloated, on a fleshing beam (a semi-circular wooden beam, that allowed the skin to be laid flat without wrinkling). A curved double-handed knife (a scudder) was used to remove the hair and any remaining bits of flesh (see Stadtbibliothek Nürnberg, Amb. 317.2°, fol. 92r). The quality of the animal hair would have degraded in the lime solution so was not used for wool, but it may still have been used for insulation or stuffing mattresses and so on.

The next stage was to stretch out the dehaired skin over a wooden frame, or harrow/hearse, to be scraped and dried under tension. From images in medieval texts, we see parchment frames depicted as rectangular shapes, but the Harley manuscript above referred to a 'circular frame'.[11] The benefits of one over the other are not apparent, but perhaps circular frames were better suited for smaller skins. It would seem more logical to favour a rectangular frame – first, because it's a lot easier creating an angular shape with wood than bending it into a circle, and second, a flayed animal skin laid out is more or less a rectangular shape. The accounts of Beaulieu Abbey list the price of making hearses (*hersiis faciendis*) at 12*d*, but do not mention the shape.[12] Anyway, circular or rectangular, the skin was attached to the frame. A later account of parchment making from 1663 (Royal Society, CLP/3i/18) explains that the frame should have nineteen wooden pegs, which are attached by cord to the corners of the skin. To attach the cord to the skin, you would need to make a 'peppin/pippin' by pushing small scraps of parchment into the edge of the skin, so it forms a button, and then wind one end of the cord around the base of the button. The other end of the cord is then held in place by winding it around the wooden peg, and the peg turned to tighten the skin.

The skin needs to be attached to the frame quickly, especially in warmer countries, as it becomes less pliable as it dries out. Once the skin is attached, it is scraped with a lunellum, a sharp semi-circular blade which thins and smooths the surface. Some parchment in manuscripts is so thick it is like card, whereas other parchment is wafer-thin. This may partly depend on the skill of the parchment maker, but animal skin also has different densities depending on where it is on the body – the skin on the neck is much thicker than the skin on the tummy – and it may have depended on the finances of the monastery whether they could afford the choicest cuts. This process of scraping the skin was hard work, but as a physical, repetitive action it can be quite hypnotic. Also, it is quite satisfying to see the matter being removed from the skin as you work your way down, and to feel it constantly changing, thinning and getting smoother under your hand. Once the surface has been sufficiently scraped, the pegs would be turned again to re-tighten the skin and then left to dry. Crucially, it is this drying of the skin under tension that flattens the fibres and makes it parchment. Unfortunately, as the skin is stretched taut, any imperfections – such as scars or bites, or a careless nick from a blade – may now grow into fully fledged holes. Often holes were stitched together by the parchment makers, sometimes extremely delicately. Very few skins would have been completely flawless, so there would either have to be skilful cutting of the finished parchment to avoid the holes, or simply writing around them by the scribe (or even celebrating them, as we saw in the previous chapter). Even the most skilfully prepared parchment can still bear traces of the once-living animal: the spine often remains visible, and the veins and pores of the skin can still be seen, providing the scribe and reader with a constant reminder of its origins.

Removing hair from a sheepskin that has been soaked in a lime bath.

Sheepskin laid over a beam and being scraped with the blunt side of the scudder to remove the hair.

Once the skin was scraped and dried, it was rewetted and rubbed over with a paste of ground cuttlefish and/or pumice. This was to smooth the surface further, soak up any remaining grease and give a nice white finish to the parchment. Once dried

Partly scraped sheepskin on a frame.

again, it would be cut off the frame and rolled up, ready to be used or sold. We can see in the manuscript image from the Hamburg Bible that monks often bought parchment from secular sources, but it might be the case that parchment was made in the grounds of some medieval monasteries, particularly the larger ones that had tanneries, such as Clairvaux and Rievaulx. The listings in the account book from Beaulieu Abbey show that they used parchment from their own animals but topped up with external purchases.[13] The records from Ely Cathedral Priory show that in

1374/5, Robert, a Cambridge parchmenter, was paid for parchment manufacture for the abbey.[14] Secular parchment makers, like tanners, were plentiful in urban environments where the high consumption of meat meant a ready supply of by-products.

A notable feature of parchment is that it retains its memory and as soon as it is cut off the stretching frame, it wants to return to its original shape, when it was wrapped around the animal. This tendency increases in humid conditions, and the parchment can buckle and warp as it absorbs moisture. Parchment is an organic material, and it will always react to its environment, so a completely flat folio is not a realistic expectation – even the heat of your hand writing over the parchment can have an effect. This is why many manuscripts would have had clasps attached to the book boards – to stop those unruly folios springing apart. Parchment is different to paper in that it can withstand high temperatures and does not catch alight, but it does shrink and warp when exposed to a naked flame. Parchment that has been exposed to water or damp can survive, although it will dry out very unevenly, and the ink may transfer onto the facing page. The biggest problem is the mould that grows in the damp folios, which can then eat away at the whole manuscript. The best conditions for parchment preservation are in a cool, non-humid environment – a shaded cloister in a Mediterranean monastery was ideal (although not so much the damp climate of northeast Europe). Parchment also provided a tasty snack for all kinds of insect larvae (grouped under the term 'bookworm'), which leave behind perfectly round holes as they burrow their way through folios. Their progress can be charted as you leaf through a manuscript and you can even identify missing or rebound quires by matching up the bored holes. There was a medieval solution to keep the bugs away: laying the herb *artemisia absinthium* (wormwood) between the books, as the nasty taste and strong smell was known to repel insects.[15]

Leather

Leather was often used as a covering for books, so it is worth mentioning here as the initial preparation process is largely the same as for parchment. Skin was soaked in lime to remove the hair and scudded over a beam. However, once the skin was dehaired, the process gets significantly more unpleasant. To soften the skin and remove any residual lime, it was soaked in a warm bath of dog or bird excrement (both would have been easily obtainable). The softening enzymes in dog and chicken poo are actually so potent that the skin can disintegrate if left in this mixture for too long. This softening process was known as bating or puering – possibly because it was the job of young boys (*pueri*) to get into the mixture and tread on the skins to further soften them. Those poor, poor boys. (For a similar example, see Stadtbibliothek Nürnberg, Amb. 317.2°, fol. 34r.) This step was sometimes followed by drenching: putting the skins into a warm bath of fermenting bran and stale beer or urine to neutralize the last of the lime.[16] Many tanneries were located near rivers on account of all the water that was needed. You can probably understand why people preferred them on the outskirts of towns or villages.

The next stage was the tanning, where the skin was placed in a weak solution of crushed tree bark (usually oak) and stirred continuously. The tannins in the tree bark leeched into the water to create a brown liquid. Once the skin had absorbed the colour evenly, it was removed, laid flat in a large vat and covered with more oak bark. More skins would be placed on top, each with a layer of bark in between them, and then the vat was filled with cold water. The skins could be in this vat for over a year. Unlike parchment, the tanning process is irreversible, and means that the leather becomes stable and stays flexible, even after it has got wet. Once the tanning process had completed, they were dried flat in a dark room and passed on to the curriers to shave, stretch, oil and dye the leather – and possibly become a handsome new binding for a manuscript.

Alum-tawed leather

Alum-tawed leather is a bit of a misnomer, as it is technically not leather. It is animal skin preserved in a mixture of salt and alum (a compound of potassium and aluminium), which (unlike the tannins in leather) washes out when wet and reverts to animal skin. However, its qualities as a strong yet flexible material made it ideal for sewing quires together when bookbinding, and also as a book covering. The bating process was followed as above for leather, but instead of being soaked in a tannin mixture, it was soaked in a mixture of alum, salt, egg yolk, flour and water. Once removed, it was left to gradually air dry over weeks, where it would become stiff as the alum salts absorbed into it. Once it was fully dry, it was stretched over a wooden pole or stake, which opened the fibres to create a soft and pliable material.

Paper

Although parchment was generally the preferred writing material for manuscripts in Europe during the medieval period, by the end of the fifteenth century it was overtaken by paper, partly because it was cheaper and partly because it was more suited to the printing press. Although it was seen first as more ephemeral than parchment, it soon became mass-produced in papermills across Europe and used for all sorts of documents. Paper was a late arrival to Europe – it had been used in China from the first centuries, made of shredded plant and cloth fibres pulped together and mixed with water, before being strained through wooden sieves. The fibres knit together during the drying process, forming a sheet of paper. This method of making paper spread out from East Asia, and by the eighth century it had been adopted by the Islamic world, which used cloth fibres. Parchment continued to be used, but paper had become the preferred writing surface by the tenth century in the Eastern Mediterranean and had spread to North Africa and Spain by the eleventh century, with paper being produced in Xàtiva on the east coast of Spain by the mid-century. From then on, paper mills started to appear in Europe. Italy seems to have been quick on the uptake, with several mills in operation by the end of the thirteenth century, and more mills appearing across Europe by the fourteenth century. These paper mills used water pressure to power huge hammers that pounded and shredded the rags to pulp in troughs. The pulp was then evenly sieved through a thinly wired wooden frame, known as a mould, which allowed the liquid to drain off. Watermarks were often woven into the wire in the frame to create an image on the paper such as an animal or symbol that would become known as the trademark of the manufacturer. The paper was then placed between layers of felt and squeezed dry with a press, coated with a size to prevent ink absorption and then hung up to dry. Different grades of paper were available, depending on the quality of the rags used.[17]

Ink

Our ancestors were using carbon ink as far back as 40,000 BCE to paint images in caves. This was a very basic ink, made from the soot of organic materials such as wood, bone or oil and mixed with water or fat. Good-quality carbon ink has a blue/black quality which doesn't discolour with age, but it can smudge easily and is easy to scrape off from the surface of a document. It was widely used in the ancient world for writing on papyrus. Pliny's description in his *Natural History* describes a dedicated manufacturing process for carbon-based ink, indicating that this was the most popular type of ink in the classical world in the first century.[18] However, a new type of ink made with oak galls came in towards the end of the classical period and a love spell from the late third-century *Leyden Papyrus v* provides one of the earliest recipes. For the magic to work, you have to write a special word on the root of a plant in ink, and then carry it around with you – everyone that meets you from then on will be thoroughly enamoured with you. The spell lists the ingredients for the ink – one dram of myrrh, four drams of truffle, two drams of blue vitriol, two drams of oak gall and three drams of gum arabic – but unfortunately no method is provided, so, alas, no love for us.[19] Analysis of the *Codex Sinaiticus* (mentioned in Chapter One) has revealed that by the mid-fourth century iron gall ink was being used. This book is one of the earliest examples of a Christian Bible, perhaps indicating that early Christianity had embraced not just the new codex format for spreading the word of God, but also a different type of ink than that used by traditional classical scribes.

So, what was iron gall ink? The clue is in the name really – it's an ink made from iron and galls (and gum arabic). Galls come in many different types, but the main ones that make ink are marble galls, Aleppo galls, apple galls and knopper galls. They are roundish growths full of tannic acid that are found on oak trees. The galls are a result of gall wasps laying their eggs onto the tree branch or acorn. When the larvae hatch and begin to feed, the tree, thinking it is being damaged, reacts by forming a protective shell over the area around the larvae, encasing the developing gall grubs in a safe cocoon. When the larvae pupate and become fully developed, they chew their way out of the protective shell and fly happily away, leaving the gall behind on the tree. Fortunately, the tree doesn't seem to mind too much that it's just been tricked into growing safe little nurseries for insect babies.

Vacated marble galls still attached to the oak tree.

Galls were well known in the classical world. In his first-century text *De materia medica*, Dioscorides describes galls as strongly astringent, and good for curing abnormal growths of the flesh, ulcers and toothache, as well as for more serious conditions, such as a prolapsed uterus or dysentery. Interestingly, among all the medical uses, Dioscorides also recommends galls steeped in vinegar or water as a black hair dye, so its potential as a dyestuff was well known, even if it wasn't widespread as an ink until a few hundred years later.

There are many recipes from the medieval period for making ink and the one below is from the same twelfth-century manuscript that contained the parchment instructions (BL, Harley MS 3915, fol. 148v). We don't know who the author of this recipe was, but this manuscript is full of artistic techniques, so it looks like these recipes and methods have been deliberately assembled as a craft guidebook. The ink recipe reads:

> First you take an earthen vase that contains eight pounds of water.
> Add half a pound of small galls and crush them well
> Boil until the mixture is reduced by half
> Take three ounces of gum arabic and grind it well
> Pour the gum into the mixture in the jar and boil it until reduced by half
> Remove the jar from the fire and take four ounces of vitriol and one pound of warm wine and mix them together in another jar and add little by little, stirring well
> Leave it to rest for a few days and afterwards, every day, stir four times with a stick.[20]

There are many variations of this recipe from the Christian and Islamic world, but the basic method stays largely the same. You take some galls, crush them, add some water and then warm the mixture to release the tannic acid into the water. Then add two ingredients, gum arabic and vitriol (ferrous sulphate), and perhaps a little bit of alcohol to act as a preservative, and you have an ink that can last thousands of years.

Gum arabic comes from the acacia tree which grows in Africa and Asia. The gum is harvested by making incisions in the bark, which fills with a thick and frothy liquid that then hardens into droplets and dries out, allowing easy collection. This resin has been used for thousands of years as a glue, as a binding agent for paint and cosmetics and as a thickener in food. It also gives an extra fluidity to help the ink to flow from the quill or pen and adhere to the writing surface. There are other tree gums that similarly work as a binder, and although European sources use the generic term 'gum arabic', it may have been substituted for local tree variants, such as cherry gum.

Vitriol was also known in the medieval period as copperas (which is today known as ferrous or iron sulphate) and was manufactured across England and the Continent. Copperas is formed naturally in caves from the exposure of iron ore to rainwater, which combines with naturally occurring sulphur to form pools of liquid. The liquid evaporates and turns into green iron sulphate crystals.[21] When these crystals are added to the tannic liquid from the crushed oak galls, a chemical reaction occurs and it immediately turns jet black. This also makes the ink bond with the surface of parchment, soaking into it and making it a much more permanent ink than carbon. Because of this knitting with the fibres of the parchment, even if the ink has been scraped off and written over, it often leaves a ghost-like shadow.

While iron gall ink became the most commonly used ink in medieval Europe, carbon ink was still used. Soot was just about the easiest thing to source in the medieval period, so making carbon ink was simple enough – collect soot from a fire, then grind with a bit of water and gum arabic, and you are good to go. There may have been a hierarchical system with ink – with the more permanent iron gall ink used for writing proper texts, and the more ephemeral carbon ink for less important jottings.

Oak galls seem to have been in plentiful supply in medieval Europe and we can see from surviving records in England that they were very cheap. Records from Ely Abbey show that in 1361, 4 pounds of galls, 4 pounds of copperas and 2 pounds of gum arabic cost three shillings and fourpence all together.[22] The *History of Agriculture and Prices in England* breaks down the prices further in an account from 1418, with 3 pounds of galls costing 2*d*, 3 pounds of copperas costing 4*d*, and 1¼ pounds of gum costing 1*s* 11¼*d*.[23] Many accounts list the ink ingredients separately like this, with galls, copperas and gum priced as individual items. This would seem to indicate that ink making was done domestically – you buy the necessary ingredients, and then go home and make up the ink yourself. It's nice to think that people might have had their own personal recipes and ratios for ink making.

However, ink is also found as a purchasable commodity. Records from Beaulieu Abbey and Ely Abbey list purchases of hard ink (*durum encaustum*),[24] presumably ink that had been dried into a solid block to be rehydrated as and when required. A solid lump of dried ink would have been easier to store, and could not get spoilt by mould, so it would have made sense to buy it in this way. It would also have been practical for travelling scribes to transport ink as a dehydrated solid to prevent spillages, and then rehydrate it when they had reached their destination. A curious addition from the accounts at Ely Abbey also includes 'beer for ink for the year' at a price of ninepence,[25] with the beer probably acting as a preservative.

Iron gall ink was also used by Islamic and Jewish scribes. Muhammad ibn Zakariyā al-Rāzī (854–925) was a Persian scholar who wrote (among other things) *Zīnat al-Kataba*, a collection of recipes and instructions for calligraphers. He has several recipes for iron gall ink, including this one for writing on codices: 'crush thirty gallnuts and cover them with three ratls of clear water. Cook on low heat until reduced by half, then strain. Stir in five dirhams good [green] vitriol and ten dirhams gum arabic. Leave in the sun for a day then write [to test it]. If the black is not good enough but leans towards brown, add more vitriol, and if it's not glossy enough, add more gum.'[26] So it would seem the same basic recipe for iron gall ink was used across the Christian and Islamic world alike. Islamic scribes also used other inks, including carbon ink, plant-based ink (made from galls or tree bark but without iron added) and mixed ink (carbon ink with iron gall or plant ink, sometimes with copper or lead added). Jewish use of iron gall ink is slightly more ambiguous, as the Talmud did not permit the use of ink that could not be erased for sacred writings. However, Hebrew scribes in their everyday lives probably used carbon ink, plant ink, iron gall ink and mixed ink.[27] It was probably the case (as with all scribes) that they made ink with whatever

Illuminated portrait of St Dunstan with writing materials, 12th century.

aterials there were to hand, what they could afford and also hat they (or their patron) personally preferred.

Ink in medieval manuscripts can range from intense black to nore mellow brown colour. This often depends on the ingre-ents used, for example, mixing galls with blue vitriol (copper ılphate) will make a browner ink. Inks, like parchment, age fferently, depending on their chemical make-up and environ-ental conditions. Also, if the ink has a high iron content, it comes corrosive over time and actually eats through the paper parchment. Parchment is slightly more stable, as it is slightly kaline and can neutralize the iron – although there are still enty of examples from parchment where the written letters ve corroded and only the outline remains. Like most things to with parchment, damp conditions make iron gall ink much ore unstable – so a cool, low-humidity environment is best for eservation.

uills

the early medieval period (and probably earlier) quills had super-ded the use of reed pens in the Christian West. However, like any of the materials used by scribes, they were so commonplace ere was no need to write down instructions on how to make one. ter all, why would a scribe need to know how to sharpen a quill nen they were already holding one in their hand? Fortunately, nnini provides instructions in his *Craftsman's Handbook*:

> If you need to know how to cut this goose quill, take a good, stiff quill and lay it upside down along the two fingers of your left hand. Then get a sharp, fine blade and snag it across the width, one finger's length up the quill and cut it, drawing the blade towards yourself, making sure that the cut is even and through the middle of the quill. And

> then put the blade back on one side of this quill (that is, on the left side, which faces towards you) and shave and thin it towards the tip and cut the curve into the other side and taper it to this same tip. Then, turn the quill around so that it faces down and rest it on your left thumb nail and carefully, little by little, shave and cut that little tip and make the nib broad and narrow as you wish, either for drawing or for writing. (ch. 14)

This is quite a good description; except Cennini leaves out the crucial vertical slit down the centre of the sharpened nib that acted as the reservoir for the ink.

Like most medieval instructions there are a lot of gaps to fill in. To start with – where do the quills come from? Geese and swans were the best source of quills as they were in ready supply in the medieval period, and they have a strong barrel (the central shaft) that sits comfortably in your hand. They also shed their feathers naturally every year in June and July. The birds were also used for meat, so feathers were probably harvested from carcasses too. The barrels can be quite soft when initially shed, so they would have been left for a period of time to harden naturally – it's possible that there was a rolling stock and that scribes used quills collected from the year before, while the newly collected ones would be stored for use the following year. Depending on what wing of the bird the feather has come from, it will curve a certain way. Most scribes are depicted as right-handed (regardless of whether this was their natural inclination), so would favour feathers from the left wing, as when held in your hand the barrel curves away from the body to the right, making it less distracting when bending forward to write.

Most scribes would have removed the feathers (barbs), perhaps sometimes leaving a tuft at the end to dust things away. The large, feathered quill in full plumage has become an iconic symbol of the pre-industrial age, but this is not an accurate representation, at least of the medieval period. If you look at most depictions of scribes holding quills, you will notice that they are bare and look more like a pen or pencil (a good example is BL, Royal MS 10 A XIII/1, fol. 2v). There are some examples where a smattering of plumage is noticeable, but these are in the minority – they also seem to be more prevalent in German and Eastern European images, so perhaps it was a cultural practice.[28] It seems practical to remove the barbs – it's easier to hold a smooth barrel. Once the barbs were removed, the waxy outer layer of the barrel (that would repel the ink) was scraped off. Slightly contradicting Cennini's account, it would be much safer to cut the quill away from the body, rather than towards. Starting about an inch from the end, the scribe would make an angled cut halfway through the barrel underside and then scoop the blade around so that the section was removed lengthways. With this section exposed, the inner membrane that would have carried the blood supply to the wing was easily removed. This membrane can release quite a pungent odour (but cats often find it a tasty treat, which is perhaps

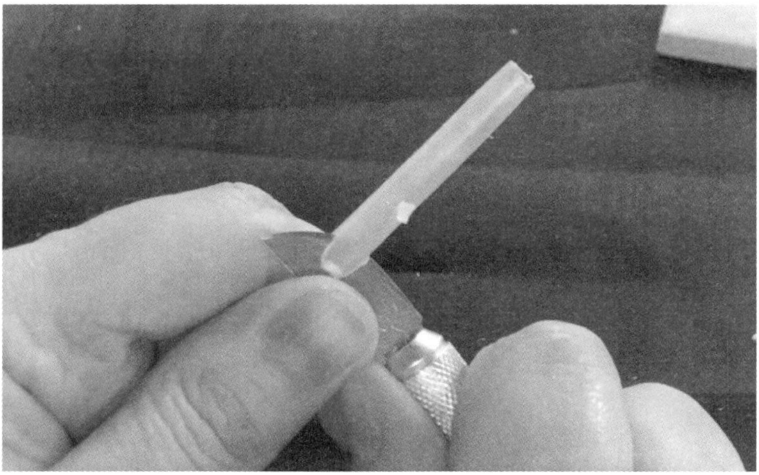

Making the first cut into a quill.

why they hung around with scribes). Then, about half an inch from the end, shoulders were cut into the halved barrel to make the width of the nib, and a slit made vertically to create the two halves of the nib. As many scribes knew, a quill needs constant sharpening and adjusting, which explains why they are so often shown with a quill in one hand and a penknife in the other. The penknife also came in handy for erasing mistakes and holding parchment in place.

Preparing the parchment for writing

Once the parchment was cut to size, it was laid flat out as a bifolium and rubbed down again with pumice and/or chalk before being ruled. In the earlier medieval period, this was done by marking horizontal lines with a sharp implement – enough to leave an indent, but not enough to cut right through the parchment (although, of course, we do see instances of scribes being a bit heavy-handed). Holes were pricked out in equal distances along the edges of the parchment with a knife, an awl or dividers (which is like a compass but with two sharp points) and then the holes were connected horizontally to make rows of lines. These prick marks can often still be seen on the edges of manuscripts, provided they have not been heavily trimmed. Vertical lines were also added to create a margin around the page. The method of marking lines with a sharp implement is called drypoint and was used in the early medieval period. From about the eleventh century onwards, a lead stick (similar to a pencil) was more common (although the use of leadpoint has been noted in the Lindisfarne Gospels for the drawing preparation).[29] The lead stick made a grey or reddish mark, known as leadpoint or plummet. Scribes were quite happy to leave these lines visible, no attempt being made to erase them once the writing had been done. The marked-out grid pattern allowed the scribe to work out where the text was

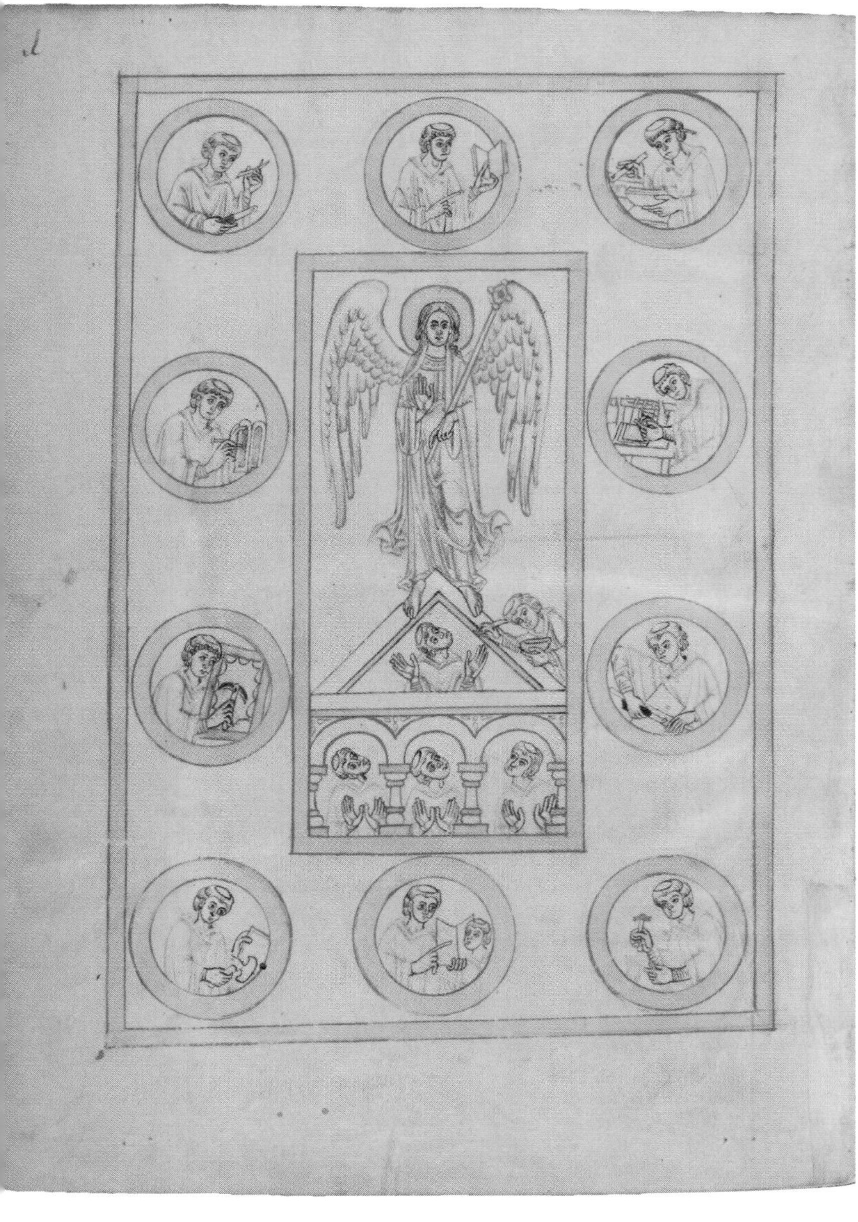

Stages of manuscript production, *Opera varia*, 12th century.

going to go and to leave gaps for decorated initials and miniatures – which were added after the writing had been done. Many of these stages are illustrated in the twelfth-century manuscript Staatsbibliothek Bamberg Msc.Patr.5.

Scribes sat at angled lecterns (this helped the ink flow better from the quill, as well as being less back-breaking), with perhaps a stand to hold the exemplar manuscript that was being copied. Also present would be a vessel to hold the ink, either an ink pot or animal horn, and a quill and a knife. As well as giving it a rub-down with pumice, scribes would apply to the parchment a light dusting of gum sandarac, a powder which absorbs ink and helps create crisp lines for the letters. Now the parchment was ready. It's incredibly difficult to know how long it would have taken to write a manuscript as it would have depended on so many different factors – the size of the parchment, the type of text, the type of script, the layout, the proficiency of the scribe, the quality of the exemplar they were copying, how many hours a day they were allowed to write – but for a really top-quality Bible you could be looking at years rather than months. Monastic conventions may have only allowed between three and five hours of writing a day, fitting around the daily prayers – although occasionally scribes worked at night (like the monk who completed by candlelight what he did not write in the sun).[30] As a very rough guide, a monastic scribe working in the eleventh/twelfth century would perhaps be expected to write around 150–200 lines per day. The number of lines ruled on a manuscript page varies, but generally falls between twenty and forty – so if we take thirty lines as an average, a scribe could produce five to seven pages a day.[31] It is estimated that Raulinus of Framlingham took ten months to a year to copy the Bible, otherwise worked out as roughly 3 miles' worth of script.[32] But don't forget that often creating a manuscript was a communal effort, with many scribes contributing to the final product.

Once the page was written, it was passed to the rubricator to add the coloured initial letters (*litterae notabiliores*) that signified a new passage of text. The scribe would often add small 'guide letters' to indicate to the rubricator what letter of the alphabet to insert, or even sometimes the colour to use. A twelfth-century manuscript from Nunnaminster has visible guide letters denoting what colour the initials should be, such as *r* for rouge or rubeus (red) and *a* for azurus (blue).[33] These *litterae notabiliores* could be red, blue, green, purple, brown or yellow, but after the thirteenth century tended to just be blue and red. They were drawn with a quill, rather than being painted in with a brush. Text headings, known as rubrics, were also added at this stage, usually in red (rubric comes from one of the Latin words for red – *ruber*). Then they would be passed to the illuminator or painter to add any images – which leads us on to the next chapter.

Five

Illumination and Painting

A German convent in the twelfth century

Gisela goes into the alcove by the cloister and takes down the earthenware jar from the wooden shelf. Scooping out a small spoonful of lapis lazuli pigment, she sprinkles it evenly on the grinding slab, puts the stopper back on the jar and replaces it on the wooden shelf. Selecting a smooth grinding stone from the bench, she adds a few drops of water and gum arabic and begins to grind the brilliant blue grains. As she moves her hand in a circular motion, she feels them rub against the weight of the grinding stone, creating a rasping sound. The familiar tang of sulphur drifts up to her nostrils as the tiny rock fragments are crushed into a smooth paste. She allows her mind to wander as she grinds, trying to picture the long journey this pigment has been on. It comes from a land far away, further than she can imagine, where this prized pigment is cut from the rocks, and travels from merchant to merchant before arriving at their monastery.

Sister Sophia bustles in to check on Gisela, making sure she is not idling. As the senior sister measures out a portion of minium on another slab, Gisela finishes her grinding. Taking her spatula, she scrapes the pigment into a large oyster shell and returns to her desk. Setting out her tools – paintbrushes, shells filled with brightly coloured pigments, a water pot and a cloth – she arranges her skirts and sits down in front of the image she is currently working on. She is careful to keep her water pot for the lapis separate – the tiny blue particles will settle at the bottom, and she will drain off the water at the end of the day to reuse the precious pigment. Today she will be starting on the figure of the Virgin Mary, decorated with the deepest lapis lazuli. Taking her finest paintbrush of squirrel tail fur, she dips it into the blue pigment and coats the brush before lifting her hand to the parchment. Careful not to place her hand on the gold illumination that fills the background, Gisela starts to paint. Frustrated with the uneven line that the brush produces, she puts the paintbrush in her mouth without thinking and licks the end to bring the bristles together in a sharp point. Feeling the grittiness of the lapis against her teeth, she sweeps her tongue around her mouth trying to dislodge the tiny granules. While she knows that the blue pigment is safe, the same cannot be said for the other colours such as the golden yellow of orpiment, or the brilliant red of vermilion, and she is mindful of the dangers of her craft.

She stifles a smile as she sees old Sister Gertrude vigorously scraping around in her ear with her earspoon and depositing a large waxy lump into her too-frothy egg glair. She watches the ancient nun in her cubicle as she carefully mixes the egg glair to a suitable consistency with a stick, the earwax magically causing all the bubbles to disappear. Before Gertrude goes any further, she pulls the heavy curtain across her cubicle. Behind the curtain she will apply the glair to the parchment, deftly removing a square of gold leaf from her pouch before pressing the gold down to adhere to the parchment. She must protect the precious metal from flying away with the breeze, which is why the heavy curtain is needed.

Gisela turns back to her parchment and takes up her paintbrush again, satisfied with the shape it now has. Her brush sweeps lightly over the image, slowly bringing to life the Virgin with the infant Jesus in her arms. She creates folds in the Virgin's drapery by skilfully applying lighter and darker shades and finishes by adding highlights in lead white. Gisela looks deeply into the eyes of the Virgin and feels a strong connection between the two of them, both bound to serve Christ. She feels her spirits rise as she lays down her brush, satisfied that she has honoured the Virgin with her artwork.

Let us head back to the manuscript production area, where our parchment folios are hanging up on a rack, beautifully scribed with brightly coloured *litterae notabiliores* and headings, all ready for decoration. Large blank spaces left by the scribe indicate where the artist needs to add the images and/or decorated initials. The artist will start the process by first sketching out an image, perhaps with a lead stick. This might have been done freehand by skilled artists, but the similarity in composition of many medieval images suggests that there was a certain amount of copying. As mentioned in Chapter Two, the portrait of Matthew in the Lindisfarne Gospels bears a strong resemblance to Ezra in the *Codex Amiatinus*. BL, Egerton MS 2019 has marginal decoration that is identical on both sides of each folio. It's possible here that a lightbox was used to copy images, illuminating the image from behind.[1] Alternatively, images could also be traced using translucent kid goat parchment, or by boiling fish glue and kid glue together, brushing a thin layer over a marble slab and then peeling the sheet off once dried.[2]

Another copying method was called 'pouncing'. The image to be copied was placed over some blank parchment, and then holes were pricked all around the outline of the image, through to the parchment underneath. The underlying parchment then served as a template. Taking this template and placing it over a new piece of parchment, ash or ground pumice was dabbed over the template so that it went through the holes onto the parchment below and left a mark. Then, after carefully removing the template, the dots were connected on the parchment underneath to create a duplicate image of the original.[3] There are also surviving 'model books' of decorated initials to help training artists. Some surviving folios from a twelfth-century Italian manuscript (Fitzwilliam Museum, MS 83-1972) contain the outlines of 22 alphabet letters, decorated with zoomorphic features, evangelist figures and interlaced vine scrolls.

Once the artist had sketched out the preliminary drawing, an outline was added in thin pigment or ink to make it more visible. Often this was done with red lead pigment, known as minium (which is where the word 'miniature' comes from). Many unfinished manuscripts still have these stages visible. BL, Royal MS I B XI has many unfinished decorated initials, finely outlined in ink but with the lead stick sketch still showing underneath, for example, on folio 44r. If the outlined image was to be illuminated, the next stage was to apply the gold.

Illumination

Gold has always been an incredibly important metal to many cultures throughout history, representing a light and radiance inextricably linked with the divine. The symbolic weight of gold became even more potent when used in Christian religious texts. The manuscripts were already sacred objects channelling the hallowed word of God, but the gold added a further layer of spiritual connection, with the dazzling shine distilling the wisdom of the holy words into the reader. We can get an idea of how visually arresting these manuscripts were from a letter from Boniface, the early medieval missionary, to the abbess Eadburg, probably of Wimborne in Dorset. He implores her to make him a manuscript:

> written in gold of the epistles of my master, St Peter the Apostle, to impress honour and reverence for the Sacred

> Scriptures visibly upon the carnally minded to whom I preach . . . I am sending by the priest Eoban the materials [gold] for your writing.[4]

Eadburg's abbey clearly had the skills capable of producing fine religious texts in gold in the eighth century. Unfortunately Eadburg's manuscripts don't survive, but the lavishly decorated Stockholm *Codex Aureus* (National Library of Sweden, MS, A 135) was made around 750 in the south of England, providing an example of what was being produced in that area at that time.

Some illuminated Bibles were so highly prized that they may well never have been used in the liturgy – rather they served as religious relics in their own right. They may have been placed on the altar or in some other prominent position and venerated as a holy object. We can see how the codex became more than just a carrier of information – it took on significance as a physical object. As well as the religious symbolism, manuscripts laden with gold (both inside and outside) were a display of wealth, so affluent patrons would commission monasteries to produce sumptuous codices – to keep for themselves or to give as gifts.

In Europe, there were few sites where gold could be mined and the Romans had largely exhausted any natural sources. Therefore it was common practice to melt down what gold was already in circulation – from coins, jewellery and decorative objects. However, the purest gold came from West Africa, imported into Europe in the early medieval period in powdered form.[5] A fourteenth-century map, the Catalan Atlas, shows Mansā Mūsā, the wealthy ruler of the Māli empire (1307/12–1332/7), seated on a throne with the following caption: 'This king is the richest and most distinguished ruler of this whole region on account of the great quality of gold that is found in his lands.'[6] The Catalan Atlas is an important visual representation of medieval trade and networks, denoting the internal and external links between Africa, Asia and Europe.

Powdered gold was known as shell gold, as it was kept in seashells. It was mixed with honey or gum arabic so that it adhered to the parchment and tended to be quite grainy in the early medieval period. It was applied by quill or copper pen,[7] or perhaps brushed on for larger surfaces. Gold could also be applied in leaf form, hammered down from gold coins into thin sheets 0.001 mm thick. Gold leaf had been used for gilding since Egyptian times, and by the twelfth century it was more prevalent in European manuscript art than powdered gold. In his textbook *On Diverse Arts*, Theophilus recommends to 'take pure gold and thin it out with a hammer on a smooth anvil, very carefully, so as not to let any break occur' (Book 1, ch. 23). Once the gold was thin enough, it was stored in a pouch ready to be applied to the parchment. An adhesive was applied first to the parchment for the gold leaf to stick to, known as a base layer, ground or size. In the earlier medieval period, this was probably plant gum or egg glair. (Glair is made from whipped-up fresh egg whites left overnight; the next day the crusty froth on top is removed and the liquid underneath is your glair.) Theophilus provides useful instructions on applying the gold to the glair:

> In laying on [the gold] take glair, which is beaten out of the white of an egg without water, and with it lightly cover with a brush the place where the gold is to be laid. Wet the point of the handle of the brush in your mouth, touch a corner of the leaf that you have cut, and so lift it up and apply it with the greatest speed. Then smooth it with the brush. At this moment you should guard against drafts and hold your breath because, if you breathe, you will lose the leaf and find it again only with difficulty. When this piece has been laid on and has dried, lay another piece over it in the same

> way, if you wish, and also a third, if necessary, so that you can polish it all the more brightly with a tooth or a stone.

The gold was applied to the parchment while the gum or glair was still tacky and built up in layers. It was a tricky business, as the gold was so thin it could be lost by the slightest breeze. Then it was polished with a burnisher to really make the gold shine. Cennini recommends 'the teeth of dogs, of lions, of wolves, of cats, of leopards and, in general, of any animal that feeds finely on meat' (ch. 135). Fortunately, there is also a vegetarian option – precious stones work just as well, such as sapphires, emeralds or rubies. Although shell gold gave way to gold leaf in the twelfth century, it was used again along with gold leaf in the later medieval period – as grinding techniques had improved and allowed artists to create delicate shimmering highlights with the powdered gold. A fragment from a Book of Hours made for Louis XII around 1498 shows the Virgin Mary and baby Jesus bathed in golden rays of light streaming down from the heavens (Victoria and Albert Museum, E.949-2003), demonstrating this beautiful effect.

After about the twelfth century, gesso started to be used as a base for gold, which was essentially plaster of Paris mixed up with other sticky things. The bulk of the plaster created a cushion for the gold to be laid on, so when applied it looked like a layer of solid gold. The raised surface also reflected the gold further. The main ingredients for gesso were plaster of Paris and anything adhesive – for example, egg glair, gum arabic, fish glue, rabbit glue, sugar and garlic juice could be used. It would certainly have had a distinctive smell. A bit of pigment was then added to the mixture – anything from red, yellow, pink, brown, blue or grey. Not only did this help the artists see where they were laying the gesso, it also provided a softer backdrop to the gold if it flaked off the parchment later. It is possible that artists used different colours to create warmer or cooler tones against the gold.[8] Once all the ingredients were added, they were ground together in a mortar and pestle to a thin consistency.

Medieval people were nothing if not resourceful. All this mixing and grinding could result in too many bubbles in the egg glair or gesso, which meant it could not be applied smoothly – but fear not, there was a handy solution. Earwax. Yes, that's right, earwax. As if the gesso was not already full enough of offensive ingredients. Many medieval craftspeople would have had a range of useful implements hanging off their belts – including an ear scoop – so all they had to do was have a quick rummage around in the old ear canal and stir the contents into the mixture. An English manuscript of miscellaneous recipes contains some instructions dating from the fourteenth century that instruct on making a ground for gold lettering with glair, white chalk, the 'ryngynge of thinne ere' (earwax) and a little bit of saffron. *The Art of Illumination* helpfully explains that 'if the glair makes a froth, human earwax will break that up at once, if you put in a little of it; and this is a secret' (ch. 23). Alternatively, clove oil also does the trick, and (unusually for this chapter) smells lovely.

Once the gesso was applied to the parchment, probably with a quill, it was left to set thoroughly, ideally overnight. The gesso would dry out and harden, so to reactivate the adhesive properties the illuminators needed to do some heavy breathing. A few deep breaths from the diaphragm over the gesso produced enough moisture for the surface to become sticky again (but not wet enough to break down the smooth surface). Ideally a piece of gold leaf would be already on the tip of the illuminator's brush, and they would lay the gold over the gesso immediately after breathing on it and brush it down. Any excess gold was collected and reused for shell gold. After the gesso had re-hardened the gold was then burnished to a dazzling shine. In some illuminated images, you can see scored lines that were incised into the

Applying gesso with a quill to an outlined miniature.

softened gesso, creating a textured pattern of squares, diagonals or lozenge shapes.

BL, Add MS 42555, fol. 54v gives a useful insight into the illumination process, where we can see the gesso has been added to the image but the gold not yet applied. This manuscript also shows the effect of the gesso when the gold has not adhered properly or has subsequently flaked off. Folio 30v is also unfinished, but some gold has been applied, for example to the king's crown. A closer inspection shows that there are several areas not covered, but the warm tones of the gesso mean that it is not so jarring on the eye. Although gold was the main precious metal used to illuminate manuscripts, other metals were used, such as silver or tin. In this same image the soldiers' swords and helmets are depicted in silver – however, silver does tarnish quite easily over time, and one of the soldiers' boots, once in silver, has now degraded to a black mess (presumably the sulphur in the gesso aided this process). Pigments have also started to be added to this image, so you get a real idea of the different processes going on here in the stages of creation.

Painting and pigments

There are so many modern-day depictions of the medieval period being really drab and brown, but in reality it would have been full of colour. Churches were painted inside and out, often quite garishly. Similarly, there's not much room for subtlety or carefully blended tones in the earlier medieval manuscripts. There are surviving instructions on how to make pigments from the earliest medieval recipe books – the *Mappae clavicula* describes how to make verdigris, lead white and cinnabar (albeit vaguely) and Theophilus and Cennini expand on these pigments as the medieval period progresses. Creating a European medieval palette would have been an industrious affair, requiring ingredients from

Unfinished illumination of a battle scene, with gold and some pigment applied, Abingdon Apocalypse, 13th century.

near and far. Some pigments could be homegrown and harvested from plants from your back garden; some pigments needed to be skilfully manufactured applying chemical knowledge; and some pigments were imported from lands far away. Artists could get the finest or cheapest pigments depending on their geographical location, trade links and financial support.

Outside of the monasteries (and perhaps even inside), artists would be trained through apprenticeships, learning the skills by starting off with the most menial tasks – like filling in backgrounds. Medieval artists were not particularly revered for their talent, they were considered ordinary craftspeople, often doubling up as mural painters or sculptors; Master Hugo of the Bury Bible was also noted for carving the double doors at the front of the church.[9] Although Hugo is known to us, for the most part medieval artists remain anonymous and many of their daily work practices are still a mystery. Where did they source their pigments, for example? Did they grind up their own pigments or buy them ready ground? Did they buy in bulk or as needed? Place names like Maddermarket Street in Norfolk indicate that the red-coloured madder was easily available to purchase there, either as a dyestuff or pigment.

We have already seen that model books existed to help training artists, and Theophilus and Cennini also provide useful instructions for beginners. Theophilus' *On Diverse Arts* has chapters on mixing pigments to make flesh colours, applying shadows and highlights and how to paint hair and beards on old and young men. Cennini expands on this, instructing on how to paint drapery, water, flesh wounds and dead people, including this important tip: 'do not apply any pink because a dead person has no colour' (ch. 161). There is another artists' manual called the Göttingen Model Book that dates from the mid-fifteenth century (Gottingen, Niedersächsische Staats- und Universitätsbibliothek, Cod. MS Uffenb. 51). This contains a step-by-step guide on painting foliage and how to create an illuminated chequered background, with written instructions followed by diagrams – an extremely useful visual aid for the young apprentice. So, from the early medieval period – with its terse few sentences in the *Mappae clavicula* on making a handful of pigments – the recording of artistic technique had developed to such an extent by the end of the medieval period that there were fully fleshed out instructions with accompanying diagrams. This may also, of course, reflect the move away from monastic manuscript production, where in-house training would be provided, to the secular, commercial workshops of the later medieval period. The rise in literacy may also have been a factor.

Like the guideletters left in the margins for the person adding the *litterae notabiliores*, we sometimes see instructions left for the artist, telling them what details or colour to add. The Bury Bible (CCCC, MS 2) had a multilingual team working on the designs, with letters left in Latin/French, English and even Greek. Multispectral imaging has revealed these instructional letters underneath the paint. Some letters, such as *A* for azurus/azur (blue) and *R* for ruber/rouge (red), suggest a Latin- or French-speaking artist, whereas elsewhere *B* is used for blewe/blue, suggesting an English-speaking artist. The Greek letter *Φ* (phi) is also used, probably for the Greek word *φοῖνιξ* (crimson/purple), suggesting either a Greek-speaking artist or an acute familiarity with Byzantine art – giving a fascinating insight into the influences of (presumably freelance) artists working on a manuscript in England in the twelfth century.[10] This letter is just about visible in the illumination of a reclining Anna following the birth of Soloman, in a small purplish section just behind her elbow (fol. 147v). A similar Bible produced at Winchester has more detailed instructions for the artist: still visible in the margin are the words, 'Make [draw] Soloman in the temple with hands extended to God' (fol. 303r).[11]

Interestingly, it is documented in the *Memorials of Bury St Edmunds Abbey* that Master Hugo could not source calfskin locally that was of good enough quality, so the abbot procured some from Ireland which he then painted on separately and stuck into the Bury Bible.[12] This gives a rare glimpse into a painter's methods: Hugo clearly had very high standards and wanted only the best-quality materials to paint on (apparently with the blessing of the abbey) – even though the parchment used in the manuscript was already quite high quality. Furthermore, creating the images separately and glueing them in gives a different approach to the collaborative nature of manuscript production. The obvious advantage of doing this is that it ensures the colours do not show through onto the other side of the folio, but it could have further implications for the workshops that developed in the thirteenth century, where perhaps images were mass-produced on individual pieces of parchment that could then have been supplied as and when needed – just paste and go.

IT'S HARD TO SAY exactly what a typical medieval palette would have consisted of, because it changed throughout the period (depending on things such as location and trade links), but the following section will identify the most common pigments. Specific names of pigments in medieval recipes are often vague or misleading (for example, dragonsblood or azure), so the pigments that are discussed here have been identified as present in manuscripts by modern multispectral imaging.[13] Technically speaking, a pigment is a colour that does not dissolve in water (for example, verdigris, lapis lazuli, vermilion). If you take a pigment and mix it in water, eventually it will settle out at the bottom and you can pour off the water and dry out the pigment.

Colours that are soluble in water are dyes – but they can be mixed with a mordant to create a lake pigment and dried to a

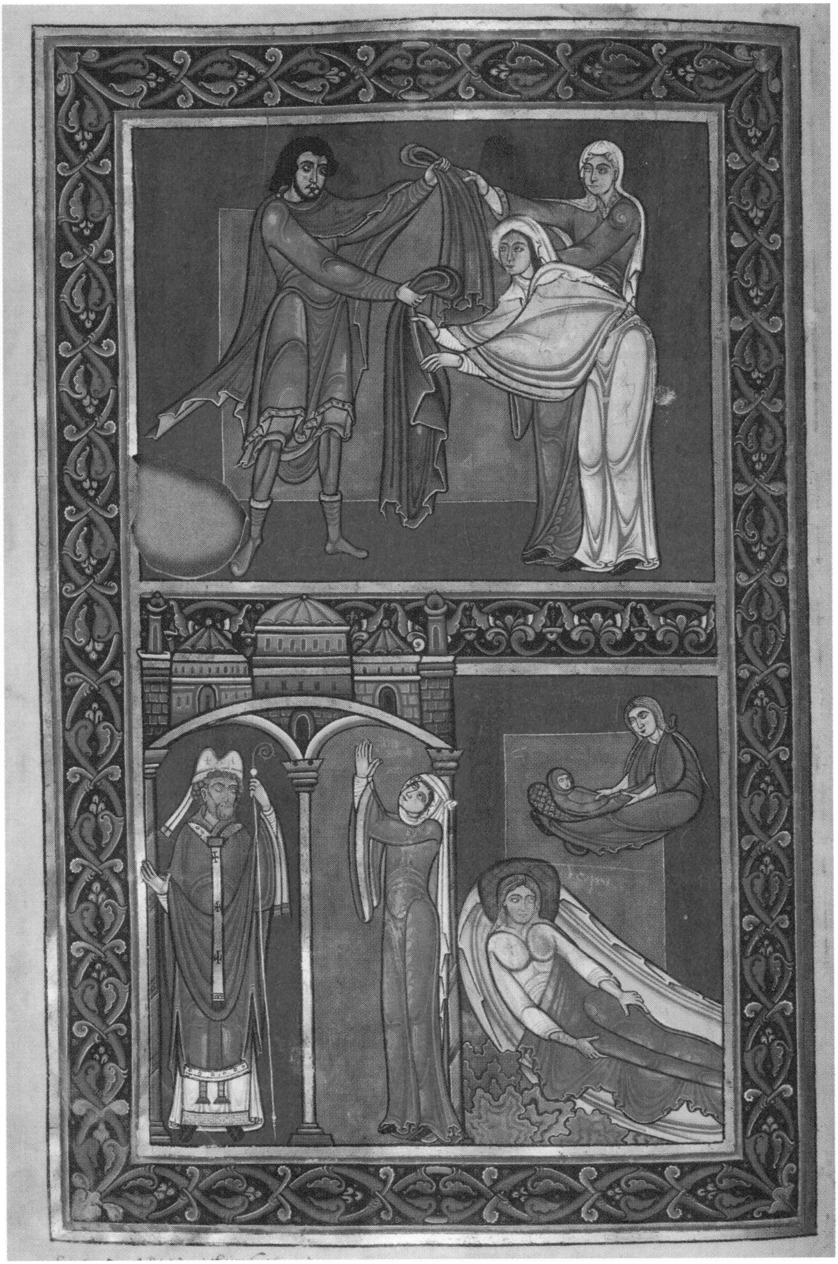

The Greek letter Φ (phi) is just about visible in the purple section behind the reclining woman's elbow, from the Bury Bible, vol. II, 12th century.

powder (for example, weld, madder, woad). Alum (aluminium potassium sulphate) was a popular mordant used for pigments and dyes (mordant comes from the Latin word *mordere*, to bite). The colour molecules, which are water-soluble, bond with the alum and the colour then 'piggybacks' on the alum, allowing it to stay in a non-soluble form and be used as a pigment. Alum was often used along with lye (also known as potash or lixivium), an alkali solution that was the basic ingredient of soap in the medieval period. It was made by filtering rainwater through wood ash. Adding the alkali solution to the acidic alum solution causes a precipitation reaction that thickens the dye and allows it to settle at the bottom and separate from the water. The colour that settles is the lake pigment, which is then dried out.

To then use as a paint, remix the powdered pigment with some water and a binder, such as gum arabic, honey, egg glair or egg yolk, and this binder helps to fix the paint to the surface. Without this binder, the pigment would just flake off the surface once dry.

Here is a brief guide to the pigments used in medieval manuscripts in Europe, grouped into colours.

Reds and Oranges

Apart from black, red was the most common colour in manuscripts, used to write the rubrics (headings) and *litterae notabiliores*.

Red ochre is a natural brownish-red pigment that comes from the ground and is made mainly of haematite (iron oxide). It is found pretty much all over the world and is one of the oldest colours used by humans for decoration. Red ochre was used as pigment through the Assyrian, Egyptian and classical periods, remaining popular throughout the medieval period and up to the present day. It's made by digging up the coloured rock or soil and washing and grinding it. When the particles are small enough, the pigment is ready to be used. For examples of red ochre in medieval manuscripts, look at the red colour on the capital letters in BL, Harley MS 7653, fol. 1v.

Madder is extracted from the madder plant (*Rubia tinctorum*) that grows in Europe. It was popular as a dye and as a pigment from at least Egyptian times. The alizarin red colour is extracted from the roots. The roots need to grow for at least three years, preferably four, and then dry out for another year before they are ready to be used for pigment, so this is not a quick process. The final colour depends on all sorts of things – such as soil quality and weather conditions – so uniform batches of colour are not easily achievable from year to year. Madder can vary in shades from brown, orange, bright red to pink. It is perfectly safe, and the roots can even be consumed as a tea. It would have been grown naturally and harvested in gardens or bought (perhaps in dried root form) at markets. To make madder, chop the dried roots into small chunks and heat gently for a few days (not too hot or the alizarin will die off). Add alum and lye, wait for the lake pigment to settle at the bottom and pour off the water. Top up again, wait for the pigment to settle and repeat until the water is clear. Pour off most of the water and then filter through a muslin cloth. Once the water has drained off, spread the muslin cloth out to allow the pigment to dry. Grind to a fine powder and add water and a binder to make the right consistency to paint. To make rose madder (a pink shade), add more alum.

Red lead is artificially made lead oxide. It was used from classical times and the orangey-red is clearly identifiable in many medieval manuscripts. It was the most common red in European manuscripts up to about the tenth century. Red lead is considered highly toxic today due to the lead content. It's made by soaking the metal in vinegar in a sealed pot and then heating the residue that accumulates. Red lead is also known as minium (this is why medieval miniatures are called miniatures, not because they are small, but because the images were initially outlined in minium). When the residue from the lead is heated, it changes from white to yellow, to orange, to red. These inbetween stages form pigments known as litharge and massicot. When massicot is detected in early medieval manuscripts, this is probably a result of the lead not being heated enough.[14] A twelfth-century manuscript (known as the Phillipps-Corning manuscript) has this recipe for making red lead and lead white:

> If you wish to make minium, either red or white, take a new pot and put lead sheets in it, fill the pot with very strong vinegar, cover it and seal it. Put the pot in a warm place and leave it there for one month. Later take the pot, uncover it, and shake out whatever surrounds the lead sheets into another earthenware pot and then set it on fire. Stir the pigment continuously and when you see the pigment become white, like snow, take away as much as you like of it, and that pigment is called ceruse. Then put the rest on the fire and stir continuously, until it becomes red, like other minium. Then take it away from the fire and leave it in the pot to cool.[15]

Examples of red lead in manuscripts include the red dots in the Lindisfarne Gospels (Cotton MS Nero D IV, fol. 91v) and the robes in the Abingdon Apocalypse (BL, Add MS 42555, fol. 75r).[16] Red lead is often discoloured or has a dark halo around it, as over time it can degrade (see BL, Add MS 34890, fol. 1r for a dark halo around the red letters).

Vermilion is a bright red pigment made artificially from mercury sulphide. It is also a naturally occurring mineral known as cinnabar, often found around volcanoes and hot springs. It was mined from pre-classical times, particularly in Spain. Its toxicity came to be known, as Dioscorides noted that ingested mercury caused the insides to rot.[17] It is likely that in the Roman period Spanish cinnabar was mined by enslaved people and/or convicts, and this cruel practice of enforced labour carried on in Almadén until the end of the eighteenth century. While they may not have had the scientific knowledge to understand how poisonous mercury was, the high illness and death rate of the miners was an acknowledged consequence.[18] However, techniques were developed to make mercury sulphide artificially and the pigment became known as vermilion. This technique, perfected by Islamic alchemists such as Jābir ibn Ḥayyān, then spread to Europe in the ninth century. The Phillipps-Corning manuscript also contains a recipe for making vermilion:

> If you wish to make vermilion, take a glass flask and coat the outside with clay. Then take one part by weight of quicksilver [mercury] and two of white or yellow sulphur and set the flask on three or four stones. Surround the flask with a charcoal fire, but a very slow one, and then cover the flask with a tiny tile. When you see that the smoke coming out of the mouth of the flask is straw-coloured, cover it again; and when yellow smoke comes out, cover it again, and when you see red smoke, like vermilion, coming out, then take away the fire, and you have excellent vermilion in the flask.[19]

However, Cennini observes that there are many different recipes for vermilion and recommends that instead of making your own 'just take what you can find at the apothecary's for your money,' giving us an idea of where to buy pigment in late medieval Italy (ch. 40). He also says that monks know a lot of vermilion recipes, indicating that monasteries were centres of production (although there is also plenty of evidence of monasteries buying vermilion from outside).[20] Once the pigment was extracted, it was ground and mixed with water and a binder. For examples of vermilion in manuscripts, see the Eadui Psalter (BL, Arundel MS 155, fol. 147r) and the angel's robes and red text in the Abingdon Apocalypse (BL, Add MS 42555, fol. 5r).[21] Like red lead, vermilion can also discolour due to degradation.

Realgar (As_4S_4) is an arsenic sulphide mineral mined with orpiment, orangey-red in colour. Like orpiment, it is highly dangerous, described by Cennini as really 'toxic . . . it is not to be kept company with . . . watch out for yourself' (ch. 48). It was not widely used.

Kermes is a red dye and pigment, used from at least Egyptian times. It was obtained from the bodies of female scale insects (*Kermes vermilio*) that fed on the sap of Mediterranean oak trees. The insects were collected and dried, then crushed to release carminic acid. Like many organic pigments, kermes pigment is hard to detect using modern methods of manuscript analysis, but the inclusion of kermes in many recipe books such as the *Mappae clavicula* suggests it was a commonly used medieval pigment. A 1431 compilation of recipes by French bibliophile Jean Lebègue, *Experimenta de coloribus*, gives the following instructions on making kermes pigment:

> Take some lye, and boil in it *rubea de grana* [kermes] until the colour is extracted, and then strain the lye with the colour through a linen cloth. Afterwards take some more lye and heat it; and put into it some finely powdered rock alum, and let it stand until the alum is dissolved. Then strain it through the strainer into the kermes lye, and immediately the lye will be coagulated, and make a

> lump or mass, which you must stir well. Pour the liquid on a new hollow brick, which will absorb the lye, and the pigment will dry out on the top. Scrape it off the brick and keep it for use.[22]

As the kermes insect was only found in Mediterranean regions, it seems to have been more prevalent in manuscripts produced in these areas. It would have been harder for artists in northwest Europe to source it, and although it has been identified in some French manuscripts, madder seems to have been a more commonly used pigment.[23] Locally sourced ingredients would always have been a cheaper option. Due to conservation reasons, it is not possible to buy kermes today.

Lac is a similar pigment, obtained from another scale insect (*Kerria lacca*) that lives on trees in South and Southeast Asia. They secrete a red resin on the branches, which is then removed and sold in flakes. It was particularly widely used in medieval Portuguese manuscripts, thanks to the Arabic and Jewish trade networks.[24] Towards the end of the medieval period, kermes and lac were superseded by *Dactylopius coccus* (cochineal) from the New World, which contained much more carminic acid. Both *Kerria lacca* and *Dactylopius coccus* are perfectly safe as they are used as food colourants.

Brazilwood, or sappanwood (*Caesalpinia sappan*), comes from a tree native to Southeast Asia. The branches contain the red dye brazilin (the Portuguese colonists gave Brazil its name after recognizing the same species of tree growing there that they knew from Asia). Brazilwood was available in Europe as a pigment and dye in the later medieval period, imported from Asia. The plant features in medieval herbals, such as a thirteenth-century copy of *Tractatus de herbis* (BL, Egerton MS 747, fol. 18r), which describes brazilwood as 'a twisted and very red tree, which like sandal wood is found in the land overseas', and is used for dyeing. The fourteenth-century *Art of Illumination* has a recipe for making brazilwood, indicating that its use as a pigment was well known:

> Take some of the best brazil wood with a knife or a piece of glass [and] scrape off as much of this wood as you want. And put it into a lye made from the wood of vines or oaks. And put this into a glazed dish which will stand the heat: And let it stand in this lye for a night or a day to soften. Then put it on the fire, and heat it to the boiling point, but do not let it boil; and stir it often with a stick. Then take account of how much scraped brazil there was, and take the same quantity of very nice white marble powder, and as much sugar alum or rock alum as there is of the brazil. And grinding them thoroughly, mix them gradually in this dish, always stirring it with a stick, until the froth which it makes subsides, and it is well coloured. And then it is strained through a clean linen or hempen cloth into a glazed or unglazed porringer. (ch. 12)

Brazilwood has also been detected in French manuscripts from the fifteenth century, so it was being used in manuscripts in Europe in the later medieval period, as trade routes and networks improved.[25]

Yellows

The main challenge with yellow is achieving a beautiful vibrant colour that doesn't fade. Many natural sources, such as plants, may yield a lovely colour initially, but they lose their radiance very quickly.

Yellow ochre is an earth pigment, like red ochre, and it was also one of the first pigments used by humans. It was used at least around 25,000 years ago in cave paintings and continued to be used as pigment through the ancient and medieval period. It is made the same way as red ochre. For examples of yellow ochre in medieval manuscripts, look at the yellow colour on the capital letters in BL, Harley MS 7653, fol. 1v.

Orpiment (*auripigmentum*) occurs naturally as a yellow mineral called arsenic sulphide (As_2S_3) and is found around hot springs and volcanic fumaroles. It was used as a pigment from Assyrian times and remained popular in the classical and medieval periods, even though it was known to be toxic. Strabo wrote about the cruel business of mining arsenic using enslaved people in Turkey in the first century BCE:

> The Sandaracurgium is a mountain hollowed out by large trenches made by workmen in the process of mining . . . Besides the great labour of the employment, the air is said to be destructive of life, and scarcely endurable in consequence of the strong odour issuing from the masses of mineral; hence the slaves are short-lived.[26]

The casual attitude demonstrated here towards the treatment of enslaved human beings is quite disturbing. Orpiment mining is also pictured in the thirteenth-century *Tractatus de herbis* (BL, Egerton MS 747, fol. 9r), seemingly being extracted in the same way. The granular deposits were then ground down to make the pigment, sometimes with glass. Orpiment can also be made artificially by mixing sulphur and arsenic either by heat or precipitation, although it remains dangerous. Cennini warns about its danger: it is 'made by alchemy and really is toxic . . . watch that you do not spatter your mouth with it lest it does you harm' (ch. 47).

It can also react with other pigments such as red lead and verdigris, blackening over time. Orpiment is found in many medieval manuscripts, including the Lindisfarne Gospels (Cotton MS Nero D IV, fol. 91v) and the Book of Kells. It dramatically fell out of use after the twelfth century, as other synthetic yellows were introduced.[27]

Lead tin yellow (*giallorino/giallolino*) is a delicate, lemony yellow that became a popular pigment in manuscripts and frescoes in Europe from about the thirteenth century. It was artificially created by heating lead and tin together, manufactured initially by the glass and ceramics industry. It is toxic due to the lead content. There is a brief description of how to make lead tin yellow in a fifteenth-century Bolognese manuscript (Biblioteca Universitaria di Bologna, MS 2861): 'Take 2lb of this calcined lead and tin [1 lb of lead and 2 lb of tin, heated at a high temperature], 2½ lb of minium and ½ lb of sand from the Val d'Arno pounded very fine; put it into a furnace and let it fine itself, and the colour will be perfect.' However, Raffaello Borghini's treatise on painting and sculpture (*Il Riposo*, 1584) recommended that artists buy it ready-made, perhaps indicating that this was a skilled process.[28] It has been identified in the Abingdon Missal created in 1461 (Bodleian Library, Digby MS 227, fol. 113v, top left foliage).[29]

Mosaic gold (*purpurino/purpurinus/aurum musicum*) is an artificially made pigment of the mineral sal ammoniac, mercury, tin and sulphur (SnS_2). It is a delightfully sparkly golden yellow, as the name indicates. It was used from the latter half of the thirteenth century in Europe, although it was used in China long before this.[30] A summary of the recipe in *The Art of Illumination* tells us to: 'heat tin and mercury and mix with vinegar and salt. Heat again and mix with heated sulphur and sal ammoniac until it turns black. Place the mixture in a jar in a furnace until a grey smoke is released. Remove the jar and break open once cooled' (ch. 8).

Cennini warns to be 'as careful as if for fire' when using mosaic gold near gold leaf, as he says if any mercury comes into contact with gold, it eats it up (ch. 173). The mercury content also made it toxic to humans. However, mosaic gold and gold leaf are often seen alongside each other, as in Fitzwilliam, MS Marley Add. 1. On folio 2v there are a group of figures with blonde flowing locks of mosaic gold against an illuminated background of gold leaf.[31] This manuscript was made during the period 1265–72, possibly in Acre (Palestine), so it could have been influenced by Byzantine or Islamic practices that then made their way to Western Europe.

Plant yellows

A variety of plants produce yellow pigments, including turmeric, weld, saffron and chamomile. They are often difficult to identify in manuscripts by spectroscopy owing to their organic nature; however, it is likely they were sometimes used – even if just as a cheap alternative when nothing else was available. Plants that grew for free (for example, weld is known as dyer's weed) and were easily extracted using a lake pigment would have been an attractive source of colour for painting or dyeing. However, these natural yellows were a lot more fugitive (that is, not lightfast) than the artificially manufactured ones.

Greens

Verdigris was the main green in the medieval period, used as a general term for any copper-based green pigment. It was easily sourced from the green patina that forms naturally on copper when exposed to the elements, which was then scraped off and used as a pigment. It was used from at least Egyptian times. The verdigris used in the medieval period tended to be copper (II) acetate, where copper was exposed to acetic acid (vinegar). The *Mappae clavicula* gives us an effective recipe for making verdigris:

> take a new pot and put sheets of the purest copper in it; then fill the pot with very strong vinegar, cover it and seal it. Put the pot in some warm place, or in the earth, and leave it there for six months. Then uncover the pot and put what you find in it on a wooden board and leave it to dry in the sun.[32]

Other methods advise using urine instead of vinegar or burying the pot in animal dung to create the necessary heat.[33] Although making this pigment is quite a straightforward process, the acetic acid can be rather overpowering, stinging your eyes and getting to the back of your throat. It is not particularly dangerous, unless you were inclined to ingest large amounts or bathe in it. Most of the green paint in medieval manuscripts will be a type of verdigris, but particular examples include the initial A and T on fol. 18v of the Lindisfarne Gospels (BL, Cotton MS Nero D IV, fol. 18v) and the sea in the Abingdon Apocalypse (BL, Add MS 42555, fol. 22r).

Vergaut is not a pure pigment, it is a forest green colour made by mixing green and yellow pigments – most commonly orpiment and woad. It was particularly popular in Northumbrian manuscripts in the early medieval period. A good example of vergaut is the green in the coloured initial in Durham Cathedral Library, MS A.II.10, fol. 2r. It seems to have fallen out of favour in the eleventh to thirteenth centuries but was then revived in English manuscripts in the fourteenth century, for example in a copy of the Life of Christ in verse (Fitzwilliam, MS 259, fols 18v–19r).[34]

Malachite is a naturally occurring green mineral made of copper carbonate found in caves along with its close relation, azurite. It is a lovely spearmint green colour. It was mined in England in prehistoric times and used by the ancient Egyptians and Romans but does not seem to have become popular as a pigment in Europe until the later medieval period. To make the pigment, take a chunk of malachite and grind it to a powder (it's quite soft). Then pour a lye solution over the powder to swill out the impurities. Malachite is found in caves in France and Germany, so it would not have been difficult to acquire in medieval Europe. The Hours of Isabella Stuart, a French manuscript produced circa 1431 (Fitzwilliam Museum, MS 62, fol. 141v), has used malachite pigment in the bottom left of the image.[35] Like verdigris, the copper content makes it mildly toxic.

Blues

Woad is a European plant (*isatis tinctoria*) that grew abundantly in medieval Europe and was a popular dyestuff, producing dark indigos to light blue-greys. It is made by harvesting woad leaves in late June/early July. First put the leaves in a pan of rainwater and heat for an hour, then cool the liquid and discard the leaves. Aerate the mixture by whisking and add alum so that the pigment settles at the bottom. Wash the pigment until the water is clear. Strain through a cloth and dry. Indigo was a very common pigment and has been identified in early medieval manuscripts such as the Lindisfarne Gospels and Tours Gospels.[36]

Lapis lazuli (also known as *ultramarinus* – beyond the sea) is a naturally occurring metamorphic rock that was highly regarded as a pigment in the medieval period for its brilliant vibrant blue. It was (and still is) exported from a particular place in Afghanistan, the Badakhshan Province. It was revered as a precious stone by the Assyrians and was used for eye complaints as well as being used as a cosmetic by the Egyptians and Romans. It has been found as a pigment in Romano-British villa wall-paintings from the first century, used by Roman artists who brought the pigment over with them.[37] The imperial trade links faded after the disintegration of the Roman empire, but in the medieval period trade was re-established between Europe and Asia. By about the tenth century we see the pigment again being used in England – transported along the land route from Eastern to Western Asia and then loaded onto merchant ships for Europe and England.

It is quite a labour-intensive pigment to make, as it comes as a very hard rock which needs to be broken down and then have the impurities (such as iron pyrites and calcite crystals) removed. Fortunately, Cennini provides detailed instructions on how to make it (ch. 62). To summarize the recipe: first the lapis lazuli is ground, then mixed into a viscous liquid of melted gum and wax and moulded into a pastille. When it has cooled and hardened, the pastille is left for a week or longer. Then it is softened and kneaded in a warm lye solution, which loosens the grains of pigment that then fall to the bottom. The lye is carefully drained off into another bowl, with the lapis pigment remaining at the bottom of the first bowl. This is repeated in successive bowls until there is no lapis lazuli left in the pastille. The impurities will either remain in the pastille or be washed off by the lye. The first bowls will yield the best grade.

Lapis lazuli is not toxic to humans. It has even been found in the preserved jawbone of a twelfth-century woman religious in Germany, who presumably was licking her brush while painting, and tiny fragments of the pigment got lodged in her teeth.[38] However, the lye solution can be very hard on your hands due to the alkalinity, causing the skin to crack. Lapis lazuli has been frequently identified, such as in the decoration of a manuscript produced at Canterbury in the tenth century (Cambridge, Trinity

College, MS B.11.2), written in a beautiful Insular square minuscule particularly associated with the scriptorium there.[39] The Dover Bible (CCCC, MS 4, fol. 242v), also coloured with lapis lazuli, was made in Canterbury in the twelfth century and on one folio depicts two lay artists within a decorated initial Z. The artist below is painting in blue, and his assistant above is grinding a pigment with a stone in one hand and spatula in the other – presumed to be lapis. Lapis lazuli is particularly associated with the Virgin Mary in medieval art – using the precious high-grade pigment to paint the Holy Virgin was symbolic of the reverence people felt towards her. Lapis lazuli continued to be the most popular blue pigment in Europe up until about the thirteenth century, when it was overtaken by the cheaper azurite – although it continued to be used.

Azurite is a naturally occurring mineral made of copper and found in caves, often with malachite. The pigment is made the same way as malachite: ground in a mortar and pestle to a powder, mixed with a lye solution to collect the impurities which are then decanted into another bowl, keeping behind

Pouring the lye solution out of the bowl while keeping the pure lapis lazuli pigment behind.

the azurite that sinks to the bottom. The azurite goes through repeated washings until the liquid is clear. Like lapis lazuli, the first pourings will be the best grade. Cennini adds a note of warning about grinding azurite too much, instructing to grind 'just a little and lightly because it has great disdain for the stone' (ch. 86). The blue from azurite comes from the light reflecting off the larger crystals, so the smaller the crystals are, the greyer and duller the pigment will look. It takes great skill to grind the pigment fine enough that it can be applied evenly, but not too fine that it loses its vibrancy. Azurite became popular in Northwest Europe during the thirteenth century (probably sourced from Germany or France) and eventually became more widely used than lapis lazuli. It is moderately toxic. The English illuminator William de Brailes was an early adopter of azurite, as it has been identified in one of his manuscripts produced around 1230–40 (Fitzwilliam, MS 330).

Egyptian blue was the first pigment manufactured by humans, used in prolific amounts in the Egyptian and classical eras. It largely disappeared in the medieval period – however, sporadic examples have been identified in medieval manuscripts. It is posited that these instances are perhaps a result of a small amount of ancient pigment being found by chance by a medieval practitioner or scraped off classical wall paintings and reused.[40] It has been identified in a handful of English manuscripts from the tenth century, including a copy of Hrabanus Maurus's *De laudibus sanctae crucis* (Cambridge, Trinity College, MS B.16.3). The flyleaf facing folio 1r has an illuminated image of a seated Pope Gregory receiving a golden book from a grey-bearded Hrabanus Maurus. The blue of Maurus's garment and the panel above Gregory's head have both been identified as Egyptian blue.[41]

Purples

The importance of purple as an imperial or ecclesiastical colour has already been discussed in Chapter One, where it was used to dye manuscript pages purple. This style of decoration continued up to the Carolingian period. Purple was then used very sparingly in the later medieval period; for example, a very delicate shade of purple is used for Christ's robes in a fourteenth-century copy of the Life of Christ in verse (Fitzwilliam, MS 259, fols 18v–19r), which is either orchil or folium.[42] Blue and red pigments were also mixed to create purple.

Tyrian purple (*purpurae*) came from the secretion of *murex* (sea snails) mainly in North Africa. It was known from Phoenician times and highly valued as a dyestuff in the classical period, due to the large amounts of sea snails that were needed and the labour-intensive extraction process. Pliny wrote about the process in his *Natural History* (Book 9, ch. 38); and Diocletian's *Edict of Maximum Prices* in 301 CE lists purple dye as being more expensive than gold, pound for pound. However, Tyrian purple has not been firmly identified in Western medieval manuscripts, and it is more likely that it was used very sparingly, if at all. It is made by breaking the snail shells to extract the hypobranchial gland, which releases a purple colour when exposed to oxygen. The glands are then boiled for several days until the right colour is achieved. This process is apparently highly offensive to the nostrils. The pigment is not toxic, and the snails can be eaten.

Orchil is a lichen that contains orcinol, found in the Mediterranean and Canary Islands. Its dye properties were known in classical times. It was made by drying the orchil out and grinding it, before soaking in ammonia (or – more authentically – 'stale pisse'), which then fermented to release the purple.[43]

Only methods of dyeing, not painting, with orchil have survived, but it is thought that it was soaked into clothlets and dried, then rehydrated by painters to release the colour. It was used throughout the medieval period, often for dyeing parchment pages, as in the sixth-century gospel books the *Codex Argentius* and the *Codex Brixianus*. It has been identified in Northumbrian manuscripts of the seventh and eighth centuries, such as the eagle's head in CCCC, MS 197B, fol. 1r. Orchil is not toxic but is no longer available as a pigment or dye due to conservation issues.

Folium (*turnsole*) is a plant native to the Mediterranean and Asia (*chrozophora tinctoria*) that grows in nutrient-poor soil in warm climates. It produces fruits in the summer that exude a purple dye when squeezed. The dye is then soaked into clothlets and dried, ready for transportation. The colour is released by rehydrating the cloths as needed. Folium has been identified in Western manuscripts from the eleventh to fifteenth centuries, often used as penflourishing decoration around initial letters.[44]

Browns

Brown wasn't that common in early medieval miniatures. However, brown ochres were available, or could easily be made by mixing primary pigments together (red, blue and yellow). The colour was used more in the later medieval period, when depicting realistic wildlife and hunting scenes became more fashionable, for example, in Books of Hours.

Blacks

The black paints used in medieval miniatures were iron gall ink and carbon ink (see section on inks).

Whites

Simple whites could be made from eggshell, gypsum or chalk – basically any calcium-based material. Sometimes the parchment was just left unpainted.

Lead white (*cerussa*) was usually made artificially, using the same initial process as red lead. It has been used since at least classical times and its toxicity was long known, as Pliny and Vitruvius both commented on its 'deadly poison' being 'injurious to the human system'.[45] Despite this, its properties both as a cosmetic and a pigment continued to be highly valued. Lead white is made by exposing sheets of lead to vinegar, scraping off the white crust that forms and heating it. The pigment was also mixed with other colours to lighten them. An example of a lead white base for flesh tones can be seen in a thirteenth-century image of the crucifixion (Metropolitan Museum of Art, 1981.322). Some of the paint has flaked off, exposing the parchment underneath. As well as mixing with other colours, lead white was used extensively as a highlighter in medieval images, with delicate white lines adding tonal range.

So, with this rainbow palette, you could produce all the wonderful vibrant colours you can see in medieval manuscripts, and the sheer scale of the operation is impressive. Some pigments could only be obtained from overseas, some required complicated and dangerous methods of extraction and some required planting years in advance. As always, those who could afford it sourced the highest-quality ingredients, but a wide variety of colours could be obtained for free from your local landscape.

Artists' tools

To make a paintbrush, Theophilus recommends the 'tail of a martin, badger, squirrel, or cat or from the mane of a donkey' (Book 2, ch. 17), but Cennini tells us that there are only two types of animal fur suitable for paintbrushes – squirrel (*vair*) tails and pig bristles (ch. 64). As pig bristle brushes were more suitable for large areas of painting, such as walls, we need only worry about the squirrel brushes. The paintbrushes were made by plucking hairs from a squirrel's tail, tying the bundle with waxed silk and feeding it through a short tube cut from a hen or dove quill. Then a sharpened stick of maple or chestnut, 23 centimetres long, was pushed into the other end of the tube and glued in place to make the paintbrush handle. Simple but effective. A paintbrush is clearly depicted in the hand of the artist Rufillus in Cologny, Cod. Bodmer 127, fol. 244r.

A miniature from an early fifteenth-century French manuscript gives an idea of the set-up for a medieval artist (BnF, MS Français 12420, fol. 86r). A female artist is seated at an easel supporting an illuminated image of the Virgin Mary. The artist holds a wooden palette in one hand and works on the painting with a brush in her other hand. An assistant stands to one side of her, grinding down a blue pigment, probably lapis lazuli as it is for the Virgin Mary. A smaller table in the foreground shows a selection of brushes neatly lined up, and pigments ready to use in pots and shell containers. Interesting finds from Carthusian cells excavated at Mount Grace Priory, North Yorkshire, indicate that the monks there not only wrote, but illuminated and painted manuscripts in their cells. Oyster shells still containing pigments were found there alongside grinding stones; tweezers for handling gold, containers for gesso and the all-important ear pick were also found.[46]

ONCE THE BIFOLIUM was scribed, illuminated and/or painted, then came the tricky business of assembling the text into a quire in the right order. Quires could be anywhere from one bifolium to twelve bifolia – although four or five bifolia was the average. Four bifolia folded in half would then form a quire of eight folios, or sixteen pages. With the exception of Britain and Ireland up to about the ninth century, bifolia were stacked alternately hair side up and flesh side up (known as Gregory's rule). This meant that when the parchment was folded in a codex format, the flesh sides would be facing each other when opened, and the hair sides would be facing each other. As the flesh side tended to be lighter and the hair side more yellow, this created a more aesthetic appearance on the open page. It is often easy to distinguish manuscripts that were made in Britain or Ireland in the early medieval period, as they followed the opposite collating method, where flesh side would face hair side on the open page and vice versa. This can be seen in the St Cuthbert Gospel.

To make sure that the quires were assembled in the correct order for binding, scribes would often leave a roman numeral or word on the last page of the quire to indicate where it came in the sequence. The word, known as a 'catchword', was the first word of the next quire, so that the collator could match the last word of one quire with the first word of the next. A thirteenth-century copy of the Law Code of King Alfonso X (BL, Add MS 20787) is a great example, with catchwords clearly visible every ten folios: for example, fol. 10r has *oraciones* written at the centre bottom of the page, which matches the first word of the text on fol. 11r. This is also extremely useful for modern manuscript users, as it enables us to work out the number of folios per quire.

Binding books

The codex is such a well-designed structure that its outer case brilliantly preserves and protects its important inner contents. However, this also means that the outside absorbs all the knocks and bruises though the life cycle of the codex, as it is handled, bought, sold, stolen, dropped in puddles, used as a doorstop, thrown at students and so on. Many surviving manuscripts will have been rebound at least once, with the old, tatty covers discarded and – unfortunately, for book historians – lost forever. Some original attached covers do still survive, often in places like the St Gall library, where the books have lived most of their life. These intact covers allow for careful study of sewing techniques, board attachment and decoration. Original bookbindings can hold a tremendous amount of information about methods, materials, trade, fashion, influence and financial status. Of all the aspects of manuscript production, information on bookbinding is the least recorded in the medieval period. It wasn't regarded as a highly skilled occupation, and as many bookbinders would have been illiterate, there was no need to write down instructions for future bookbinders. Therefore, most of our knowledge of bookbinding comes from direct observation of the bindings themselves. It is unfortunate that the only way you can fully understand how a medieval manuscript has been bound is by taking it apart – not a practice that would be wildly popular in libraries today. However, there have been occasions when precious manuscripts have needed to be rebound for preservation reasons, such as the Book of Dimma, an eighth-century Irish gospel book (Dublin, Trinity College, MS A.IV.24).Although its original binding was long gone, disbanding the manuscript revealed important clues about the quire arrangement and original sewing methods. The manuscript was then resewn using the traditional medieval bookbinding methods.[47]

An original 12th-century bookbinding.

St Cuthbert Gospel, the earliest known original bookbinding from Europe, early 8th century. This manuscript was found in Cuthbert's tomb during his translation in 1104.

Early codices were made from single quires, with papyrus sheets folded inside each other and sewn together. As the codex became more popular, a multi-quire method was adopted, known as the Coptic binding technique (although this technique was not restricted to Egypt). Text blocks made of papyrus leaves were divided up into sections (quires), folded in the middle and stacked together. Holes were punched through the middle of the opened quires (an even number, normally four or six), refolded and restacked on top of each other. The quires were then sewn together with a chain (or link) stitch. Every time the stitch exited a punched hole, the needle would loop behind the stitch below on the previous quire and then go back into the original exit hole. This linked each stitch to the corresponding one on the quire below. Once the quires were all sewn together, they were attached to boards made of wood or pasted-together papyrus.[48]

As the codex format and Christianity spread throughout the Western world, a new technique developed in the eighth century. The parchment was folded, arranged into quires and pricked through the spine, as the method above. However, instead of just sewing each quire to the preceding one, leather or cord strips (sewing stations) were placed horizontally across the spine and sewn onto the quires, providing a much more stable structure. The text block was sewn by either clamping it between the knees with the spine facing up, or on a wooden sewing frame, with the text block laid horizontal and the sewing stations held in place (see Staatsbibliothek Bamberg Msc.Patr., fol. 1v). Once the whole text block was sewn together, the excess length of the strips could be threaded into wooden book boards, thus creating a fully integrated structure. This method became known as flexible sewing. It created a much stronger unit, with less pressure on the joint between the spine and the connecting edge of the book board – the constant opening and closing of a book means that this hinge takes the most abuse. The best material for sewing stations was alum-tawed leather, a material that was both supple and hard-wearing – ideal for bookbinding. The structure was further reinforced by the addition of endbands. These were extra cords sewn onto the spine at the top and the bottom of the codex, sometimes covered in brightly coloured thread.

Although sewing methods could differ, this flexible technique became the main type of bookbinding across Europe up to the nineteenth century – although the St Cuthbert Gospel (BL, Add MS 89000), an English manuscript from the eighth century, has a chain stitch binding. The gospel is the earliest European codex with its original binding still intact and illustrates how different binding techniques were used throughout the Christian world. While flexible sewing onto stations became the norm throughout Europe as the medieval period progressed, in Africa and the Byzantine world the chain stitch continued to be the favoured method.

Hard wooden covers (or even any covers at all) were not mandatory. Some surviving manuscripts are bound simply in parchment covers, known as limp bindings. They are perhaps the equivalent of our modern-day paperbacks. Wooden covers were often made from oak or beech in Europe, although examples of fruit tree, poplar and plane have all been found.[49] Again, it would have been down to personal preference, finances and what was available, although a hardwood was probably favoured over a softwood. The best cut of wood was on the quarter – that is, sawn or cleaved lengthwise from a quartered section of the trunk, which prevents the wood from warping. Once the desired shape was cut, it was trimmed and shaped with an adze.[50] The covers were attached to the text block by boring or chiselling holes into the wooden boards and threading the alum-tawed leather strips through these holes. Once pulled tight, they were kept in place by hammering wooden pegs into the holes and trimming the pegs flat with the board. The wooden boards

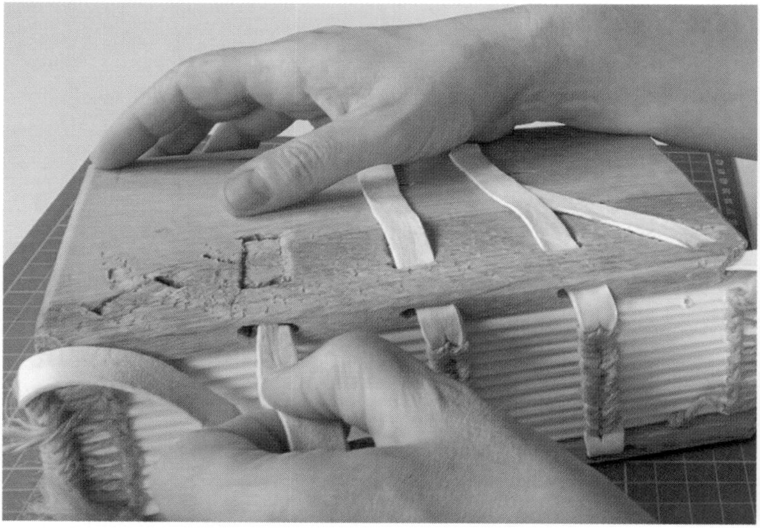

Threading the alum-tawed leather straps through the book board to attach the text block to the covers.

might then be covered with dyed leather – green and red were particularly popular colours in the twelfth/thirteenth century. Further decoration might be added by 'blindtooling' – applying a heated tool to the leather to create lines or patterns.

Bosses were round raised discs hammered onto the covers to add extra protection – with books being stacked in book chests, and constantly lifted onto hard surfaces, bosses stopped the covers coming into direct contact with other abrasive materials. Book clasps were popular as a way of keeping unruly parchment from springing out of its covers and ranged from functional to elaborate. European clasps tend to be affixed on the bottom board and attach to the top board, whereas English book clasps are generally the other way round.

However, if you really wanted to show off, you could ramp up the book furniture and go for a full-on treasure binding. Treasure bindings were around from at least the classical period, thoroughly irritating Jerome, who lamented manuscripts being

A treasure binding from the *Codex Aureus* of St Emmeram, 9th century.

'decked with jewels'. Medieval examples are no more subtle – with chunky covers dripping in gold and silver, encrusted with precious jewels. For example, the ninth-century *Codex Aureus* of St Emmeram (Munich, Bayerische Staatsbibliothek, Clm 14000) was produced for Charlemagne's grandson Charles the Bald in 870. The top cover is a three-dimensional golden sheet framed with sapphires, emeralds and pearls, attached to a wooden board underneath. There is a central panel with Christ seated on a throne hammered in relief into the gold, surrounded by more gems. Further gold relief images of the evangelists and Bible scenes fill the four corners. There is a lot going on.

Embroidered covers for codices were also popular, although unfortunately very few survive. A rare example from the fourteenth century is the Felbrigge Psalter (BL, Sloane MS 2400), a manuscript that was written in France but came to be owned by Anne Felbrigge, a member of the Poor Clares at Bruisyard, Suffolk. The brown leather covers of the psalter have been inlaid with two embroidered panels in *opus anglicanum* (English work) – which at the time was the absolute pinnacle of skilled needlework in Europe. Although the images depicting the annunciation and crucifixion are faded and tatty now, they were sewn in coloured silks of red, green, blue, grey, yellow and white, and must have been a fine sight.

Less attractive, but certainly more functional, were chains attached to books and bookshelves – to stop them 'accidentally' falling into people's pockets or bags. The chained library at Hereford is an excellent example of how they would have looked – although this is not an authentic medieval survival. However, we know that book chains were used in the medieval period, as the Ely accounts list 'iron chains for books' at a cost of 16*d* in 1300–1301.[51]

Another type of cover popular in the later medieval period was the girdle book – a portable codex that could be hung on your belt and easily accessed. The text block was made in the normal way and attached to wooden boards, but the leather cover was left long on the bottom edge of the codex, so that it could be gathered up into a tapered knot and then hung from your belt or hand. The codex would be carried upside down but would then swing easily into the hand the right way up. Girdle books were popular among the clergy as they allowed quick access to Bible verses, and also among women who liked to carry their Books of Hours this way. See Yale, Beinecke Library, MS 84 for an original fifteenth-century girdle book.

There are also some examples of innovative and unusual bookbinding shapes, like heart-shaped books. The *Chansonnier Cordiforme* (BnF, MS Rothschild 2973) is a late fifteenth-century French music book that is in the shape of a heart, with the spine edge forming one of the long sides of the heart. Another French manuscript (BnF, Latin MS 10536) is teardrop-shaped, so that when it is opened, the two halves form a heart shape. There is even a round book, known as the *Codex Rotundus* (Hildesheim, Dombibliothek, MS 728), also made at the end of the fifteenth century, probably in Flanders. This small book, measuring 3 centimetres thick and 9 in diameter, is almost perfectly round, with 266 beautifully illuminated pages. Its red-and-gold covers are held together with three clasps. Even more unusual, and slightly later than the medieval period (1555), is a Book of Hours in the shape of a fleur-de-lys (Amiens, Bibliothèque municipale, Fonds Lescalopier MS 22), made for Henry II of France.

Not much is recorded about bookbinders. There are some mentions in monastic texts indicating that bookbinding was done in-house by the monks or nuns – the *librarius* was in charge of the maintenance of the books, mending and binding books when necessary.[52] The guidelines for St Albans included bookbinding among the activities for monks involved in manuscript production: 'instead of manual work, [they] should be occupied with certain exercises according to their ability, namely, studying, reading and writing, correcting, illuminating, as well as binding.'[53] The customary of St Peter's Abbey, Westminster, mentions that the precentor was previously only allowed to leave the cloister for the purpose of bookbinding or making ink – giving the impression that these activities were done in a separate area, or perhaps even off-site completely.[54] The accounts from Ely list an in-house purchase in 1301 – 'leather and thread for binding books' – but in 1396/7 a payment of four shillings is listed to 'pay to John Dalling for two weeks for binding and repairing/amending books'. John Dalling was also the 'present scribe' at Ely, hired for sixty shillings a year – giving an indication of the freelance opportunities for scribes, and the doubling up of manuscript production jobs.[55] We know that there were secular bookbinders in the thirteenth century living on Catte Street in Oxford – a Lawrence Ligatur (Bookbinder) lived there around 1220 and a William Ligatur lived on the other side of the street between 1266 and 1281.[56] As books became more commercially produced, they were often sold unbound or in temporary bindings, to allow the discerning customer (or poor student) to then choose their own bindings according to their finances.

Six

The Twelfth-Century Renaissance

Catte Street workshop, Oxford, 1215

Sara wakes to the sound of the church bells and silently rises, careful not to disturb the children beside her. She dresses quickly and lifts the latch, looking back to check on the still slumbering Eleanor and William before softly closing the door behind her. With a light tread on the stairs, she descends into the ground floor workshop where her brother Elias is already beginning to set up for the day. Greeting him with a smile, she helps him open the shutters, letting the morning light flood into the studio. Sheets of parchment full of text and illumination sit on the workbench ready to be painted and the sun's rays immediately light on the golden outlines of the images. Sara is momentarily dazzled by the sight, and the radiance of the warm hue lifts her spirits and takes away the chill of the early morning. Elias shouts out to the other residents in the street setting up their businesses for the day, greeting them with hellos and friendly jibes. Elias owns the tenement just opposite and he rents the downstairs out to Thomas the scribe, who is setting out samples of his script on the table in front of the shop window, hoping to attract customers with his fine hand. His next-door neighbour, Laurence the bookmaker, has already put examples of his bound books out on display and started work, sewing quires onto strong leather supports with his neat and precise stitching. Catte Street was becoming known for its skilled manuscript makers, and although much of their work came through the parchmenter Robert, putting their work on display was a good way of attracting any potential new patrons wandering through.

Since the death of her husband, Adam, Sara had taken over the running of their illumination workshop. Although it had been hard at first, especially with three little ones, the community had supported her and her workshop had maintained its good reputation. She and Elias had been taught the skills of illumination and painting by their father who had travelled to France, Italy and even Sicily as a jobbing artist, picking up commissions where he could. He had seen the wonderful sights there and had spoken with artists taught in the Byzantine way, learning from them and sharing tips. When he came home to Oxford, he had set up his own workshop just a few doors down, and young Sara and Elias could often be seen sitting at a workbench, paintbrush in hand, while their father watched over them. Elias had always been better at illumination, he understood how to handle the gold and how to tease it into position, whereas Sara had shown a flair for painting, instinctively knowing how to bring an image to life. Now her father and mother had gone, as had her husband, so it was Sara running the business, with Elias as supervisor and illuminator. They also had two apprentices, Henri and Jean, who came from Paris. An old acquaintance of her father's had got in touch and asked if Sara could take them on, and always keen to learn more about practices and techniques from overseas, she had readily agreed. The apprentices shared the other room upstairs with her eldest son, Simon, and she now hears them banging about upstairs as they get ready.

She walks through to the hall at the back of the workshop and kindles the flames of the hearth. Once the fire has taken, she opens the back door onto a small plot of land where she grows the plants that provide the reds, yellows and blues she uses in her paintings. Washing her face in the water from the barrel, she is interrupted by her cat Isabel, mewling and weaving round her legs. Sara briefly scratches under her chin before collecting the eggs from the chickens and going back inside. Gathering her basket and purse, she checks with Elias what they need for the workshop and goes out into the street, walking down to St Mary's church and turning right onto the high street. It is already getting busy as she ducks between traders still setting up their stalls and customers looking for an early bargain. Her first stop is the spicery, to pick up some saffron to make a particularly delicate hue of yellow she needs for a miniature she is working on. She lingers by the stall after the purchase to inhale the mingling smells of ginger, cinnamon and pepper, before walking past All Saints church along to the goldsmiths. Examining the samples of gold leaf, she selects two dozen sheets of a particularly radiant gold, knowing that her current patron wants their illuminations to be of fine quality (and that she would be reimbursed accordingly). With her workshop purchases made, she moves down past the butchers slaughtering the sheep and pigs, careful to avoid the straw, shit and blood on the ground. Crossing over the junction, she buys provisions for lunch and dinner – bread, cheese, fish, leeks and apples. Now her main purchases are done, she walks back eating some of the bread, swinging her basket and enjoying the sun on her face, soaking up the bustle of the marketplace before going back to the workshop.

As she enters the workshop, she sees Henri and Jean working quietly and studiously on the workbench, learning how to form the new initial letters that Sara has been working on. It was her idea to design a set of letters in a certain style, so that patrons would know which workshop the manuscript had come from. Already she has seen how Henri likes to give letters an extra flourish, and she hopes that he will not be too extravagant in his execution of the initials. At the back of the workshop, Elias sits at the table with the children, who are swinging their legs and eating bread and pottage left over from yesterday. Suddenly noticing their mother, the children launch themselves at her, full of crumbs and sticky fingers, and she gathers them in her arms laughing.

Once the children have been fed and washed, she sets them to their daily tasks. Simon is learning illumination from Elias, and William and Eleanor are sent over the road to Thomas for some writing lessons. Finally, Sara sits down at her bench to carry on with the psalter she is decorating. It is for a wealthy London patron, so she is doing all the illustration herself. With any luck, the patron will be satisfied with the psalter and tell his friends, leading to more commissions. Admiring the beautiful finish on the gilded decorated initial, she dips her paintbrush into the oystershell full of vermilion and starts to fill in the figure of Solomon. Isabel wanders in and sniffs around, before curling up at Sara's feet. An air of concentration fills the room, broken occasionally by the odd muted shout or dog barking in the street outside. In this contented, creative atmosphere, the workshop inhabitants pass their day.

These next two chapters will examine how manuscript production developed from the eleventh century to the end of the medieval period in Europe. These centuries saw huge change, with the rise of the commercial manuscript industry, the growing use of paper as the main writing material and the adoption of a movable type printing press. We also see the beginning of personal book ownership among the urban elite, separate from the monastic houses. This is all against a social, religious and political backdrop of invasions, plagues, climate shifts, crusades and heresies. However, it was also a period of extended peace and prosperity. Threats of invasion from Viking, Hungarian and Muslim factions had dissipated from European borders by the eleventh and twelfth centuries, allowing for greater population growth and land cultivation. The Church was still the dominating and centralizing force, with Latin the universal language among the educated. Internally, sophisticated systems of government administration developed, and externally, greater trade networks developed, resulting in an influx of disposable income and the rise of the merchant class.

There was also an intellectual explosion, with new developments in philosophy and science, known as the twelfth-century renaissance. Many taught at cathedral schools or monasteries went on to develop their intellectual talents, influenced by Greek and Arabic texts. Over the course of the early medieval period, many ancient Greek authors, such as Aristotle, had disappeared from European circulation, as he was considered heretical by some of the early Church Fathers. Once the older classical copies of Aristotle in circulation fell into disrepair and were not recopied, they essentially disappeared from the European Christian library. Muslim scholars, in their intellectual veracity, had translated these texts into Arabic from ancient Greek in the early medieval period, and over centuries had reflected and commented on them. Ibn Rushd (Averroes) was an Arabic polymath whose commentaries on Aristotle and other philosophical works were renowned throughout the Islamic world. Despite the religious wariness between Muslims and Christians, there was scholarly exchange between the two cultures in the eleventh and twelfth centuries, with European intellectuals travelling to centres of learning in Muslim states, such as Toledo, Spain. It was here that European scholar Michael Scot (1175–*c.* 1232) learnt Arabic and translated many texts into Latin, including Aristotle and Ibn Rushd, which were then transmitted through educated networks in the Christian world.

Sicily in particular, having been invaded first by Muslims then by the Normans, was a melting pot of Byzantine, European and Islamic cultures, leading to new exchanges in astronomy, law, mathematics, science and medicine. The increasingly embarrassing crusades to the Holy Land (1096–1291), led by Western Christians trying to reclaim Jerusalem from the Muslims, did at least show those European soldiers a different way of life, opening their eyes to a world beyond Western Christianity. These new transport routes and settlements along the way to Jerusalem gave more opportunities for Europeans to travel and experience new sights and sounds, creating a new sense of internationalism. This exchange of cultures and scholarly learning, along with the extra money flowing around from trade, meant that from the late eleventh century a prolific number of new texts were being produced, on a greater scale than had been seen before. As the lay audience developed more sophisticated tastes, it drove exciting innovations in art and book production. Unfortunately, the plague that came along in the mid-fourteenth century rather derailed this period of prosperity in Europe, but manuscript production continued nonetheless.

Manuscript production in northwestern Europe looked a lot different in 1500 to how it did in 1050. Up to about the twelfth century, manuscripts were produced mainly by monastic houses, albeit with the help of visiting scribes or artists. These manuscripts could often be identified by certain 'house styles', such as at Canterbury and Durham, with a uniformity of script or decoration. However, after the thirteenth century this seems to peter out, indicating a lack of investment in keeping the traditions of the monastic scriptorium alive.[1] Monastic life also underwent significant change too. Although the Benedictine order had been dominant in the early medieval period, from the eleventh century other orders started to emerge. The Cistercians branched off from the Benedictines in the late eleventh century, wanting to follow a stricter observance of the *Rule*. This new order spread rapidly throughout Europe, with crusade-enthusiast Bernard of Clairvaux (1090–1153) becoming one of its most well-known members. The Cistercians had strict regulations, with one of their statutes insisting that newly established houses could not be used until they were furnished with a set of liturgical books, including a missal, a *Rule of St Benedict*, a martyrology, a psalter, a hymnarium, a collect, a lectionary, an antiphon and a graduale.[2]

This inevitably led to a greater demand for book production. However, the Cistercian's defining feature was austerity, to contrast against those decadent Benedictines who liked lavishly decorated churches and beautiful manuscripts. Bernard was particularly offended by 'the silliness' of the fantastic creatures carved into stone of the church, not to mention the expense.[3] This attitude is further reflected in a Cistercian statute that prohibited any outer decoration of books in gold or silver or buckles or cloth (*c.* 1109–19) – no doubt the early Church Father Jerome would have thoroughly approved of this move. A later statute (*c.* 1145–51) only allowed one colour to be used for initial letters and forbade any use of images or crosses in manuscripts. They relented slightly in 1202, allowing rubrics to be decorated in any colour, apart from gold or silver.[4] So while the Cistercians were anxious to avoid any ostentatious ornamentation on the binding of their books, or illuminated images within the books, it seems they were happy to allow some colour and simple (or even ornate) decoration of letters. This means that Cistercian manuscripts can often be easy to identify. The Grande Bible de Clairvaux (Troyes Bibliothèque municipale, MS 27) produced at Clairvaux around 1145–65 has no illumination or images, but it has large ornate initials intricately decorated in monochrome colours of red, blue or green.

The Carthusians were another order that found Benedictine life too comfortable and wanted to get back to basics in the manner of the early Christian hermits in the desert. Bruno of Cologne founded a hermitage in the beautiful Chartreuse mountains with six companions in 1084, devoted to a life of isolation, poverty and prayer. Each monk lived in a small cell divided into several rooms, where they worked, prayed, ate and slept alone, occasionally meeting in the communal areas. The order gained popularity throughout Europe, establishing male and female priories called Charterhouses. Their self-imposed isolation restricted their pastoral duties, so one of their statutes instructs that 'because we cannot preach the word of God with our mouths, we must do it with our hands' (*ut quia ore non possumus dei verbum manibus predicemus*). They regarded books as 'eternal food for their soul', reinforcing the earlier Christian belief that accurately reproducing manuscripts was a spiritual vocation. Carthusians were taught to write at the monastery, and the inhabitants were permitted writing materials in their cells, with the chance to restock their parchment and ink during the communal Sunday cloister meetings.[5]

Oyster shells containing pigments and tools for applying gold have been found in excavated Carthusian cells at Mount Grace Priory, indicating that they were not as strict as the Cistercians about colourful decoration, illumination or depicting figures. Surviving from the fifteenth century is a beautiful illuminated missal produced by the Spanish Carthusian monastery of Porta Coeli, Valencia, probably for their own community (Morgan Library and Museum, MS M.450). Although other orders increasingly relied on secular scribes and artists for their manuscripts in the later medieval period, the Carthusians remained true to their calling and continued to produce beautiful manuscripts into the early modern period.

Other orders were keen on a less cloistered way of life and preferred to go out into the community to preach, heal and help the poor and destitute. By the thirteenth century, urban life had developed significantly, and those with a religious calling felt that they would do more good by being actively out in the world rather than hidden away in a monastery praying the canonical hours. These became known as the mendicant orders, choosing a life of poverty, travelling and preaching to emulate the life of Jesus. The four main mendicant orders were the Augustinians, the Carmelites, the Dominicans and the Franciscans. With all these monks and nuns wandering around doing good in the lively urban streets, you may wonder who was now wielding the quill and parchment.

THINGS HAD STARTED to shift towards a more commercial market in the twelfth century, with universities being established and a rise in urban living and consumerism. Centres of learning were nothing new – the ancient Greeks had their gymnasiums, where they enjoyed physical exercise along with discussions of philosophy, and libraries had been around since the Mesopotamian era, with collections at Ninevah and Alexandria enticing scholars from far and wide. In the eighth century, Charlemagne had established the palace school at Aachen that was run under Alcuin's tutelage, and they both promoted a programme of education reform, focusing on the liberal arts – the Trivium (grammar, rhetoric, dialectic) and the Quadrivium (music, arithmetic, geometry and astronomy). By the eleventh and twelfth centuries, other centres of learning, later to become universities, started to emerge in Europe. Bologna in Italy was the place to learn law, and Paris and Oxford became known for theology. The word *universitas* was originally applied to any group or guild of professionals, but over time 'university' came to mean specifically a scholarly instruction. These early centres were still very much of a religious bent and focused on providing further education for clergymen after they had attended cathedral school (and even for monks, who now had much greater freedom to travel with the new mendicant orders, although women were completely excluded from this). These universities started off as informal gatherings of masters and students, without structural organization or designated teaching buildings. Often classes were held in a nearby church – but as these centres attracted more students (and money), boarding houses and formal buildings were built, and the universities became recognized as official scholarly institutes, focusing on theology, law, philosophy and medicine.

As these places grew, so did the demand for books, and secular manuscript makers stepped into this gap nicely, embracing the opportunity to develop their skills. Being much less restricted than the religious orders, they were able to quickly set up workshops around the centres of learning. We know from surviving tenement records and trade registers from Catte Street in Oxford and the Rue Neuve Notre-Dame and Rue de Ecrivains (Street of the Scribes) in Paris that the manuscript-making community often lived together. Medieval urban tenements were usually long and narrow, with the ground floor used as a shop or workspace and the one or two floors above for living quarters. There was sometimes space for a small garden to grow plants – useful not just for cooking, but for herbal remedies or dyes and pigments. These tenement records date back to the early thirteenth century, and we can see that in Catte Street around 1220 there were illuminators, parchmenters and bookbinders who owned or rented tenements. Moreover, we can see from witnesses to their documents that their communities consisted of many family members and friends involved in manuscript production.

Around 1210 Sara Bradfot and her husband, Peter the Illuminator, sold back some land in Catte Street to her father, Adam Bradfot. Sara's brother, Elias Bradfot, later gave this tenement to the hospital of St John, which was confirmed in 1267 by Simon Bradfot, son of Sara and Peter. Around 1220, Elias also sold a tenement to a parchmenter on the other side of Catte Street, in between Laurence Ligator (bookbinder) and Emma Rideratrix (strapmaker). Witnesses to deeds from Catte Street include Thomas Scriptor (scribe), Roger Pergamener (parchmenter) and many illuminators.[6] The term 'parchmenter' probably wasn't used for a parchment maker, but someone who sold parchment, and possibly acted as a project manager for manuscript production. They received commissions from clients and coordinated scribes and illuminators to complete the project (later they were known as stationers, or in France as a *libraire* or *stationarius*).[7] It is fascinating to imagine how a close-knit community like this would have lived and worked together, exchanging ideas and innovations, having friendships and relationships (and disputes), all bound together by their shared trade.

We can also see these manuscript production networks arranged in a similar way in Paris. Alexandre (parchmenter), Guillaume de Poitiers (bookseller), Robert (illuminator), Robert de Chevreuse (bookseller), Richard (scribe), Emery (bookseller), Guillaume (illuminator) and Adam and Alain (parchmenters) were all based on rue Neuve Notre-Dame circa 1230–45.[8] Family connections were commonplace, such as Herbert the parchmenter, son of Henri the parchmenter; and Jean le Noir and Bourgot, a father and daughter team who worked as illuminators on the rue Erembourg de Brie (now rue Boutebrie) around 1358.[9] Women such as Petronilla de Péronne swore oaths (to obtain a licence to practise) alongside their husbands, indicating that they were both in charge of the business.[10]

Thanks to this urban development, it would have been easier to obtain materials, not just from neighbours, but from the busy marketplace that attracted merchants. With all these craftspeople living so closely together, it is easy to see how they would have worked together to produce books – and not constrained by the monastic tradition, this close-knit society could organically develop new and innovative techniques. Also, because the scribes and artists weren't tied to the monastic hours of prayer, their output could possibly have been much higher. Of course, something was then lost, in that the transaction became commercial rather than spiritual, although monastic production still continued alongside the urban workshops. However, the book industry needed to keep up with the growth of the universities and provide a much wider variety of student texts – such as canon and civil law, philosophy, theology and the arts – that were not generally produced by the monasteries.[11]

Yet as we all know, students are usually broke and the medieval period was certainly no different. An Oxford student in the early twelfth century wrote a letter home to ask for more money, complaining 'the city is expensive and makes many demands; I have to rent lodgings, buy necessaries, and provide for many other things.'[12] Poverty-stricken students would have been in no position to purchase the more expensive books, but the new merchant class were keen to wave their money about and commission lavish illuminated manuscripts. Psalters (books of psalms) and Books of Hours (personal prayer books that followed the canonical hours) were particularly popular among the laity, and we have many surviving examples from the thirteenth century onwards, often beautifully decorated. Private reading became an accepted practice, particularly among a growing audience of women. This increase in production led to greater literacy and to exploring new ways of thinking – psalters and Books of Hours were even used to teach the alphabet and calendar to young children.[13] How lovely to be the child of a well-off merchant, sitting on your mother's lap and learning to read from a manuscript decorated with beautiful images, tracing the outlines of letters with plump little fingers until they make sense!

Illuminated manuscripts were also popular as gifts – between betrothed couples, from wealthy landowners to religious institutions and from scholars to universities and libraries. This conspicuous consumption – lavish books decorated with family crests and then distributed to the wider community – highlights a shift away from the monastic ideal of creating books to celebrate the word of God. Yet there can be no doubt that the growth of the commercial manuscript industry created new opportunities for artisans and paved the way for the stunning works of art that we see in manuscripts by the end of the medieval period.

FOR ABOUT THREE HUNDRED YEARS, from 800 until 1100, Caroline minuscule remained the most prevalent script in Europe (albeit alongside some regionally independent scripts, such as the Insular scripts in Britain and Ireland, Beneventan in southern Italy and Visigothic in Spain). Manuscript production trotted along quite nicely, with monastic experimentation in decoration and layout, and the occasional use of professional scribes and artists when needed. Manuscripts by the twelfth century were fairly standard, with grammar, punctuation and word separation generally conforming to the same pattern.[14] Centres of monastic book production grew and receded as necessary, depending on demand for texts.

By the end of the eleventh century, a new script was developing in French and English manuscripts called Romanesque (or Anglo-Norman or Protogothic). This script was rapidly adopted across England and France, although it took longer to spread into central Europe, Italy and Spain. It is somewhat of a transitional script between Caroline minuscule and full Gothic, and so often lacks a uniformity and coherence across European regions. Rather than the lovely languid roundedness of Caroline minuscule, Romanesque script was more compressed and angular. The circular bowls of *o*, *b* and *d*, for example, were replaced by ovals, and letters such as *m* and *n* get 'feet' or seraphs. Letters such as *ct*, *et* or *st* were often joined together with a ligature. This more upright script meant that scribes could fit more words on a page, which no doubt was an advantage to a thrifty monastery.

Contractions and suspensions were also used as a space-saving (and time-saving) device. Like the *nomina sacra* in the early Christian texts where certain words were abbreviated, this was taken further in the Romanesque period and almost became a whole vocabulary in itself. Simple contractions were still marked with a line above, for example, dominus was dn̄s, but other symbols were used to denote common Latin word beginnings such as 'con' and word endings such as 'us', 'ur' and 'rum'. 'Per' and 'pro' were also abbreviated by marks on their descenders. With

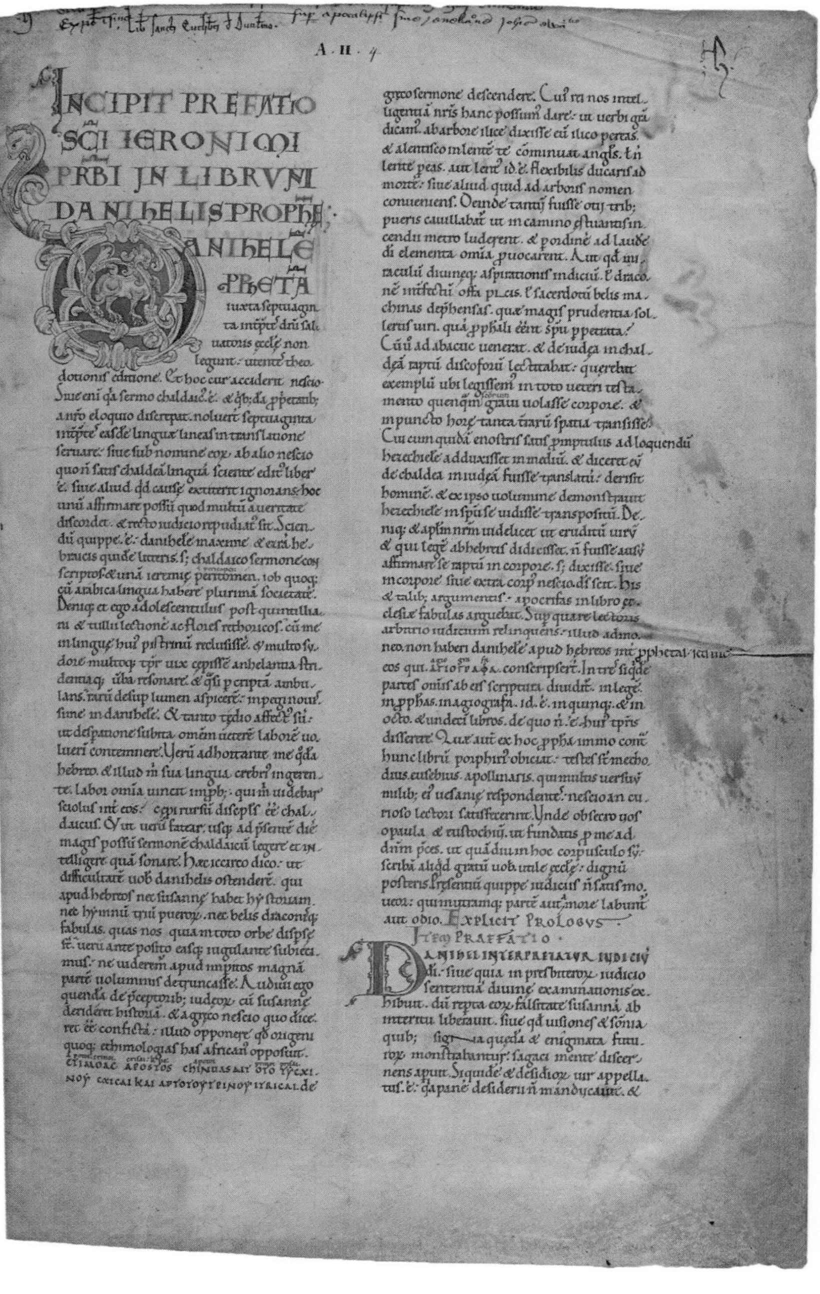
INCIPIT PREFATIO SCI IERONIMI PRBI IN LIBRUM DANIHELIS PROPHE

Romanesque script in the Carilef Bible, 11th century.

practice, these contractions can become easy to decipher, but heavily contracted text can be quite a headache.

When done well, Romanesque script represents a beautiful transitional point – perfectly readable and easy on the eye. The roundedness of Caroline minuscule feels sometimes a bit too relaxed, and full Gothic goes too far in its angularity and crampedness (to the point of being illegible) – so Romanesque script is definitely the happy place in between. A particularly good example of Romanesque script can be seen in the Carilef Bible (DCL, MS A.II.4), produced just after the Norman conquest (1066). The newly installed Norman clergy in England instigated a surge in book production – and Durham in particular, under the new management of Bishop Carilef, began an exciting and extensive programme of book manufacture. It is likely that the scribe and the artist of the Carilef Bible were based in Normandy (as they have been identified in other Norman manuscripts), but it is not certain whether they were hired professionals or Norman monks.[15] Many texts were produced in Normandy in the post-conquest period and then distributed to new Norman-run houses in England, leading to a certain uniformity in the manuscripts produced in this period. Other beautiful examples of Romanesque script can be seen in the Rochester Bible from the early twelfth century (BL, Royal MS I C VII), and a mid-twelfth-century manuscript from western France (Tours, Bibliothèque municipale, MS 321). This script was not confined to England and France, as we can see in the late eleventh-century Romanesque Bible of Burgos, Spain, and the copy of *Liber Scivias* authored by German abbess and visionary Hildegard of Bingen (the twelfth-century original was lost during the Second World War, but fortunately had been faithfully reproduced earlier that century).

Romanesque decoration

Preceding the new script was the Romanesque artistic style. As a very rough guide (and this varied from place to place), this artistic period was 1000–1200, and encompassed architecture, sculpture and painting. Drawing inspiration from classical Rome, the many churches that were built across Europe at this time had distinctive architectural features such as rounded arches and thick columns. Particularly good examples of Romanesque architecture remain at Durham Cathedral in England, Angoulême Cathedral in France, Speyer Cathedral in Germany and the Basilica of Sant'Ambrogio in Milan. This new architectural style can be seen in manuscript images. Scenes from Byzantine iconography also grew fashionable, particularly relating to the life of Christ. The Virgin Mary was a popular image, as was 'Christ in Majesty', depicting Jesus seated on a heavenly throne, one hand holding an open book and the other making a blessing. He is often enclosed in an almond-shaped frame (known as a mandorla), surrounded by the evangelists and other holy figures (see, for example, the Stammheim Missal, Getty MS 64, fol. 85v). The dazzling golden sheen of Byzantine icons and mosaics, seen in Sicily and the Holy Land, was incorporated into Western illumination, with gold leaf used for the background in miniatures to create images of eye-catching radiance. The colours used were very bold and bright, albeit without much blending or subtlety. There was also a greater uniformity in the use of pigments, and lapis lazuli and vermilion, favoured by European artists, now became commonplace in English manuscripts. The sumptuousness of colours can particularly be seen in the Bury Bible, painted by Master Hugo, with the generous application of lapis lazuli in its decorated initials and biblical scenes. The expressive faces of the painted figures and the drapery that clings to the body as if still wet (known as 'damp-fold' style) in this manuscript are distinctive features of Romanesque art. Landscape features tended to be somewhat abstract, with trees often cartoonishly simplified, with large blobs of foliage (looking a bit like lollipops). Roman rounded arches often frame human figures, with two-dimensional buildings in the background. Miniatures are frequently surrounded by a painted frame containing delicate patterns of scrolls or acanthus leaves. Good examples are the St Albans Psalter, the Missel de Saint-Denis (BnF, Latin MS 9436) and the Stammheim Missal (J. Paul Getty Museum, MS 64).

The fluidity between English and French scribes and artists remained in place all through the twelfth and thirteenth centuries, with an artistic style developing called the 'Channel style'. English and French artists moved freely between each other's workshops at this time, allowing for an alignment of styles so synchronized that it is almost impossible to tell visually which are English- and which are French-produced manuscripts. White lions, concentric circles, swirling acanthus leaves and biting animals were all popular Channel-style motifs.[16]

DECORATED INITIALS really came into their own as an art form during this time, so it is worth first explaining the different types. Of course, they had been a feature of manuscripts for a long time – we have seen initials from the early medieval gospels featuring strange creatures and interlaced patterns, such as in the Lindisfarne Gospels. These types of initials made up of animal shapes are known as zoomorphic. Initials made up of human shapes are called anthropomorphic, for example in BL, Arundel MS 91, fol. 40v, where two vertical figures and one horizontal figure form an L. Historiated initials are ones that depict a scene that can usually be identified: for example, the Winchester Bible shows a historiated initial with the prophet Jeremiah in a large letter V, for the passage beginning Verba Jeremiah (the words

Christ in majesty, Stammheim Missal, 12th century.

Historiated initial of the prophet Jeremiah in the Winchester Bible, 12th century.

of Jeremiah) on fol. 148r. The vividly coloured initial depicts Jeremiah looking troubled, surrounded by lush grapevines, while the Lord, stretching down from heaven, puts his finger on Jeremiah's lips. The unfurled scroll held by Jeremiah reads (in Latin), 'Behold, I cannot speak, for I am a child'. The other scroll, held by the Lord, reads 'Behold, I have put my words in your mouth', which are direct quotes from the Book of Jeremiah (1:6–7). The historiated initial gives a visual narrative scene as a precursor to the biblical text that follows. The scrolls further elaborate the message and were often used in this way to add text to images – almost like a speech bubble. Inhabited initials (which were particularly popular in Romanesque manuscripts) are decorated initials that may include humans or animals, but that do not depict any particular scene or narrative. For example, if you look at the opening pages of many psalters from the twelfth and thirteenth centuries, they have a large *B* to start the opening words of psalm one, *Beatus vir*. These large initials became increasingly decorative, with foliage interwoven in tight, concentric circles, often terminating with lions' heads and other biting animals in the Channel style (see, for example, BL, Harley MS 5102, fol. 1r).

We need to make a distinction here between the large, decorated initials that may be illuminated and/or painted to start new sections and the smaller, coloured initials that are much less elaborate and more integrated with the text. These are often called penworked or penflourished initials (also *litterae notabiliores* or *litterae florissae*), as they were done with a quill, often by a rubricator. In the eleventh and twelfth centuries, they can be found in a variety of eye-catching bright colours including blue, green, red, purple, pink, yellow and tan (for example, in the Bury Bible). The penworked initials in a mid-twelfth-century martyrology from Canterbury (BL, Royal MS 7 E VI) go a step further, combining different colours in the same initial, with geometric patterns and descending acanthus leaves. By about the thirteenth century, the flamboyant colours calm down a bit, and most penworked initials just alternate in red and blue. These coloured initials, as well as being decorative, also provided easier navigation of the text – although the two-colour format somewhat loses the sheer joyfulness of the earlier multicoloured initials.

By the late Romanesque period, the layout of the manuscript page started to coalesce around a structure that essentially 'framed' the central text within a grid of lines and images. From the late twelfth century, we see law texts in Bologna with added sprays of red and blue penwork at the bottom of the page, in horizontal or vertical patterns, sometimes embellished with florets or human heads (for example, in Paris, Bibl. Sainte-Geneviève, MS 168, fol. 232v).[17] It is not known why this decoration appeared, but perhaps it helped readers to mentally 'fix' the page in their head – many hard-up students would not have been able to buy texts, so would have to commit passages to memory. This decorative trend spread across Europe, and, in some cases, the penflourishing got a bit carried away with itself. There are some examples thought to have been produced at an Oxford workshop in the early thirteenth century, possibly on Catte Street, where a group of artists developed an extraordinary style of *litterae florissae* that eventually bordered on self-parody. The Golden Psalter (BSB, CLM 835, fol. 82v), a deluxe manuscript that has extremely high-quality miniatures and decorated initials, has some of this garish penflourishing, but to appreciate the full extent of the penflourishing extravaganza, you need to see a manuscript now held in Lincoln Cathedral (Lincoln Cathedral, MS 147, fol. 15v). It is fascinating to see this experimentation with style. Even though it ultimately goes nowhere, it shows how workshops were thinking about new forms of decoration and how they were given the freedom to try things out.[18]

Several manuscripts have been linked together because of their penflourishing decoration, but the close links that existed

Beatus vir illumination in a psalter in the Romanesque style, 12th–13th century.

between England and France at this time, resulting in the 'Channel style', means it is very difficult to identify specific workshops. However, by looking closer at the style of the coloured initials and examining the shape of certain letters, it is possible to suppose that these manuscripts with the same penflourishing and coloured letter shapes originated in the same workshop. The artists in a certain workshop worked to very specific templates when forming their coloured letters, in particular the letter *A*. There are six different models for this letter that are repeated over and over in about six manuscripts. From the identification of the style of *litterae florissae* in these manuscripts, it is possible to trace them to a specific group of artists in a workshop in Oxford at the turn of the thirteenth century.[19] It is tempting to link them with the workshop of Sara Bradfot and her husband Peter the Illuminator, but even if that might be a stretch, we know that the Oxford manuscript makers were a tight-knit community, so it is quite possible they at least knew each other.

Texts in the Romanesque Era

Religious texts remained the staple of book production, but we will now look at the range of texts being produced in the Romanesque period. The eleventh century saw a trend in the manufacture of 'giant Bibles' – enormous tomes of two, three or four volumes that were written in Romanesque script and illuminated with beautiful biblical miniatures and decorated initials. The Carilef Bible (DCL, MS A.II.4) is an excellent example, although like many other multi-part giant Bibles, only one of its two original volumes survives today. Other giant Bible examples include the Bury Bible (CCCC, MS 2), the Winchester Bible, the Arnstein Bible (BL, Harley MS 2798 and 2799) and the Montpellier Bible (BL, Harley 4772 and 4773). The general size of the giant Bibles hardly made for an intimate reading experience. That, of course, was the point. They

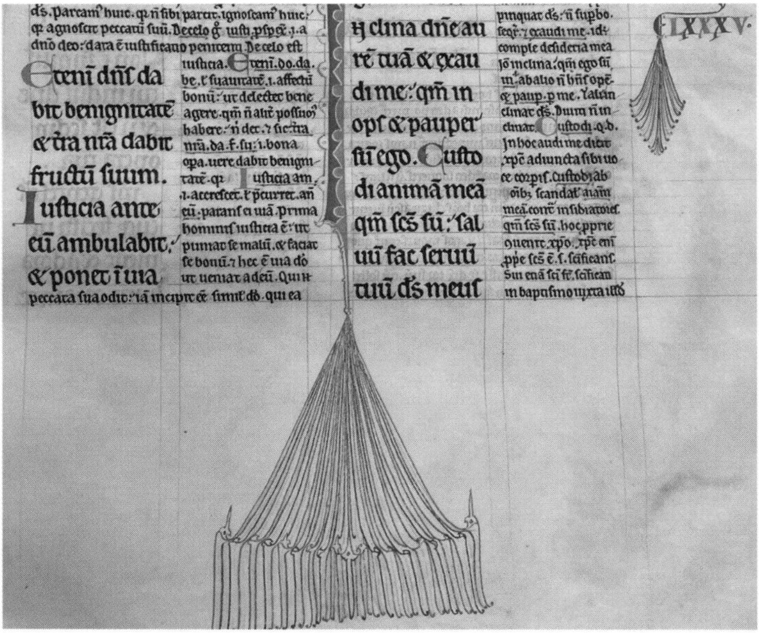

Example of extreme penflourishing (*litterae florissae*) a manuscript of Peter Lombard's *Sentences*, 12th–13th century.

were intended to be opened on a large lectern and read aloud from in public groups, as a shared experience. And very much in keeping with the earlier medieval jewelled bindings, giant Bibles were also statements of importance – the Bible contained the word of God, so it needed something big and impressive to represent its status. And don't forget, the affluent person who commissioned the Bible would also bask in that reflected glory, having a chance to show off their wealth and their generosity. Not only would this good deed add to their status down on earth, it would also smooth their passage into the afterlife.

The Winchester Bible, along with the Bury Bible, is considered one of the finest examples of Romanesque art. It is also the largest surviving English Bible from this period, measuring 58.3 by 39.6 centimetres. It was written by one scribe, probably a monk at Winchester, with six contributing artists who were likely freelance.[20] The manuscript is made up of 468 folios of calfskin parchment, and is now bound in four volumes, although originally it was probably a two-volume Bible. It was produced (on and off) between 1150 and 1190, commissioned by the extremely wealthy Henry of Blois, Bishop of Winchester, for the cathedral, and it still resides there today. The artwork consists of three full-page illustrations (perhaps more originally) and numerous decorated initials, which are regarded as the pinnacle of Romanesque design. Generously illuminated in gold and painted in pigments of lapis lazuli, vermilion, red lead, verdigris, yellow ochre, carbon black and lead white, the historiated initials beautifully visualize the stories of the Old and New Testament. For example on fol. 169r, a large illuminated letter *H* shows the prophet Baruch reading in front of King Jechonias in the top section, and in the lower section we see the people of Babylon also listening, which narrates the Bible section Baruch 1.3: 'And Baruch did read the words of this book in the hearing of Jechonias the son of Joachim king of Juda, and in the ears of all the people that came to hear the book.'

However, what makes this manuscript even more interesting is that much of the decoration is incomplete – which allows us to see the stages of production. In some cases, we can even see instructions to the artists left visible on the page.[21] From the many unfinished initials we can chart the artistic process of the manuscript – first the initials were sketched out, then the outlines defined in ink. Next the gesso was added before the gold or silver leaf was applied. The last stage was the painting. Often one artist started the image and another finished it – showing the different stages of production. It is not known why the Winchester Bible was left unfinished, but it probably became too expensive to complete – particularly after the death of Henry in 1171. In some unfinished images, it looks as if the artists have simply downed tools the moment the money ran out. However, the six artists who contributed to this Bible display the range of artistic influence in this period, including Byzantine styles. Perhaps some of the artists had travelled to Sicily and seen the golden Byzantine mosaics, which led in turn to the heavy use of gold in the backgrounds of manuscript illuminations.[22] The artists in the Winchester Bible have also been identified in many other English manuscripts of the period, indicating the itinerant nature of manuscript illumination.[23] It is even suspected that at least two of them were involved in the planning and/or creation of the wall paintings in the Royal Monastery of Santa María de Sigena in northeast Spain, further supporting the idea of this peripatetic lifestyle.[24] It's also worth remembering that freelance manuscript artists and illuminators might additionally be goldworkers, sculptors and/or mural painters.

THE TWELFTH CENTURY also saw a new development in Bible commentary, where notes or glosses were added to the main text, almost like a footnote today (although the glosses often took up more space than the main text). This enabled the reader to read the main text and surrounding explanatory text at the same time. The glosses themselves were also standardized texts, the two main ones being the *Glossa Ordinaria* composed by Walafrid Strabo in the ninth century and the *Glossa Interlinearis* composed by Anselm in the early twelfth century. It was up to the poor scribe to fit all these texts together on the page, which would require real logistical planning. Scribes often wrote the gloss in a smaller script with a finer-cut nib to visually separate the texts, and employed paragraph symbols (paraphs) to make location of the corresponding text easier. A Bible from the second half of the twelfth century (BL, Burney MS 29) demonstrates how the different texts can fit together effectively, with the main Bible text well spaced out in the central column, interspersed with an interlinear gloss in a smaller text, surrounded by the *Glossa Ordinaria* in the margins marked with paraphs. The popularity of biblical glosses reflects the theological scholasticism that developed alongside the universities.

PSALTERS HAD ALWAYS been produced for religious members, but from the twelfth century onwards they became popular among the laity. Featuring the 150 psalms as well as a calendar, litany of the saints (prayers) and canticles (hymns), the format of the psalter lent itself well to spectacular decoration. One of the best examples is the St Albans Psalter, associated with the anchoress Christina of Markyate (*c.* 1096–*c.* 1155), who fled from her forced marriage as a young girl and lived in a priory cell in Markyate (near St Albans), devoting her life to God. The psalter was possibly commissioned by her spiritual companion and protector, Geoffrey de Gorham, Abbot of St Albans. It was written by six scribes of varying skill, but all in a Romanesque style, sometime between 1124 and 1139. Some of the scribes have been identified in other St Albans manuscripts, but the unidentified ones may have been hired scribes who were just passing through (as we know that St Albans often hired freelance scribes and artists).[25] There were four artists who worked on the psalter – the Alexis Master, the most accomplished of the artists, and three lesser artists who painted the initials, the calendar illustrations and the final two miniatures at the end of the psalter. Like the Winchester Bible and the Bury Bible, the St Albans Psalter is considered one of the finest English Romanesque manuscripts.

Psalters normally begin with a calendar, which gives a good opportunity here to talk about the format of calendars, and why they were so important to medieval people. They were primarily a record of the major feast days in the Church year, such as Christmas and the saints' days, but they were also computus tables, allowing the user to work out when Sundays fell and even Easter, which was celebrated on a different day each year. The calendars in psalters tend to be fairly straightforward, with a page allotted for each month, starting in January (although technically the Church year started on 25 December or 25 March). Each month is often decorated with two sets of images, representing the zodiac year and the agricultural year (labours of the month), so the page for January will normally illustrate the zodiac sign for Aquarius (the water bearer), and a feasting figure, often two- or even three-headed and in front of a fire, for the labour of the month. The feasting image signifies the feast days in January (medieval Christmas went on until Twelfth Night/5 January), and the multiple heads represent looking back to the old year and ahead to the new (BL, Add MS 62925, fols 1r–6v).

The number of earth days and lunar days is usually written at the top of the calendar page: for example, January has thirty-one earth days and thirty lunar days. The main body of the calendar will list the days of the month and the corresponding saints' feast days. There are often additional columns to the left containing numbers or letters. Sometimes, but not always, the first column contains golden numbers, which run from one to nineteen. They are supposed to tell the reader when the new moon will appear so that they can calculate Easter each year, which was a movable feast. Despite its importance, this wasn't always strictly accurate, and the golden numbers in many calendars and martyrologies do not make computational sense. The next column will list the Sunday (or dominical) letters – seven letters from A to G, representing the days of the week. Every year a different letter will be the Sunday letter: for example, if the Sunday letter for 1214 was 'E', you just need to find all the Es in the column to work out the Sundays. The system moves backwards, so the Sunday letter for 1215 would be 'D' (although leap years slightly confuse this).

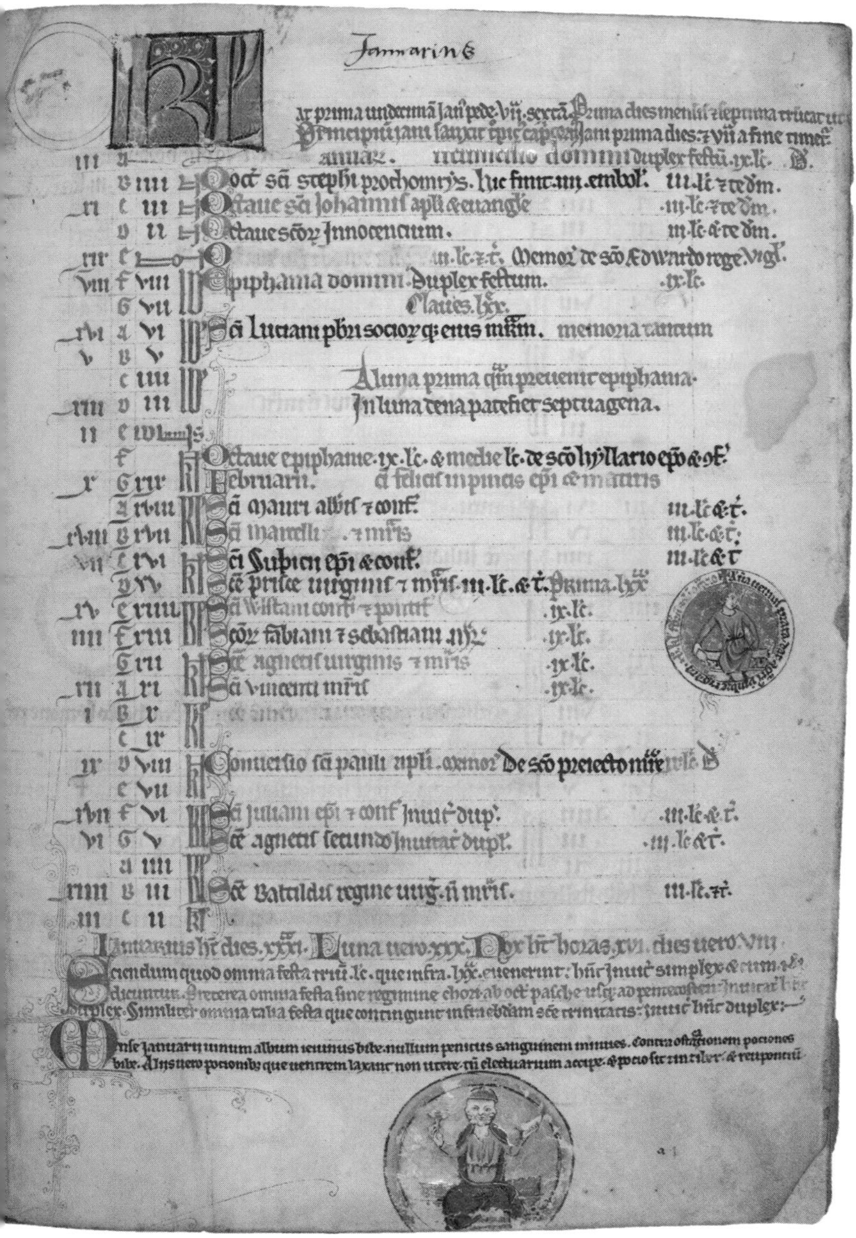

Month of January in a medieval calendar, the Rutland Psalter, 13th century.

The next two columns list the days of the week following the Roman calendar, which divided the month into nones, ides and kalends. The nones was the fifth or seventh day of each month, the ides was the thirteenth or fifteenth of each month, and the kalends was the first day of each month. So, for example, once the kalends of January (1 January) had passed, you began counting down to the nones (5 January in this case). So, 2 January = IIII nones, 3 January = III nones, 4 January = II nones, 5 January = nones. Then you began counting down to the ides (13 January in this case), so 6 January = VIII ides, 7 January = VII ides, and so on. Once the ides had passed, you began counting down to the kalends of February (1 February), so 14 January = XIX kalends, 13 January = XVIII kalends, and so on. Medieval calendars were certainly good for a mental workout. However, it was much easier to navigate the year by feast days, and as 1 February is also St Brigid's Day, it would have been much more common to say St Brigid's Day, rather than the kalends of February. And memory and the landscape would probably have been more relevant than calendars in measuring the passing of the year for most people, particularly those who worked in agriculture.

The main column of the calendar contains the medieval feast days (or holy days/holidays), of which there were about forty to sixty in a year. On these days, work was forbidden – so you can understand why a medieval person would want a note of these. Obviously going to church was the main event on these days, but there would also be bonfires, games, plays, parades and, of course, feasting. Really important days, such as the feast day of St Brigid, might be written in the calendar in red. The feast days might vary depending on your local saints, or who was the popular saint at the time, so calendars can be a useful tool for dating or locating manuscripts that we don't know much about. For example, if there is an original entry for Thomas Becket, who was martyred on 29 December 1170, it's a pretty clear indicator that the manuscript was made after that date. However, the manuscript may have been made before that date and the entry added afterwards, in which case you might be able to tell by the different script or colour of the ink. Even more telling would be if the name of Thomas Becket was scrubbed out, because after the English Reformation Henry VIII insisted his name be erased from manuscripts. So, if Thomas's entry has been defaced, it indicates that the manuscript was still in circulation in the Tudor period. Other additions were often made too – of favourite saints, or significant events, or obituary entries for family members, so they can also be a deeply personal view into what was important to the manuscript owner. In the St Alban's Psalter, there are obituary entries for Christina's parents and her brothers. These additions were not made by Christina herself but were made shortly after her death by one of the scribes at St Albans, which offers a reminder of the importance of family connections and the close communities that existed in the medieval period.

After the calendar in the St Albans Psalter come a series of full-page miniatures depicting the life of Christ. Known as cycles, these narrative images were intended to immerse the reader in religious history as a spiritual exercise, to meditate on and to bring their own imagination and knowledge to the story. The images in this cycle are particularly notable for the active roles of women in the scenes. While this reflects the increased visibility of women such as the Virgin Mary and Mary Magdalen in Romanesque art, it may also have a personal meaning, if this psalter was originally intended for Christina of Markyate.[26]

After the narrative cycles in a psalter came the actual psalms. These often began with a large decorated initial *B* for the opening psalm: *Beatus vir, qui non abiit in consilio impiorum, et in via peccatorum non stetit, et in cathedra pestilentae non sedit* (Blessed is the man who has not followed the advice of the impious, and has not stood in the street among sinners, and has not sat in the

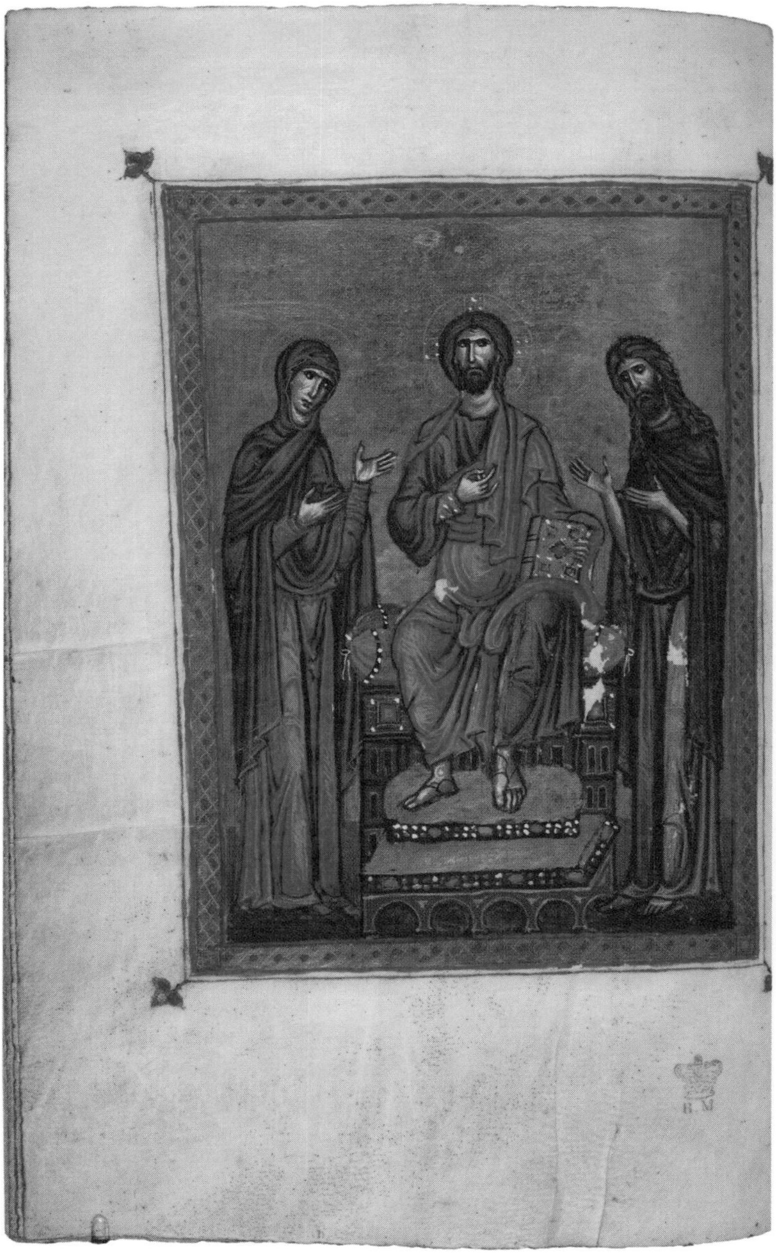

The lavish Melisende Psalter made in Jerusalem, 12th century.

ory book cover inlaid with turquoise from the Melisende Psalter depicting
enes from the life of David on the upper cover, 12th century.

company of complainers). A particularly lavish psalter, like this one, might then have historiated or inhabited illuminated initials for the beginning of each psalm (all 150 of them), whereas a more modestly produced psalter might just have a large coloured initial for each psalm. Smaller coloured initials then indicated the beginning of each new line. Psalters (and many other manuscripts) of the twelfth century are often wonderfully colourful affairs.

Psalters in the twelfth and thirteenth centuries often start each new sentence of a psalm on a new line. This can leave a long empty space on the line above where the previous sentence finishes. Innovative scribes or rubricators filled these lines with what we rather unimaginatively call 'linefillers'. They are pen drawings of swirling patterns, geometric designs or animal/human figures, normally in red or blue ink, and they are quite simply doodles to fill up the space. They range from simple squiggles to ornate illuminated portraits: for example, a twelfth-century psalter (BL, Add MS 38819) features very basic linked-circle linefillers in alternating red and green, whereas the lines in the slightly later Ormesby Psalter (Bodleian, MS Douce 366) have intricately decorated patterns interspersed with ink and gold dragons, fish and hybrid human/animal forms. This form of decorating the page with strange little creatures is perhaps a precursor to the amusing marginalia seen from the mid-thirteenth century onwards.

Another psalter of note, the Melisende Psalter (BL, Egerton MS 1139), was produced in Jerusalem around the same time as the St Albans Psalter. It was probably made for Melisende, Queen of Jerusalem during the occupation by the Christian crusaders in the twelfth century. Melisende was the daughter of the Armenian noblewoman Morphia of Melitene and the French crusader King Baldwin II, so she grew up in a multicultural environment. The psalter was probably produced by the monastery at the Church of the Holy Sepulchre (the site where Jesus was crucified and buried in the tomb), which was also a centre of book production at the time. The psalter is a blend of Eastern and Western styles – the script is a delicate Romanesque used in English and French manuscripts, but each line starts with a large gold letter (rather than the multicoloured initials of twelfth-century Western manuscripts) which is typical of the Byzantine style.

The cycle of illuminated miniatures of the life of Christ was a feature of Western psalters (like the St Albans Psalter), but the cycle scenes in the Melisende Psalter relate more to the Greek liturgy, and the shimmering gold backgrounds resemble Greek icons. We know that the artist of the miniatures was called Basilius because he signed the last miniature on fol. 12av 'Basilius me fecit' (Basilius made me) on the stool under Jesus's feet. Although Basilius is a Greek name, the signature is written in Latin – again indicating the fusion of Latin and Greek influences in this manuscript. The psalter's bindings are just as deluxe as the script and illumination – it was originally covered in ivory panels exquisitely carved and inlaid with turquoise and other coloured gemstones.

So, we see in the twelfth century the fusion of cultures – the close development between script and art in England and France after the conquest, and the influence of the Byzantine style on Western manuscript art. The intellectual barriers between Islamic and Christian scholars lessened to the extent that Islamic texts were translated into Latin and dispersed throughout European networks, allowing for wider philosophical thought and scientific advancement. It's understandable then that this period is referred to as the twelfth-century renaissance.

ANOTHER TYPE OF MANUSCRIPT that gained popularity in Europe in the late twelfth century was the bestiary – an encyclopaedic compilation of animals, some real, some fictitious. They contained a short passage of information about the animal, often

The basilisk in the Aberdeen Bestiary, 13th century.

with an accompanying illustration in a framed box. The bestiary was based on the early Christian *Physiologus*, a Greek text written in Alexandria in the second or third century that used animal lore to provide a Christian allegorical interpretation. For example, the death of the mythical phoenix, a bird that dies by spontaneous combustion and is then reborn from the ashes, represents the death and rebirth of Jesus; the pelican, believed to unintentionally kill its young but then revive them by piercing its breast and sprinkling blood over them, is symbolic of the sacrifice of Jesus shedding blood upon the cross to save us.

Medieval bestiaries expanded on this format, adding further knowledge to the descriptions of the animal kingdom. The advances in manuscript decoration meant that illuminated images often accompanied the descriptions, although (unfortunately but sometimes hilariously) realistic depictions of lions and other unfamiliar animals still remained beyond the remit of artists in the northwest of Europe.[27] The Aberdeen Bestiary (Aberdeen University Library, MS 24) is a particularly deluxe example, produced about 1200 for a wealthy patron, possibly in Canterbury.[28] It has a dazzling array of illuminated miniatures and decorated initials, as well as smaller gold initials surrounded by a frame of red and blue ink (known as champ initials). Besides the delightful depictions and information on familiar animals such as bees, bats and turtledoves, it also includes mythical creatures such as leucrotas, basilisks and phoenixes. A leucrota is described as 'a swift animal born in India. It is the size of an ass with the hindquarters of a stag, the chest and legs of a lion, a horse's head and a mouth split open as far as its ears. It has a continuous jawbone instead of teeth.' A basilisk is described

> as a ruler, because he is truly the king of serpents, so that seeing him, men flee, because he kills them with his smell, for if he even sees a man he kills him. Indeed, no bird flying along passes his sight unhurt, but although it is some distance away, it is consumed, burnt up by his mouth. Yet he is overcome by weasels, which men insert in those caves in which the basilisk hides. So when he sees a weasel he flees, and the weasel pursues and kills him, for the Father of all things never makes anything without a counterforce. In addition, the basilisk is a half-foot long, with white stripes.[29]

So, if you are ever being attacked by a basilisk, just remember to chuck a weasel at it.

The Aberdeen Bestiary also contains important details about its production – for example we can see preliminary sketches in the margins, such as on fol. 93v, where two faint drawings have been left in the side margin depicting the dangers of fire-bearing stones. The illuminated miniature on the page clearly reflects details from the sketch. Instructions for colours have also been jotted underneath the top sketch, indicating that 'bis' (grey) and 'mine' (minium) be used.[30] Prick marks can also be seen around some of the figures, for example, Adam and Eve in fol. 3r, indicating that this image was copied using the pouncing technique, where ash was sprinkled over a template to create the outline of a new image on the parchment underneath. The prick marks are clearly visible on the blank side of the folio. The animal stories inside bestiaries would have been a delight to readers young and old, and no doubt would have fuelled many imaginations. However, like most things in Europe in the medieval period, they were fundamentally embedded with a Christian message.

GRATIAN'S *DECRETUM* was a compilation of Church law for the students studying law at the new university at Bologna. It began to circulate in the mid-twelfth century and was the work of monk and teacher Gratian, who had sifted through thousands of extracts from Church writings to create a legal textbook. The text soon became popular in Italy, France and England, as scholars sought to obtain copies and the new secular workshops around universities happily obliged in producing them. Church law (or canon law) was different from civil law and dealt with the moral and ethical side of the law, such as marriage, property and inheritance.

Many copies of the text are also surrounded by glosses, with extraneous commentary on the text. Generous margins would have been left empty around the main text at the point of production for later owners to add their own notes (see, for example, BL, Royal 9 C III). The *Decretums* were often decorated as well, with embellished initials and illuminated miniatures depicting the issues discussed in the text. A late twelfth-/early thirteenth-century manuscript, possibly produced in a Catte Street workshop, is decorated in the Channel style with the distinctive swirling concentric circles, white lions and biting heads (CCCC, MS 10, fol. 12r).

THE TWELFTH-CENTURY RENAISSANCE saw the expansion of scientific texts for students and scholars, particularly with the recent introduction of Arabic texts on algebra, astronomy, astrolabes and medicine. Adelard of Bath (*c.* 1116–1142) translated Al-Khwārizmī's *Zīj al-Sindhind* (astronomical tables of Siddhanta), an eighth-century work containing tables for the movements of the sun, the moon and the five other planets known at the time, based on the Persian and Indian astronomical methods. The original Arabic text is now lost, only surviving in Adelard's Latin version (see, for example, Bodleian Libr., MS Auct. F.1.9). Adelard also helped popularize the Arabic notation for numbers and zero in Europe, rather than the old system of Roman numerals – which made counting a lot easier.

Yet scientific texts had always been in circulation in the Church in the early medieval period, and the monasteries maintained their interest in this subject and continued producing them. For example, one of the earliest manuscripts with anatomical images was produced in a Benedictine monastery in Prüfening, Bavaria, in 1165 (BSB, Clm 13002). It shows five squatting figures illustrating the five systems of the body according to Galen – the veins, arteries, bones, nerves and muscles – with each figure surrounded by text.

Wee charts were a popular reference guide in medical textbooks, as uroscopy (examining urine, particularly the colour, to diagnose illness) was a serious business. There is a colourful circular diagram in a thirteenth-century manuscript (Oxford, Bodleian Library MS Savile 39, fol. 7v) depicting twenty different colours of wee alongside their diagnosis. Medieval physicians are often depicted holding up a matula (a flask for collecting urine) and examining the contents intently, giving them an air of great learning. Even more closely related to matters of the body was John Arderne's medical treatise on anal fistulas, complete with eye-watering diagrams of bottoms and the various instruments used.[31] Many of these new scientific texts needed new formats to encompass the diagrams for astronomy and anatomical procedures. In the thirteenth century, volvelles appeared in manuscripts, which are astrological charts with revolving discs of parchment or paper that work similarly to astrolabes. The parchment can be revolved to work out the position of the moon and the sun, which, in the case of BL, Egerton MS 2572, fol. 51r, allows the physician to predict the best time to give medical treatment.

The Romanesque was one of the most exciting and expansive periods in book history. By the mid-twelfth century, manuscript production had seen a dramatic shift from monastic to commercial enterprise, with students and the wealthy laity providing a market for a greater range of reading material. Manuscripts became items of conspicuous consumption, growing ever more ornate during the twelfth and thirteenth centuries, with decorated initials, linefillers and penflourished initials. The standard of artistic style was also dramatically raised, moving away from the more symbolic depictions of the early medieval period. The damp-fold technique, where figures were painted with clothes clinging to the body, created dynamic and more realistic images with a palpable sense of movement. Improvements in parchment manufacture meant that thinner leaves allowed more quires to be bound into a manuscript and the increased angularity of Romanesque script meant that much more text could be written on those leaves. Manuscript making had become a serious business. The march of progress went on, and as we shall see in the next chapter, the demand for texts eventually sowed the seeds for the decline of manuscript production.

Seven

The End of the Scriptorium

A workshop in Mainz, *c.* 1450

Johannes nervously smiles at the group of people crammed into his small studio, eager to see his invention. The wooden structure in the middle of the room dominates everything else, tall and imposing. Word has got around about his new 'fast writing machine', and now he has smoothed out all the workings, Johannes is ready to unveil his creation. As a young boy he was frustrated by how long it took to laboriously write text on a page and dreamt of a machine that could somehow do it for you. Inspired by the screw presses that squeezed the liquid out of grapes with a heavy weight from above, for years he worked on a version that would do the same, pressing paper onto metal lettershapes below that would leave an imprint on the page. Imagine the hours of scribal labour it would save, not to mention a new standardization in transmission, where corrupt handwritten texts no longer had to be relied on. He has spent days painstakingly engraving letters into hard metal and then pressing them into softer metal, thereby creating a mould. By pouring molten lead into these moulds, he could produce unlimited amounts of standard, uniform type – unthinkable to a scribe whose hand tired after a long day, with their writing getting untidier and more illegible as their attention wandered. Johannes has faced many setbacks in his project, such as getting the wooden machine to exert the right pressure on the metal type and finding the right ink to adhere to the letters. He has tried many different substances, but at last he found an oil-based carbon mixture that coated the type sufficiently.

The room is stuffy and dimly lit with oil lamps. People are starting to shuffle and whisper impatiently, so Johannes signals to his assistant Stefan to begin. Stefan goes to the workbench, spreads some ink onto a marble slab and starts to roll the ink pad onto the ink, covering the surface with an even layer. The light picks up the glistening texture of the ink, and once Stefan is satisfied with the distribution on the pad, he goes over to the pressing machine. The metal type is secured in a wooden frame at the bottom of the machine that protrudes out on a sliding bed. Stefan expertly presses the ink straight down onto the top of the type, coating it evenly. Now Johannes takes over, placing a single sheet of damp paper carefully onto the type, lining it up exactly with the wooden frame underneath. He places a square of packing material over the top and slides the well-oiled bed directly under the screw press.

The room is now silent with expectation and people are craning their necks to see what will happen next. Johannes firmly grabs the wooden arm of the screw mechanism and pulls hard, bracing his foot against the base for extra leverage. The upper plate comes down, applying pressure to the paper and the inked type underneath, squeezing the two surfaces together. With a final creak of protest, Johannes releases the wooden arm and slides the bed back out. Removing the packing, he holds his breath as he peels the paper away from the type, praying that the ink is clear and evenly spread. Although he and Stefan have practised and perfected this process for months, there is still much that can go wrong. But Johannes need not have worried, as he holds up the sheet of perfectly printed text to the amazed audience. Many that had been sceptical and suspicious before were now excitedly examining the neat type and talking about the possibilities that could unfold. Johannes looks at Stefan, who grins back at him. Feeling the relief flood through him, Johannes at last feels that his invention was worth all the hard work and endless refinements, and that now, other people besides him can see the potential that this could have for book production. Looking round the room, feeling the excited hubbub that he has created, he feels on the verge of something big.

The Romanesque and Gothic styles blended gradually into each other, to the point where it is impossible to say when one ended and the other began (certainly in manuscripts). Architecturally, the Romanesque rounded arches gave way to Gothic pointed arches, which were much stronger and could endure more weight, allowing cathedrals to be built higher, with much thinner columns. The increased amount of space and light in cathedrals in this period was revolutionary. However, this kind of definitive feature is harder to pinpoint in manuscripts – but (with caveats) we will say that full Gothic script starts to appear by the mid-thirteenth century (and although it started to come in, that does not mean it was universally adopted everywhere at once). One distinguishing feature of Gothic script is the fully compartmentalized *a*, with the top loop touching the lower bowl, forming two enclosed sections. The Gothic period is generally associated with universities and the new urban classes, which ties in with the rise of the commercial book trade around this time.

Commercial workshops were firmly established by the thirteenth century, with family businesses operating from permanent premises. However, like the scriptoria in monastic houses, very little evidence survives of what they looked like. Illuminating power-couple Jeanne and Richard de Montbaston lived and worked on the Rue Neuve Notre-Dame circa 1338–53 as illuminators and *libraires*. One of their most well-known works, a copy of the poem *Roman de la Rose* (BnF, MS Fr. 25526), is a skilfully executed illuminated manuscript, full of lively, colourful images mostly painted by Jeanne. As well as many eyebrow-raising illustrations (including nuns picking penises growing from a tree and a monk and a nun in several compromising positions), there are also some images of manuscript production. At the bottom of fol. 77r, a woman sits at a table grinding some pigment by candlelight, while at a desk in front of her a man writes on parchment. On the verso side of the folio, a seated man plans out decorated initials on parchment, while in front of him a seated woman illuminates the manuscript with gold. In the background we can see folded parchment, already scribed and hung over racks to dry, ready to be selected for decoration. It is believed that this woman and man represent Jeanne and Richard de Montbaston themselves.[1] Not only does this give us a delightful insight into workshop life and processes, but it offers a fascinating glimpse into how a wife-and-husband team worked together. A comparison with a copy of the *Légende dorée* (BnF, MS Fr. 241) produced by Richard de Montbaston shows just how synthesized their artistic styles were. It's possible to imagine their conversations and their input into each other's work, looking over each other's shoulders to comment and encourage. Although we cannot speculate too much on their private life, the evidence we have shows a real creative partnership.

Unfortunately, by 1353 Richard had died, but we know from the oath she took that year that Jeanne carried on the business. Widows often took over the business after their husbands had died, as we can see from individual oaths registered in their name, or from the property rents they continued to pay. With opportunities to manage their own workshops in the thriving manuscript industry in England and France, it must have been an encouraging time for female artisans – although women were far from equal in society. The accomplished French writer Christine de Pizan (1364–*c.* 1430) understood this inequality only too well and used her platform at court to write texts celebrating women and their contribution to society. 'The Book of the Queen' (BL,

Harley MS 4431) is a fifteenth-century illuminated manuscript containing selected texts by Christine de Pizan for Queen Isabel of Bavaria, possibly partly written by Christine herself. The manuscript also features multiple images of Christine – presenting her book to the queen, writing in her *scriptoriolium*, addressing Louis d'Orléans and so forth – providing a great example of the inner life of medieval women and manuscripts.

Although, of course, Christine operated in a higher social sphere than most workshop manuscript makers. Many of the scribes and artists were producing text and images of extremely great quality and beauty, but inhabited different worlds to their elite patrons and knew that they were unlikely to see their works again once they left the workshop. Again, divisions can be drawn between the monastic scriptorium making the product in-house for their own community (or a community that they knew, or at least were on an equal footing with), and the impersonal

Jeanne and Richard de Montbaston working together in a copy of the *Roman de la Rose*, 14th century.

transaction of the manuscript from workshop (or workshops) to elite household, with neither party perhaps ever meeting each other.

To demonstrate just how streamlined commercial manuscript production had become, a system of copying was in operation in some university towns called 'pecia'. It was a system designed to mass-produce books at a low cost, mainly for students, but also tutors, preachers and the wider cultural community. This system started in Italy in the early thirteenth century, but soon spread to other university towns, particularly Paris. *Libraires* (stationers) working for the universities would be given an officially approved exemplar, which was divided into sections and numbered. Anyone wishing to obtain a copy of the text could then rent out a section or piece and copy it themselves or hire a scribe. So, for a class of students who all needed access to a text for their course, this system enabled different sections of the text to be copied on a rotational basis. We know that this system existed from marks left in manuscripts and lists of pecia exemplars rented out by *libraires*. Pecia marks can be seen in the margin to note the number of the section: for example, BL, Arundel MS 435 has 'xvii. p.' written in the right-hand margin of fol. 36r, to signify that this is the seventeenth piece of the text. Some surviving lists of pecia manuscripts from Paris give information on the title of the text, how many pieces it was divided into, and the rental price of each piece.[2]

These pecia manuscripts tend to be very basic, with text in black ink and chapter headings, initials and paraphs in the standard blue and red colouring, but rarely any decoration. Clearly, the emphasis was on the functionality of the text for the student – no point in adding all the bells and whistles. In terms of the general layout of scholarly manuscripts, they became much easier to navigate in the thirteenth century, with the increased use of tables of contents, rubrics, running heads and chapter divisions.

SCRIPTS CONTINUED TO EVOLVE, and Romanesque (or Protogothic) script developed into Gothic. No one reads full Gothic script for a visual treat. It is so tightly packed, so indistinguishable, so angular, that it makes your brain have a fight with your eyes. It might look neatly ordered and crisp from a distance, but once you start trying to read the actual words, it stops being pleasant. The Romanesque script that was prevalent in the twelfth century starts to become more upright and compressed in the thirteenth century, with extreme angularity. Letters start to 'bite' into each other, sharing strokes between them – so, for example, if writing '*de*' the long downward stroke of a *d* would also serve as the back stroke for *e*. The feet on the minims also became more pronounced and diamond-shaped, developing into a script called textualis quadrata (see, for example, the *Grandes Heures de Jean de Berry*, BnF, MS Lat. 919). The ampersand becomes less popular, replaced with a Tironian *et* '7', and the writing begins not on the top ruled line of the page, but on the second ruled line. Contractions were a normal part of the text. Textualis quadrata was a high-end script, used for deluxe manuscripts – as was textualis prescissa, a script identical to quadrata, except that instead of the diamond-shaped feet, the minims would end exactly flush with the baseline (a lot harder than you might think – it required real precision by the scribe). The prescissa script had a limited existence, only being used in England between about 1200 and 1350. Good examples are the De Brailes Hours (BL, Add MS 49999) and the Luttrell Psalter (BL, Add MS 42130). For less grand manuscripts, a rotunda script was more commonplace – and, as it sounds, it was a bit more relaxed and not so angular. This type of script was used widely in Italy, where the full Gothic style of the fourteenth century was never really embraced.

Scribes were well aware of how ridiculous this tightly compressed Gothic text looked, and they had a mock sentence that

autem populus eius et oues
pascue eius.
Aue maria grã plena dominus
tecum.
Hodie si uocem eius audie-
ritis nolite obdurare corda ue-
stra: sicut in exacerbacione secundum diem temptacionis
in deserto ubi temptauerunt
me patres uestri: probauerunt et
uiderunt opera mea.
Dominus tecum.
Quadraginta annis pro-
ximus fui generacioni huic
et dixi semper hii errant corde:
ipsi uero non cognouerunt
uias meas quibus iuraui i-
n ira mea si introibunt in re-
quiem meam.
Aue maria grã plena dominus
tecum.
Gloria patri et filio et spi-
ritui sancto.
Sicut erat in principio et
nunc et semper et in secula se-
culorum amen.
Dominus tecum.
Aue maria grã plena dominus
tecum. Hympnus.
O quam glorifica lu-
ce choruscas stirpis
dauitice regia proles subli-
mis residens uirgo maria supra celigenas ethereos omnes.
Tu cum uirgineo mater
honore angelorum domino
pectoris aulam sacris uisceri-
bus casta parasti natus huic
deus est corpore xpi.
Quem cunctus uenerans
orbis adorat cui nunc rite ge-
nu flectitur omne a quo nos
petimus te ueniente abiectis
tenebris gaudia lucis.
Hoc largitor pater luminis
omnis natum per propriũ

Gothic textualis quadrata script, *Grandes Heures de Jean de Berry*, 15th century.

was mainly composed of the letters *m*, *n*, *u* and *i* – *mimi numinum niuium minimi munium nimium uini muniminum imminui uiui minimum uolunt*. It's a nonsense phrase, translated as 'The very short mimes of the gods of snow do not at all wish that during their lifetime the very great burden of (distributing) the wine of the walls to be lightened'[3] – but the Latin sentence is simply a visual joke on how hard Gothic script was to read. The minims all run into each other so that it is impossible to tell whether you are looking at (for example) an *m*, an *i* and an *n*, or an *n* and an *i*. There is a thirteenth-century French manuscript that includes this sentence, written in Gothic rotunda (Gottfried Wilhelm Leibniz Bibliothek, Niedersächsische Landesbibliothek, MS IV, 524, fol. 3r). The manuscript is a florilegium, or anthology of various texts, including a satire on the Church, so this mockery of Gothic script seems to have been copied out by the scribe for fun. Scribes also amused themselves with the script in other ways, by elaborately flourishing the majuscule letters with decorative lines and even tiny heads. One scribe from the early fifteenth century, known as the 'Dog Head Scribe', made the letter *E* into a zoomorphic representation of a dog, complete with collar and sticking-out tongue that formed the middle bar of the *E* (BL, Royal MS 2 A XVIII, fol. 7r). Other scribes copied this trend, and it became quite a phenomenon in the first half of the fifteenth century in England, thoroughly enlivening the text.[4]

Gothic script continued to be used for religious and deluxe manuscripts in Europe up to the sixteenth century – and in Germany this script was the basis of the blackletter type used in printing up to the twentieth century. However, other scripts were available, such as anglicana – a Gothic cursive script for everyday documents used in England and France from the second half of the thirteenth century. It has distinctive letterforms such as its *g* shaped like an eight and a generously flourished *w* (see BL, Harley MS 1701, fol. 72v). This was then taken over by secretary hand, another cursive script that first developed on the Continent and spread rapidly by the end of the fourteenth century. This can be recognized by its single compartment *a*, and *g*, which looks like it has horns (see BL, Add MS 12042, fol. 1r). These were the scripts used for quick writing, for legal and administrative work. Other hybrid (or bastard) scripts developed for luxury manuscripts. The most accomplished was Bâtarde, a Gothic cursive that bears similarities to normal Gothic, but written at a slant, as you can see in a fifteenth-century copy of the Chronicles of Jean Froissart (Getty MS Ludwig XIII 7).

The last major development in script in the later medieval period was the Humanist script. This was developed mainly in Italy by scholars of the Humanities, such as Poggio Bracciolini (1380–1459) and Niccolò de' Niccoli (1364–1437). These Renaissance Humanists wanted to revive the classical culture, and they studied and copied classical texts on philosophy and literature. Bracciolini sought out and gave new life to many classical texts that had previously been hidden away in monastic libraries, such as the only copy of Lucretius' *De rerum natura* (On the Nature of Things). Many of these texts were written in Caroline minuscule, and the Humanist scholars started to replicate this older medieval style of writing when they copied out the texts – so Caroline minuscule became intrinsically associated with the study of the classical world. It has been suggested that the Humanists genuinely thought that these Caroline minuscule texts were actually the original classical texts, but that seems unlikely. These were learned men who travelled around looking at a lot of texts – and there were a lot more genuine ancient texts and scrolls in circulation then, so they would surely have been familiar with many types of script.

So, based on the Caroline script, the scholars then developed the Humanist script – which couldn't have been further away from Gothic script if it tried (which was probably the point). It was called *litterae antiquae* (ancient letters), whereas Gothic was called *litterae modernae* (modern letters). Bracciolini is generally considered the creator of Humanist minuscule, and de' Niccoli as the creator of the cursive version, which became what we know today as italic. Although Humanist is regarded as a secular script rather than monastic, Bracciolini worked for the papacy for fifty years and served as a papal secretary. He never took holy orders, but his links with the Church surely helped enhance the prestige of this script, which had been readily adopted by the papal court.

Humanist script is beautiful. Clear, spacious and elegant, it is an absolute joy to behold. Deluxe examples of this script include the *Bentivoglio Hours* (NAL, MSL/1902/1707), made in Bologna around 1494–1503, and a Book of Hours (BL, Add MS 35318) produced by a Parisian workshop circa 1530, which shows the spread of the Humanist style to the rest of Europe. Even though printed books were in circulation by the end of the fifteenth century, deluxe manuscripts continued to be produced for those who could afford them – for example the psalter of Henry VIII that was made circa 1540–41 (BL, Royal MS 2 A XVI). The Humanist script influenced the development of the early printing presses, with printers adopting the letter style (alongside Gothic/blacktype). The cursive script was adapted into the italic typeface developed by printer Aldus Manutius, so these medieval handwritten scripts live on, despite changing technologies. Although we look back at this time knowing that the printing press was just about to revolutionize European book production, the medieval scribes had no idea of this – and we can see that there was still a real drive to change and improve scripts even in the early fifteenth century, with the development of the Humanist script.

THE ART IN MANUSCRIPTS naturally developed alongside the Gothic script. The peripheral designs in the margins, in the form

Il dit vray est quil nest chose plus certaine que la mort je le dy a ce propos que le roy de navarre ne cuidoit point quant il morut estre si pres de sa fin. Car sil le sceust il se fust advise et neust point mis en termes ne avant ce quil mist Il se tenoit en la cite de pampelune en navarre la lui vint en ymaginacion et voullente de prendre sur son pais par taille la somme de deux cens mille frans et manda son conseil et leur dist quil convenoit quil fust ainsi. Son conseil nosa dire non car il estoit moult cruel. Adont furent mandes a venir devers le roy les plus notables hommes des cites et bonnes villes de navarre a pampelune tous y vindrent nul ne losa delayer. Quant ilz furent la tous venus et assembles ou pallays du roy lui mesmes sans autre moyen remonstra la querelle car ce fut ung roy qui fut moult soubtil en sa nature et dist ainsi tout conclud quil lui faisoit besoing et convenoit avoir la somme de deux cens mille francs et vouloit que une taille sen fist et monstra

Gothic cursive script, *Chroniques of Froissart*, vol. III, *c.* 1480–83.

AD TERTIAM
VERSVS.

Deus in adiu-
torium meum
intende. Do
mine ad adiu
uandum me fe
stina Gloria.
patri. ī fine all'a
Crucifige crucifige clamitant
hora tertiarum: illusus indui
tur ueste purpurarum: caput eius pū
gitur corona spinarum crucem por
tat humeris ad locum penarum. V.
Adoramus te christe et benedicim⁹
tibi. R. Quia per sanctam crucem

Humanist script, *Bentivoglio Hours*, 15th–16th century.

of penflourishing, line fillers and extended limbs of decorated initials, gradually started to form a defined border around the text. We can see in the work of William de Brailes, an Oxford illuminator who worked on Catte Street around 1230–60, how his decoration encases the written text within his horizontal penflourishing at the bottom of the page and elongated ascender and descenders on his coloured initials along the vertical edge (BL, Add MS 49999). By the turn of the fourteenth century these borders had become a distinct frame, existing in their own right, beautifully decorated with foliage and figures (for example, BL, Yates Thompson MS 8, fol. 7r). This border framework became part of the standard layout for manuscripts in the fourteenth and fifteenth centuries.

Enclosing the text in a frame compartmentalized it from the border, creating two visually separate spaces on the page. This space around the edges allowed artists free rein, and they filled the borders with all sorts of surreal and subversive images. More commonly known as marginalia today, these were previously referred to as 'grotesques', and dismissed by earlier scholars as a nonsense not worth giving attention to. Grumpy old Bernard of Clairvaux (talking about sculpture that was of a similar style to manuscript art) said in his *Apology*:

> What is the point of this ridiculous monstrosity, this shapely misshapenness, this misshapen shapeliness? What is the point of those unclean apes, fierce lions, monstrous centaurs, half-men, striped tigers, fighting soldiers and hunters blowing their horns? In one place you see many bodies under a single head, in another several heads on a single body. Here on a quadruped we see the tail of a serpent. Over there on a fish we see the head of a quadruped. There we find a beast that is horse up front and goat behind, here another that is horned animal in front and horse behind.

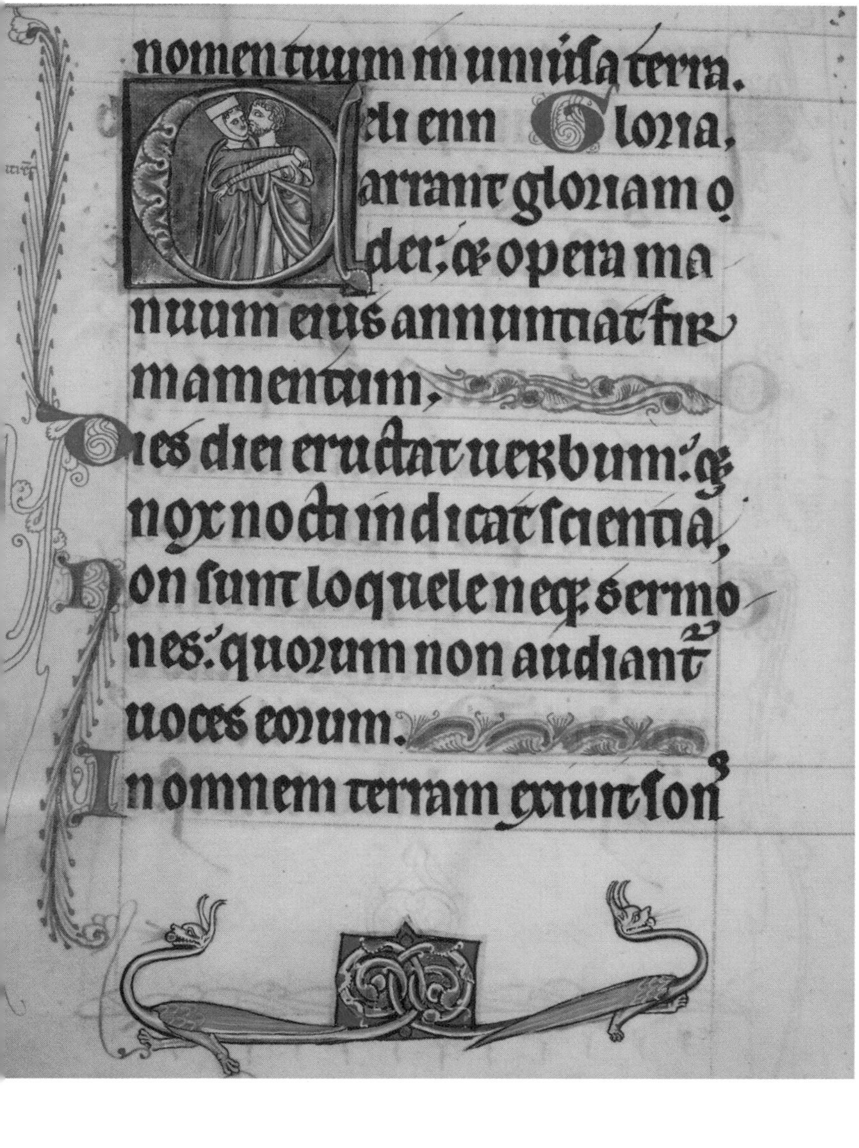

Beginnings of borders around the text in the *De Brailes Hours*, 13th century.

However, it is exactly this ridiculous monstrosity that delights the reader. They are colourful, entertaining, impossible and frequently rude. As well as bare bottoms galore – passing wind, defecating, blowing trumpets, having arrows shot into them – there are startling images of religious figures, such as nuns suckling monkeys, naked bishops, robed monks incubating eggs in a nest and animals dressed up in ecclesiastical garb.[5] Other popular themes include killer rabbits and fighting snails, apes performing human tasks, animals playing musical instruments and weird combinations of human/animal hybrids interacting with each other. It's an absolute riot.

The Luttrell Psalter is a fourteenth-century illuminated manuscript made for Geoffrey Luttrell (1276–1345), a lord of the manor in Lincolnshire. We know it belonged to him because the text contains these words: *Dns. Galfridus Louterell me fieri fecit* (Lord Geoffrey Luttrell had me made), followed by a miniature of him mounted on a horse (fol. 202v). The psalter is written in a Gothic textualis prescissa, with the minims ending neatly and precisely on the horizontal line, written by one single scribe. Some of the letters are delicately flourished with trailing tendrils, made with the corner of the nib to allow the thinnest of strokes. Colourful linefillers decorate the empty horizontal gaps between the psalms. The text is framed within borders made up of geometric or swirling patterns, or creatures with elongated necks or bodies, trailing off into foliage. The areas outside of the borders are teeming with activity, particularly in the space at the bottom of the page. Strange hybrid creatures – such as the head and torso of a bishop attached to the bottom half of cow-like creature (fol. 34v), or a bald, bearded head with no torso set on bare naked legs with bright orange dragon's heads for shoes (fol. 62v) – cavort nonsensically around the edges. As well as these amusing creatures, the psalter also depicts everyday agricultural scenes, which has provided important information on medieval farming equipment and rural life.

So, what were these kaleidoscopic marginalia for? It seems a juxtaposition to have such sacrilegious images in a book of psalms. Yet the Ormesby Psalter, similar to the Luttrell Psalter in style and date, was owned by a monk of Norwich and given to the cathedral for communal use after his death – so even the Church didn't seem to have a problem with the irreverent images on the edges. Perhaps the spiritual text and the coarse images on the page are a reflection of normal medieval life, with the profane and the sacred living alongside each other. The everyday smelly, dirty life of a peasant contrasts against the ethereal beauty of cathedral architecture soaring up to the heavens, but both were everyday realities. Even a finely dressed bishop would struggle to avoid the stench of animal dung while moving about the city. These images are often an inverted version of the medieval world too, where things are upside down and back-to-front. For example, rabbits are often shown wearing armour and fighting humans (even decapitating them) – a parallel universe where rabbits are the hunters and humans are the hunted. Some images may also be poking fun at medieval society, for example the nun nursing her child-monkey ridicules the idea of monastic celibacy and the purity of the nun who is supposed to epitomize the Virgin Mary. It becomes a parody of the Virgin Mary giving birth to Jesus, with the monstrous birth symbolizing the nun's sin.[6]

The marginalia also inadvertently signify the passage of time and how the scribal profession had changed throughout the medieval period – whereas once it was the vocation of members of religious orders, the commercialization of manuscript production meant that now many scribes were independent professionals. They are often gently mocked in marginalia – an early fourteenth-century manuscript depicts a scribe as a monkey, preparing parchment for writing by rubbing pumice over it (Oxford, Bodleian Library, MS Bodl. 264, fol. 84r). A missal also from the early fourteenth century features a hapless human scribe

Borders framing the text from a breviary, 14th century.

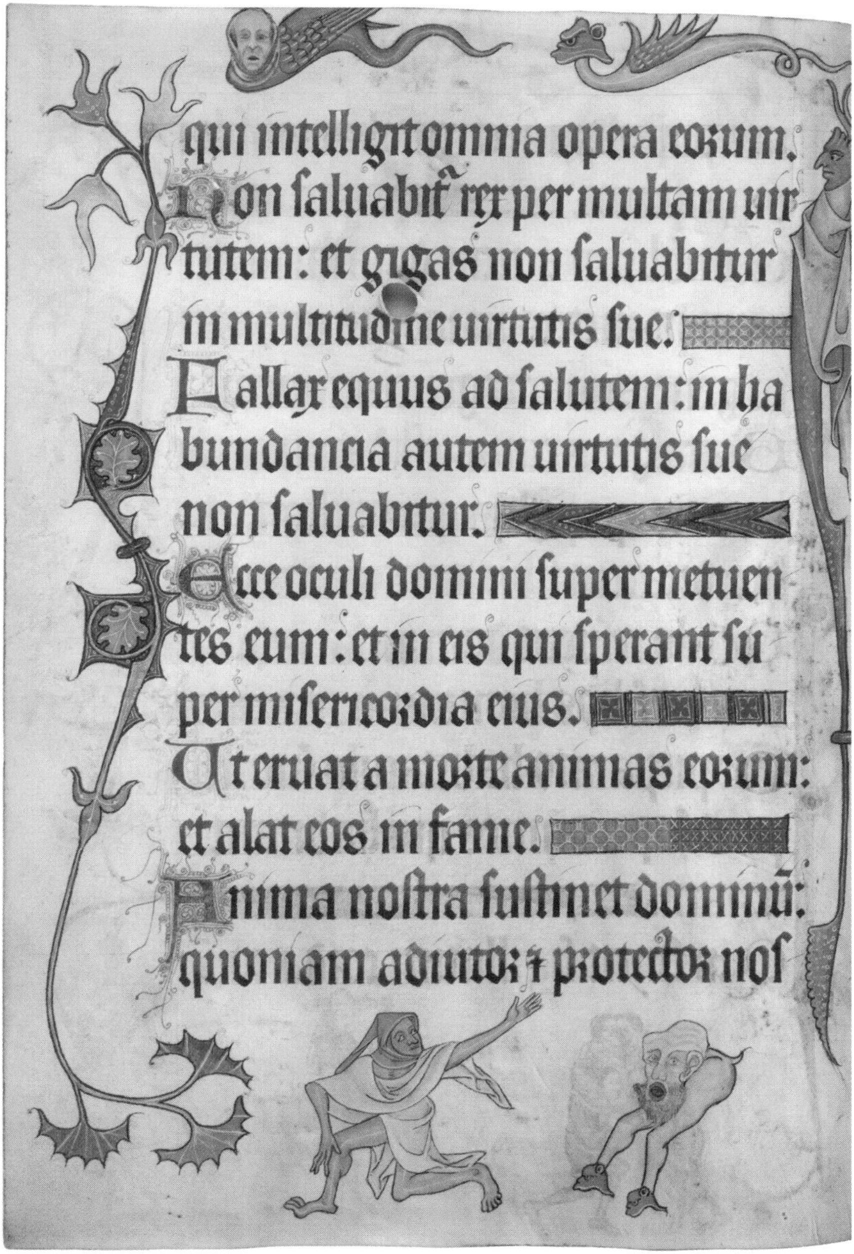
qui intelligit omnia opera eorum.
Non saluabitur rex per multam uir
tutem: et gigas non saluabitur
in multitudine uirtutis sue.
Fallax equus ad salutem: in ha
bundancia autem uirtutis sue
non saluabitur.
Ecce oculi domini super metuen
tes eum: et in eis qui sperant su
per misericordia eius.
Ut eruat a morte animas eorum:
et alat eos in fame.
Anima nostra sustinet dominū:
quoniam adiutor ⁊ protector nos

Marginalia in the Luttrell Psalter, 14th century.

surrounded by monkeys, mimicking him writing, drinking ink out of an inkhorn and treating him to a view of their splayed buttocks.[7] In this case, the scribe and the mooning monkey might simply be a playful response to a phrase that is on the text of that page – the sentence *liber est a culpa* (he is free from guilt) has been split over a line on the last word, thus reading *liber est a cul*. This can be translated into something completely different – 'the book is from the bum'. Suddenly then a new meaning emerges from the image, with a literal visual translation of the Latin.[8] There are probably hundreds of contemporary jokes and subtleties of medieval life embedded into marginalia that we completely miss, but perhaps sometimes it was also just artists enjoying the freedom of creativity. The decorated initials and miniatures would have followed a prescribed formula, with patrons expecting to see set pieces with little room for deviation, so this free space in the margins might have been a welcome respite to just let loose a bit.

AFTER THE FASHION for the huge Bibles of the twelfth century, the thirteenth century went in the opposite direction and small, pocket Bibles became the favoured option. This reflects the rise of the mendicant orders, who eschewed the cloistered life and preferred to go out into the wider world to preach. Rather than being flattened by a giant Bible, it made more sense to have a portable version that could be easily carried around in your saddlebag or held in your hand. Pocket Bibles were also easy to wear as girdle books (a book with an extended binding that could be tucked into a girdle or belt).[9] The earliest pocket Bibles start to appear around 1230 and were produced mainly in France, but also in England and Italy, and to a smaller extent, Spain.[10] They contained the Old and New Testament written in a tiny script on wafer-thin parchment. Parchment production techniques had advanced to such a level that it was possible to scrape the animal skin so thin that it was almost translucent – something that took extreme skill and understanding of the material. The thinness of the parchment meant that a greater number of quires could be sewn together, and thus a greater volume of text could be contained in one volume. A standard quire in a manuscript is normally made up of four bifolia, which are folded to form eight folios – with this thinner parchment it became usual to use six bifolia to form quires of twelve folios. Pocket Bibles were still pretty substantial though, made up of about five to six hundred folios.

Pocket Bibles were roughly 15–20 centimetres high – some were as small as 11.5 by 9 centimetres, with each line little more than 2 millimetres high (BnF, MS Lat. 10422). The developing Gothic script saved on space as the upright, compressed letters allowed more text per line, as did the excessive use of contracted words. They were normally written in a two-column layout. It is no wonder that some people struggled with this cramped script! Luckily, though, by the end of the thirteenth century spectacles were starting to be used. Rather than having side arms that hook over the ears like we have today, medieval glasses balanced on the nose, possibly by pinching the bridge of the frames together. A stained glass window in All Saints Church in York from 1410 shows a figure with glasses peering over someone's shoulder, and an altar woodpanel in a German church from around the same time depicts an apostle wearing these type of glasses while reading.[11] Even more interestingly, some physical imprints of glasses have been found in manuscripts, where the owner probably left them in a book and over time the outline of the frames transferred onto the parchment. This evidence of glasses alongside books shows that they were definitely being used for reading in the later medieval period.[12]

Pocket Bibles were not just popular with roaming friars; they were also owned by students and the wealthier urban elite. Many of the surviving Bibles are illuminated with beautiful, decorated initials and penflourished coloured initials. A particular workshop in Paris, known as the Aurifaber workshop, was known for producing particularly high-standard Bibles between 1250 and 1290. The workshop produced a deluxe pocket Bible around 1270, measuring 15.5 by 10 centimetres, that probably belonged to Louis IX (St Louis) (BnF, Latin MS 10426). The tiny Bible is beautifully decorated with historiated initials of biblical scenes and delicate blue and red penflourished coloured initials. However, after the thirteenth century, there is a sharp drop in the manufacture of these items – probably because the demand had been met and everyone who needed one now had one, but other contributing factors include the famine and plague that spread across Europe in the early fourteenth century, and the subsequent economic recession.[13]

Although the majority of pocket Bibles were made in Paris in the thirteenth century, they are not to be confused with Paris Bibles, which were revised Bibles produced around 1220–30 (although it is quite possible that a pocket Bible was also a Paris Bible). The study of theology at the urban universities influenced this new version that had a revised Vulgate text, with the books arranged in a new order (which is still the standard order we use today). The text was divided into standard chapters and running heads that helped navigation (for example, CCCC MS 437). The Paris Bible represents a new uniform style of Bible that became widely adopted across Europe and formed the structure of our modern Bible.[14] Paris Bibles were not commissioned by patrons, but were produced commercially 'off the peg' in workshops and did not contain any personalized details.

BOOKS OF HOURS were small, private books of devotional prayers that followed the monastic hours of prayer, allowing people to incorporate the canonical hours into their everyday life.

ocket Bible from the Aurifaber workshop, 13th century.

They were a natural development from the psalters and pocket Bibles of the twelfth and thirteenth centuries for a lay audience that was growing in literacy, and were particularly popular with women. They began to be produced in the mid-thirteenth century and remained in demand up until the sixteenth century (one of the most famous surviving examples is the Book of Hours belonging to Anne Boleyn, which is also witness to the developing love affair between her and Henry VIII through their added messages to each other in the margins).[15] A Book of Hours typically contained a calendar, followed by gospel readings, the Office of the Virgin Mary, the Penitential Psalms, Suffrages to Saints and the Office of the Dead. As they were normally commissioned, the contents could be deeply personal to the patron, who would choose what to include. However, whatever the variation, almost all of them would include the Office of the Virgin and other readings that followed the canonical hours. The beginning of each canonical hour (that is, matins, lauds, prime and so on) was usually marked with a miniature or historiated initial illustrating a scene from the life of the Virgin Mary.

The Taymouth Hours (BL, Yates Thompson MS 13) is a great example not only of a typical Book of Hours, but of a late medieval manuscript in general. It dates from 1325 to 1350 and was made in England, possibly London. It was definitely made for a woman, possibly of royal descent, as a crowned woman features in four of the miniatures (fols 7r, 18r, 139r, 188v). It starts with a calendar, each month showing two roundels representing the zodiac and agricultural year. The text is a Gothic textualis quadrata script, enclosed with borders decorated with foliage and curling tendrils. This format continues into the main text on fol. 7v, where from then on the bottom of every page is decorated with lively marginalia, depicting various medieval themes such as chivalric romance, saints' lives and hunting scenes.[16] There are illuminated initials (champ initials) and linefillers on every page – the high gold content indicating the quality of the manuscript. The text alternates with larger and smaller script – the small script indicates the response to the psalm or prayer.

Each new section is punctuated with an illuminated miniature – for example the prayers start on fol. 7v, showing a crowned woman kneeling before a priest who is giving communion. The most important section is the Hours of the Virgin, which starts on fol. 60r, with the annunciation scene, where Mary is told she will bear the son of God. The miniature takes up the whole page, indicating its importance. The Hours start at matins (in the very early hours of the morning), so the devout owner of this manuscript would have turned to this section to begin reading. Lauds was the next prayer time, at the break of day, and this section begins on fol. 71r, with a half-page miniature of the Visitation, when the pregnant Mary visits her (also pregnant) kinswoman, Elizabeth. The wholesome image is somewhat upstaged by the marginalia at the bottom of the page, which show a woman holding a disembowelled hare by the legs and feeding its innards to a dog, who greedily laps them up. Perhaps this is a subverted image to contrast against the purity of the precious cargo inside Mary's belly, as Elizabeth greets her with the words, 'Blessed is the fruit of thy womb, Jesus.' Also, in the medieval world, hunting dogs were representative of male genitalia, while hares were representative of female genitalia and fertility, so there's possibly a whole other subtext going on here.[17]

Each canonical hour in this Book of Hours starts with an illuminated image, making it easier to navigate. It was probably unrealistic for a busy medieval woman to strictly devote herself to the canonical hours round the clock – particularly in the middle of the night – so prayers might have been 'doubled up' to fit in with her lifestyle. Books of Hours often also show physical marks of devotion, where images have been kissed or touched repeatedly by their owners. A fifteenth-century manuscript owned by

Beginning of the Hours of the Virgin from the Taymouth Hours, 14th century.

Book of Hours with trompe-l'oeil effect, 16th century.

the Trygg family has a miniature of the crucifixion that has been completely rubbed or kissed away by the devout owner, indicating just how precious and treasured these books were.[18] Let us hope that only a minimal amount of potentially toxic pigment was ingested while smooching with the parchment. But on a more serious note, it shows how manuscripts continued to be not just carriers for words, but sacred and personal items within their own right, with mental and physical connections formed with the material object.

As the fourteenth and fifteenth centuries went on, Books of Hours became increasingly sophisticated in their artwork, with images developing greater depth and subtlety. The range of pigments available increased, and the blending of colours created beautiful delicate images (as opposed to the more 'stripey' colour application of the twelfth and thirteenth century).[19] Workshops in France, Belgium and the Netherlands were absolutely at the height of their production during the fifteenth century. Borders in Books of Hours were delicately filled with intricate foliage and realistic depictions of flowers, insects and fruit, creating a trompe-l'oeil effect (BL, Add MS 35313). The early fifteenth-century *Très Riches Heures du Duc de Berry* (Chantilly, Musée Condé, Bibliothèque, MS 65) is surely one of the best examples of late medieval manuscript art, with the images bursting with beauty and elegance. This Book of Hours was created by the Limbourg brothers, three Dutch siblings whose mastery of illuminated miniatures was recognized throughout Europe. Unfortunately, the brothers all died before the manuscript was completed, but the work lives on as testament to the sheer beauty of manuscript illumination.

Books of Hours were devotional books, but not part of the official liturgy, so the Church had no control over their creation. Books of Hours were a purely commercial product, but were personally tailored to the individual, allowing them to choose what went into it. It's easy to see how books were regarded as deeply personal objects, or how commissioning a manuscript for someone else could be a significant act, drawing on the receiver's individual tastes to incorporate them into an intimate gift.

INNOVATION IN MANUSCRIPT production slowed down towards the end of the medieval period. The codex format had been perfected in the early medieval period, so there was not much to improve upon (and indeed, remains largely the same today). Parchment production continued to develop, and methods may have become more refined, but by the fifteenth century paper had become a cheaper alternative. However, paper was used in much the same way – pricked, ruled and written on by scribes, either monastic or professional, so this did not fundamentally change the process of book production. The Humanist script that developed in the early fifteenth century was the last significant event in manuscript production, although artistic techniques continued to improve, as we can see in the magnificent Books of Hours that were produced. Monasteries continued to produce manuscripts, but commercial, independent workshops had established themselves around the university towns and become the main source of production. Also, the increased number of manuscripts in circulation meant that bookselling was a healthy business to get into. So, books continued to be written by scribes, decorated by artists, and assembled in the same way as they had always been through the medieval period in Europe.

That all changed, of course, with the development of the European printing press in the mid-fifteenth century. Printing was not a new invention – people in China had been using woodblocks for printing on silk since the second century, and many East Asian countries were using woodblock text on paper by the eighth century (for example, the ninth-century Diamond Sutra scroll found near Dunhuang in northwest China is said to be the earliest complete and dated printed text). Woodblock printing basically consisted of carving out an image or text onto a block of wood, coating it in ink and pressing a suitable surface on top to 'stamp' the image on. By the ninth and tenth centuries, printing techniques were used in the Arabic world, although it is not known whether they were influenced by East Asia or developed independently. The method was known as *ṭarsh* (printblock), producing printed amulets of religious texts on small strips of paper that people carried for protection. These *ṭarsh* amulets seem to have been printed up to the fifteenth century.[20]

Woodblock printing was quite laborious, as a whole page of text had to be carved out on a piece of wood. By the eleventh century, moveable type was being used in China, where individual characters or letters were carved in clay and rearranged in different sequences, so that you could print any text almost on demand. It was this moveable type technique that Johannes Gutenberg of Mainz (*c.* 1400–1468) developed, using metal letters that had been made in a mould. The individual letters could be selected and arranged into a wooden frame to create a text and then be disassembled for use on another text. The press that Gutenberg fashioned was based on the grape and olive presses used in Europe, using a screw mechanism to squeeze the top surface (paper) down onto the lower surface (holding the inked metal type) to transfer the ink from the metal type onto the paper. It seems that Gutenberg developed this press independently from the techniques used in the East, and once entrepreneurial Europeans saw how quickly texts could be printed, the press quickly caught on – although unfortunately Gutenberg was not given the recognition he deserved at the time.

The metal type that Gutenberg used was based on the Gothic script, and his Gutenberg Bible, which was the first major text printed in Europe, was printed both on parchment and paper in

1455. The printed Bible kept very much to the standard manuscript structure, with folded bifolia gathered into quires and the text laid out in two columns, although the copies were sold unbound, with empty spaces for rubrication, coloured initials and illumination. In this way, it mimics the stages of manuscript production, where the text was added first, then passed to the rubricators and artists to decorate. Although parchment continued to be used for printing luxury items (such as a copy of Vesalius' *Epitome* printed in 1543, BL, C.18.e.4), paper became the preferred medium for printing, as the oily surface and imperfections of parchment made it harder to print on. Gutenberg also developed a new type of ink, as a water-based ink like iron gall was no good because it soaked into the paper. The moveable type needed a sticky ink that would adhere to the surface, so an oil-based printing ink made of carbon was used (which is technically more of a varnish than an ink). The paper also needed to be slightly damp and treated with a size (such as starch) to hold the ink better.

The printing press changed everything. Suddenly, books could be mass-produced on a scale never seen before and, as it coincided with the beginning of the Renaissance, it meant that new ideas and knowledge could spread quickly to a far larger audience. Incorrupt texts could be a thing of the past (in theory – not so much in practice), with no more scribal errors copied ad infinitum. But what of our poor parchment and iron gall ink, that had been so fundamental to the exchange of knowledge for the last thousand or so years? A Benedictine monk named Johannes Trithemius was sceptical about the new technologies and wrote the text *In Praise of Scribes* in 1492. His seventh chapter was titled 'That monks should not stop copying because of the invention of printing', declaring:

> The word written on parchment will last a thousand years. The printed word is on paper. How long will it last? The

> most you can expect a book of paper to survive is two hundred years. Yet, there are many who think they can entrust their works to paper. Only time will tell . . . Printed books will never be the equivalent of handwritten codices, especially since printed books are often deficient in spelling and appearance. The simple reason is that copying by hand involves more diligence and industry.[21]

Manuscripts were made with the expectation of longevity and remained in circulation as long as they had a purpose, but eventually all books come to the end of their lifecycle. Rather than be destroyed (although some were), they were taken apart and reused, often as scraps for reinforcing bindings in new books, whole pages for flyleaves, or even as limp bindings. After the Reformation, thousands of religious texts were no longer relevant and there was a real glut of excess material used as binder's waste for the new printed books. Many fragments of older parchment texts are visible beneath damaged spines in printed books from the early modern period, where they have been added to reinforce the structure, giving a tantalizing glimpse into the medieval past. (In fact, redundant texts had always been recycled in the medieval period, with older parchment reused in manuscripts.) However, the strength and flexibility of parchment lent itself to a wide range of non-book uses, including lining clothes (such as hats and hems), purses, boxes and even pie tins.[22] At the very least, parchment could always be boiled down into glue – although of course, then it disappears without a trace. Book boards were also detached and reused as new covers, as we can see in the multiple channels carved on the inside of some fourteenth-century boards (Bodl. Libr., MS Rawl. D. 1225)

Although an oil-based ink was used for printing, iron gall ink remained in use for handwritten documents – there were still plenty of letters, charters and ledgers written with quill and ink, and there would always be a need for scribes, right up to the twentieth century. But European book production – once firmly in the domain of the monastic houses – had moved decisively into a new world by the end of the medieval period. From the early days of Christianity, where texts written on papyrus proclaimed the good news about Jesus, to the foundation of monasteries in Europe and the output of the medieval scriptoria, manuscript production had been a drive to spread the word of God. It coalesced around the idea of writing-as-sacred-task, a religious duty, a prayer to God in itself. With the rise of urban living and the foundation of the universities, manuscript production moved into the commercial sector, with independent scribes and workshops meeting the increased demand for new texts. This fundamentally changed the framework of manuscript production – it was no longer a religious transaction with God, it was a financial transaction with a customer.

While of course the workshop manuscripts are often things of absolute beauty, something perhaps is lost in knowing that they were not created with a higher purpose in mind. Although we know that the members of religious orders liked to complain about the mundanity of their daily scribal duty, there is something far more profound about manuscript production in the early medieval period, when scribes were feeling their way through this new medium, keen to share knowledge and fulfil their religious duty. We can imagine the parchment of the manuscript somehow soaking up the atmosphere and daily rhythms of the monastery, and picture the scribe writing diligently, perhaps lifting their head up to rest their weary eyes on the greenery in the cloister garden. Something about the order and the imposed silence on monastic life imbues the manuscript with a halo of reverence, which contrasts against the image of an urban workshop, set amid the noise, smells and bustle of a later medieval city. Although many people today assume the medieval period to be a time of stagnancy and lack of innovation (set against a backdrop of mud), in reality it was vibrant, forward-thinking and constantly evolving.

Without those parchment makers perfecting their craft through repeatedly scraping the stretched animal skin, without those scribes putting in endless hours of back-breaking work hunched over a desk, without those illuminators and artists delighting in intricate designs, and without those bookbinders expertly sewing the quires together, it would not have paved the way for an embedded book culture and the new technology resulting in the printing press. Consider this book in your hand (or any book in general) – is it really that different from a medieval manuscript? Books are still in the codex format that became popular in earlier centuries, with folded pages between covers. They are normally divided into chapters, maybe with subheadings. The first letter of each chapter might be in a larger font, sometimes even a little bit fancy, like a decorated initial. The typeface might be Times New Roman, based on the Humanist script that in turn was based on the Caroline minuscule script. They might also have an index and footnotes. These are all things that were used in medieval manuscripts and that still make up our standard book format today. The familiarity of holding a book in your hand – a smaller book nestling comfortably in your palm, or the comforting bulk of a larger textbook hugged against your chest – is a feeling that would have been experienced in exactly the same way a thousand years ago. And the anticipation any avid reader feels when opening a book for the first time – wondering what new worlds or intellectual journeys await them inside – that hasn't changed, nor has the rustle of the page turning as you flick with anticipation onto the new leaf. We end our journey now with a reminder of the passage of time and how the written word can have a far longer life than the person that created it – a Greek scribe writing in the ninth century reaches the end of his set text and, perhaps channelling all those many other scribes through the medieval period who feel a joint sense of pride and relief, writes the words: 'the hand is exhausted, but the writing remains.'[23]

Conclusion

So, is the art of manuscript making lost forever? Were the materials of parchment, quill and ink just a necessary stepping stone in the history of writing between papyrus scrolls and the printed book? It might seem so today, when we can print a whole text out from a computer in the comfort of our own homes or order a book on the Internet in the morning that arrives in the evening. We imagine a romanticized version of monastic scribes, sitting at their desks in the serenity of the cloister, psalms being chanted in the background – but maybe in reality they were sitting there dreaming of a world where book production was a fast commercial process. Perhaps they would have happily swapped their skilful craft for an automated system.

And yet something so vital to us as human beings has been lost in the move away from completely natural, handcrafted items that were treated with reverence, to the mass-produced printed items we handle every day without a thought (and I am aware of the irony of that sentence as you read this in a printed or electronic book). The concept of the book as a physical object would have had far more resonance to a medieval person, as people then had much more interaction with the materials that went into that book – materials that might even have come from their local landscape. Parchment is a rare material now, but to medieval Europeans, the look, smell and feel of parchment would have been as familiar as paper is to us. Even if they were not literate, the sight of slaughtered animals and skins pegged out onto frames would have been a common sight. Those in rural communities would be living side-by-side with sheep, pigs and cattle, knowing full well the worth of their carcass, not just for meat but lots else besides – and even those in urban communities would have seen the livestock being slaughtered on market day. The butchers, parchment makers and tanners were highly skilled, learning their trade over years through practice and physical exertion, with the body remembering the physical rhythm of the task. The scribes writing on the parchment would have known the effort that went into making parchment and would not have taken the material for granted.

Then think about the oak galls that went into the ink. If collected locally, crushing and boiling them, the air filling with the sweet smell of woodlands, could trigger the memories of wandering among the local oaks foraging for the galls. Or if the galls were bought at a marketplace, perhaps their mysterious journey from overseas might spark the ink-maker's imagination of distant places. Most people today have not experienced the rich tang of tannins that fills the air when a stoppered jar of iron gall ink is opened, but scribes would have known it well. The quills probably came from local geese and swans, there for the taking in moulting season. Then the pigments, possibly from the earth itself: red, yellow and green ochres dug up from the ground. Or the woad, weld, folium and madder, grown in the ground and tended carefully over years until ready to harvest, cutting up the leaves or roots just metres away from where it grew and transforming it into vibrant colours to paint with.

How would that feel, particularly in the early monasteries, knowing that these materials were locally harvested? The cattle that you saw grazing in a field from the monastery window, the galls that grew on oaks nearby, the geese that you saw swimming in the pond each day, and the plants that you watched grow through the year. All those natural ingredients, transformed into writing materials, to write the word of God as an act of prayer. It must have been an incredibly close connection to their natural world, and hard to overstate what an unbelievably precious thing it was. If a manuscript stayed in the monastery that created it, it was then imbued with the communal memory of the house, knowing that the manuscript was produced not just from their natural landscape, but by the hands of their fellow brothers or sisters, or their monastic predecessors. The basic process of manuscript production remained pretty much unchanged – and it's a reminder that people in the past were completely reliant on the natural world and its cycle. The finished manuscript occupies a profound position, not just as a carrier of knowledge, but as a truly unique manifestation of natural resources and human hands.

Those of us who handle manuscripts today are lucky enough to experience some of this ourselves. We touch the same parchment that came from living creatures, hundreds, perhaps thousands of years ago, that still contain visible traces of that animal's life – the spine and veins and skin imperfections. We know nothing of these animals, but we can see where insects bit them. We hold the same skin in our hands that the parchment maker did, and then the scribe – not to mention the multiple readers that came after them, but before us. Touching those pages, forming a tactile human connection across the years is a deeply moving experience. Handling any book for most people is a truly sensory experience, engaging sight, sound, touch and smell, and we are still doing it in exactly the same way that the medieval people did. I can sit in a reading room with a manuscript propped up in front of me on a book rest, but in my mind's eye I can imagine all the people over the years sitting in the same position reading the same manuscript, albeit in different clothing and surroundings.

So, manuscript making may be redundant as an industry, but the survival of those manuscripts is just as important as ever. We need those reminders of our past in a tangible form, to make that physical connection with those people and their landscape. Their little moans in the margins, their smudges of ink and crossed-out mistakes – these are human things that we can relate to, no matter how long the passage of time. Next time you are passing some livestock, or some ancient woodlands, or even a long-established market, just spare a thought for the human ingenuity that went into transforming those random materials into the beautiful, breathtaking manuscripts that still exist today. May they live on to delight further generations.

GLOSSARY

Ascenders – the long strokes of lower-case letters such as *b*, *d*, *h* and *l* that go above the main parallel lines of writing.

Bifolium (*pl.* bifolia) – a sheet of parchment or paper that is folded in half to create two folios.

Binder – a sticky substance that is added to ink or pigment to thicken it and help it adhere to the parchment e.g. gum arabic, egg white.

Book of Hours – a popular medieval prayer book for laypeople, containing sets of prayers to be said throughout the day, similar to the canonical hours.

Byzantine empire – the eastern part of the Roman empire (including Greece and Turkey). Mainly Christian from the fourth century, it remained one of the strongest powers in the medieval world until it fell to the Ottoman empire in 1453.

Canon tables – reference lists that indicate parallel passages in the gospels. They appear at the start of the gospels, often in table form, resembling decorated architectural columns.

Canonical hours – also known as the Divine Office or the Liturgy of the Hours. These were set times of the day when monks and nuns came together to chant prayers. The Hours were matins (3 a.m.), lauds (5 a.m.), prime (6 a.m.), terce (9 a.m.), sext (12 noon), none (3 p.m.), vespers (6 p.m.), and compline (7 p.m.), although this might vary depending on where you were and what time of year it was.

Caroline minuscule – a rounded script promoted by Alcuin and Charlemagne to encourage a scribal uniformity of written texts. It was widely used in Europe *c.* 800–1200.

Carolingian Empire – an empire named after Charlemagne that covered most of central Europe *c.* 800–888.

Carpet page – a highly decorated page in the opening material to each gospel. Popular in Insular manuscripts, carpet pages were composed of intricate, geometric patterns that incorporated animals and hybrid creatures.

Champ initials – small gold initial letters often encased in a penflourished box of blue or red ink.

Channel style – an artistic style that developed in the twelfth and thirteenth centuries in England and France. Popular motifs were white lions, concentric circles and penflourished initials.

Chi Rho – a monogram of Christ, combining the Greek letters X (chi) and P (rho). These letters are the first two letters of Christ in Greek (ΧΡΙΣΤΟΣ).

Christian East – centred around Byzantium (Constantinople), this branch of Christianity included Asia Minor, Greece and the Balkan Peninsula.

Christian West – centred around Rome, with the pope as the head of the Church. This branch of Christianity covered most of Western Europe.

Cloister – a continuous covered walkway in a square, often found in monasteries. The cloister was a space permitted only for monks and nuns, and it acted as a physical and metaphorical barrier to the outside world, as the inhabitants had to pass through the cloister to go to church, and to return to their spiritual life.

Codex – the modern book format, with folded leaves of paper or parchment sewn into a text block, encased between two outer covers.

Colophon – a note left by a scribe that might record the scribe's name, or the place the text was written.

Decorated initial – a colourful (and sometimes illuminated) large letter to indicate the beginning of the text. Decorated initials may contain a variety of historical or biblical scenes, interlaced patterns or zoomorphic creatures.

Descenders – the long strokes of lower-case letters such as *j*, *p* and *q* that go below the two parallel lines of writing.

Evangelist – one of the four gospel writers, Matthew, Mark, Luke and John. They are often depicted with their symbol: Matthew (man), Mark (lion), Luke (ox), John (eagle).

Exemplar – the text that is being copied from. As more copies of an original text were made, more and more errors would be introduced, resulting in a corrupted text. These corruptions can prove useful in tracing the original exemplars of texts.

Folio – a single leaf of parchment or paper (both sides).

Gesso – a hard surface to which gold is applied in illuminated manuscripts. A mixture of plaster of Paris and sticky substances, it is applied to parchment and left to dry. The adhesive properties are activated by breathing on the dried gesso, allowing the gold to bond to the raised surface.

Gloss – extra text written around the main text, providing a commentary or explanation. Often in a smaller script to differentiate from the main body of writing.

Gothic script – a script that developed in the thirteenth century across Europe. The script is angular and cramped, allowing more text to fit on the page.

Humanist script – a script developed as an alternative to Gothic in Italy in the fifteenth century. Based on Caroline minuscule, it is rounded and far easier to read than Gothic.

Incipit – the beginning words of a text.

Insular – refers to England, Ireland, Scotland and Wales. Insular script developed in the early medieval period, distinctive for its wedged ascenders and decorative red dots.

Laity – the general population, non-monastic and non-clerical.

Lay brother/sister – a person who lives or works at a monastery but has not taken holy orders.

Librarius – (also armarius or precentor) monastic person in charge of loaning out books, overseeing manuscript production and correcting copied texts.

Majuscule – a script where the letters fit between two parallel lines, with no ascenders or descenders above or below. These are often (but not always) upper-case letters. For example, *B*, *M*, *L*.

Manuscript – a handwritten text. Comes from the Latin for hand (*manus*) + written (*scriptus*).

Marginalia – notes or drawings added to the margins of a book around the main text.

Miniature – a painted image in a medieval manuscript. Named after the red pigment 'minium', which would have been used to paint the initial outline. It has nothing to do with the image size.

Minuscule – a script where the letters extend beyond the two parallel writing lines with ascenders or descenders. These are often (but not always) lower-case letters. For example, *b*, *d*, *g*, *p*.

Ottonian empire – an empire that covered Germany, Switzerland, northern and central Italy circa 919–1024.

Palimpsest – parchment that has been scraped to erase the original text so that it can be used again to write a new text. Sometimes traces of the underlying text are still visible to the naked eye.

Pandect – all the Christian books of the Bible in one volume.

Papyrus – a writing surface made from papyrus stems that grew along the River Nile. The stems were stripped, pressed and dried to create sheets that could be pasted together to form a roll. The word 'paper' comes from papyrus.

Parchment – a writing surface made out of animal skin, usually calf-, goat- or sheepskin. The skin had the hair removed before being stretched and scraped on a wooden frame.

Parchmenter (*parchmener/libraire/stationarius*) – a person who traded in parchment (but did not make it). They may also have acted as project managers for manuscripts, commissioning the scribes, illuminators and bookbinders for patrons.

Penflourishing (*litterae florissae*) – the extended decorated lines and swirls added to a coloured initial letter, made with a quill.

Psalter – a book of psalms.

Quire – a section of a manuscript, commonly made up of eight folded bifolia to form sixteen folios. Quires were stacked on top of each other and sewn together to form the text block.

Recto – the right or front side of a page.

Romanesque script – also called Anglo-Norman or Protogothic. This script developed out of Caroline minuscule, becoming more angular and upright. It was used in the eleventh to thirteenth centuries.

Secular – non-monastic.

Stationer – *see* Parchmenter.

Stylus – implement made of wood, bone or metal to make an impression in a wax tablet.

Text block – pages of a book, bound in quires and sewn together to form a single unit.

Uncial script – a majuscule script used from the fourth to eighth centuries. Many of the earliest surviving Christian texts are written in uncial.

Verso – the reverse or back side of a page.

Vulgate Bible – the most popular Bible version in Western Christianity. Originally translated by Jerome (and possibly Paula) from Hebrew and Greek into Latin in the fourth century.

Wax tablet – a rectangular wooden board filled with wax and used with a stylus.

Zoomorphic – an image that incorporates animal forms into its design.

REFERENCES

One The Beginnings

1 Felix Reichmann, *The Sources of Western Literacy: The Middle Eastern Civilizations* (Westport, CT, 1980), p. 88.

2 Michael H. Harris, *History of Libraries in the Western World*, 4th edn (London, 1995), p. 34.

3 Richard B. Parkinson, *Papyrus* (London, 1995), pp. 9–10; Pliny the Elder, *Natural History*, Book XIII, chs 22–6.

4 William John Tait, 'Rush and Reed: The Pens of Egyptian and Greek Scribes', in *Proceedings of the XVIII International Conference of Papyrology*, ed. B. G. Mandilaras (Athens, 1988), pp. 477–81.

5 The most common binder is gum arabic from the tree *Acacia senegal*, but the Egyptians may have used other locally sourced plant gums. Other binders possibly used for ink and pigments include glue, egg white or honey (Richard Newman, Raymond White and Margaret Serpico, 'Adhesives and Binders', in *Ancient Egyptian Materials and Technology*, ed. Paul T. Nicholson and Ian Shaw (Cambridge, 2000), pp. 475–94, at pp. 476–80).

6 Pliny, *Natural History*, Book XIII, ch. 21.

7 Anna Willi, *Writing Equipment: Manual of Roman Everyday Writing*, 2 vols (Nottingham, 2021), vol. II, pp. 33, 41, 69–87.

8 Kim Haines-Eitzen, '"Girls Trained in Beautiful Writing": Female Scribes in Roman Antiquity and Early Christianity', *Journal of Early Christian Studies*, VI/4 (1998), pp. 629–46, at p. 637.

9 Karel van der Toorn, *Scribal Culture and the Making of the Hebrew Bible* (London, 2007).

10 Yoram Nir-El and Magen Broshi, 'The Black Ink of the Qumran Scrolls', *Dead Sea Discoveries*, III/2 (1996), pp. 157–67; Yoram Nir-El and Magen Broshi, 'The Red Ink of the Dead Sea Scrolls', *Archaeometry*, XXXVIII/1 (1996), pp. 97–102.

11 Larry W. Hurtado and Chris Keith, 'Writing and Book Production in the

Hellenistic and Roman Periods', in *The New Cambridge History of the Bible*, vol. I: *From the Beginnings to 600*, ed. James Carleton Paget and Joachim Schaper (Cambridge, 2013), pp. 63–80.

12 Colin Roberts, *Manuscript, Society and Belief in Early Christian Egypt* (London, 1979), p. 24.

13 Jerome, *On Illustrious Men*, no. 113.

14 Kim Haines-Eitzen, *Guardians of Letters: Literacy, Power, and the Transmitters of Early Christian Literature* (Oxford, 2000), pp. 64–8.

15 Harry Y. Gamble, *Books and Readers in the Early Church* (London, 1997), p. 71.

16 Eusebius, *Ecclesiastical Historia*, Book VI, ch. 23. Translation from Haines-Eitzen, '"Girls Trained in Beautiful Writing"', p. 631.

17 Jerome, *On Illustrious Men*, no. 75.

18 Eusebius, *Vita Constantini*, Book IV, ch. 36, www.newadvent.org.

19 Haines-Eitzen, *Guardians of Letters*.

20 See, e.g., Oxford, Sackler Library, P. Oxy. 4494 and Bodleian Library, MS Gr. th. e. 7 (P).

21 Michael J. Kruger, 'Manuscripts, Scribes, and Book Production within Early Christianity', in *Christian Origins and Greco-Roman Culture*, ed. Stanley E. Porter and Andrew W. Pitts (Leiden, 2012), pp. 13–40.

22 David H. Wright, *The Vatican Vergil: A Masterpiece of Late Antique Art* (Oxford, 1993), p. 2.

23 Ruth Siddall, 'Not a Day without a Line Drawn: Pigments and Painting Techniques of Roman Artists', *In Focus Magazine: Proceedings of the Royal Microscopical Society*, II (2006), www.rms.org.uk.

24 David H. Wright, *The Roman Vergil and the Origins of Medieval Book Design* (London, 2001), p. 44.

25 Hurtado and Keith, 'Writing and Book Production', p. 75.

26 Samuel Rubenson, 'Asceticism and Monasticism, I: Eastern', in *The Cambridge History of Christianity*, vol. II: *Constantine to c. 600*, ed. Augustine Casiday and Frederick W. Norris (Cambridge, 2007), pp. 637–68, at pp. 646, 649–50.

27 Elizabeth A. Clark, *The Life of Melania the Younger* (New York, 1984), p. 46.

28 Andrew Cain, 'Jerome's *Epitaphium Paulae*: Hagiography, Pilgrimage, and the Cult of Saint Paula', *Journal of Early Christian Studies*, XVIII/1 (2010), pp. 105–39, at p. 111.

29 Andrew Cain, ed., *Jerome's Epitaph on Paula: A Commentary on the Epitaphium Sanctae Paulae* (Oxford, 2013), pp. 355, 362.

30 Works dedicated to Paula include Micah, Nahum, Zephaniah and Haggai, and her influence is also mentioned in the prologues to Hosea, Joel and Amos.

31 Megan Hale Williams, *The Monk and the Book: Jerome and the Making of Christian Scholarship* (London, 2006), p. 185.

32 John Chrysostom, Homily 32 on the Gospel of John; Augustine, *Contra Faustum Manichaeum*, Book 13, ch. 18.
33 Vitruvius, *De architectura*, Book 7, ch. 13, https://penelope.uchicago.edu.
34 Sophie Rabitsch, Inge Boesken Kanold and Christa Hofmann, 'Purple Dyeing of Parchment', in *The Vienna Genesis: Material Analysis and Conservation of a Late Antique Illuminated Manuscript on Purple Parchment*, ed. Christa Hofmann (Vienna, 2020), pp. 71–101, at p. 83.
35 Peter Schreiner and Doris Oltrogge, *Byzantinische Tinten-, Tuschen und Farbrezepte* (Vienna, 2011), pp. 109–11.
36 Jerome, Prologue to Ezekiel.
37 M. B. Parkes, *Pause and Effect: An Introduction to the History of Punctuation in the West* (Aldershot, 1992), pp. 15–16.
38 Anna M. Silvas, ed., *The Rule of St Basil in Latin and English: A Revised Critical Edition* (Collegeville, MN, 2013), pp. 46–7.
39 Clare Stancliffe, *St Martin and His Hagiographer* (Oxford, 1983), p. 25.

Two Monasticism and Manuscript Production in the West, 500–1050

1 *Cassiodorus: Institutions of Divine and Secular Learning and On the Soul*, trans. James W. Halporn (Liverpool, 2004), Book 1, ch. 29 (p. 162).
2 Ibid., Book 1, ch. 4 (p. 161); Book 1, ch. 20 (p. 152); Book 1, ch. 21 (p. 153); Book 1, ch. 3 (p. 118).
3 Ibid., Book 1, ch. 30 (p. 165).
4 Ibid., Book 1, ch. 15.
5 Isidore, *Etymologies*, Book VI, ch. 14.
6 Maria Caritas McCarthy, *The Rule for Nuns of St Caesarius of Arles* (Washington, DC, 1960), p. 171.
7 *Regula ad virgines*, ch. 18; *Vita S. Caesarii*, Book 1, ch. 58. Caesarius, *Caesarius of Arles: Life, Testament, Letters*, trans. William E. Klingshirn (Liverpool, 1994).
8 The period up to the Norman conquest in England will be referred to by geographical region, or more generally as the early English medieval period. For more on this, see Mary Rambaran-Olm and Erik Wade, 'What's in a Name? The Past and Present Racism in "Anglo-Saxon" Studies', *Yearbook of English Studies*, LI/1 (2022), pp. 135–53.
9 Caecilia Davis-Weyer, *Early Medieval Art, 300–1150: Sources and Documents* (Toronto, 1986), pp. 47–8.
10 Richard Gameson, *Codex Amiatinus: Making and Meaning* (Jarrow, 2018), p. 4.
11 Lisa M. Bitel, 'Monastic Identity in Early Medieval Ireland', in *The Cambridge History of Medieval Monasticism in the Latin West*, vol. 1, ed. Alison I. Beach and Isabelle Cochelin (Cambridge, 2020), pp. 297–316.
12 'The Cathach of Colum Cille: The Story of an Ancient Irish Manuscript', online exhibition curated by the Royal Irish Academy Library, www.ria.ie.

13 The folio size of the Cathach is 27 x 19 cm, so you should be able to get two or possibly three bifolia out of one skin.
14 Adomnán, *Life of Saint Columba*, ed. William Reeves (Edinburgh, 1874), Book I, ch. 19; Book II, ch. 15; Book III, chs 16, 34.
15 Ainoa Castro, 'What is "Visigothic Script"?', www.litteravisigothica.com.
16 Lorraine H. Olley, 'Benedict Biscop: Benedictine, Builder, Bibliophile', *Theological Librarianship*, VII/1 (2014), pp. 30–37, at p. 33.
17 Richard Gameson et al., 'Pigments of the Earliest Northumbrian Manuscripts', *Scriptorium*, LXIX (2015), pp. 33–59.
18 Dáibhi Ó Cróinin, 'The Original Lindisfarne Gospels?', in *Manuscripts in the Anglo-Saxon Kingdoms: Cultures and Connections*, ed. Claire Breay and Joanna Story (Dublin, 2021), pp. 1–15.
19 Richard Gameson, *From Holy Island to Durham: The Contexts and Meanings of the Lindisfarne Gospels* (London, 2013), p. 93.
20 Natasha Dukelow, 'The Book of Kells: Image and Text/The Chi Rho Page', https://blogs.ucc.ie.
21 Katherine L. Brown and Robin J. H. Clark, 'The Lindisfarne Gospels and Two Other 8th Century Anglo-Saxon/Insular Manuscripts: Pigment Identification by Raman Microscopy', *Journal of Raman Spectroscopy*, XXXV/1 (2004), pp. 4–12.
22 Michelle P. Brown, *The Lindisfarne Gospels: Society, Spirituality and the Scribe* (Toronto and Buffalo, NY, 2003), pp. 216–17.
23 Jiří Vnouček, 'The Parchment of the Codex Amiatinus in the Context of Manuscript Production in Northumbria around the End of the Seventh Century', *Journal of Paper Conservation*, XX/1–4 (2019), pp. 179–204, at pp. 201–2.
24 Gameson, *Codex Amiatinus*, pp. 20–21.
25 Gameson et al., 'Pigments of the Earliest Northumbrian Manuscripts'.
26 Gameson, *Codex Amiatinus*, p. 49.
27 Bede, *Ecclesiastical History*, Book IV, chs 1–2.
28 Mary Rambaran-Olm, 'A Wrinkle in Medieval Time: Ironing out Issues Regarding Race, Temporality, and the Early English', *New Literary History*, LII/3 (2021), pp. 385–406, at p. 396.
29 Jacqueline I. McKinley, Jörn Schuster and Andrew Millard, 'Dead-Sea Connections: A Bronze Age and Iron Age Ritual Site on the Isle of Thanet', in *Celtic from the West*, vol. II: *Rethinking the Bronze Age and the Arrival of Indo-European in Atlantic Europe*, ed. John T. Koch and Barry Cunliffe (Oxford, 2013), pp. 157–83, at pp. 166–8.
30 Alison Hudson, 'Radical Object: A North African Book in the Early Medieval British Isles', *History Workshop*, www.historyworkshop.org.uk, 12 November 2019.

31 Stacey Graham, 'The Transmission of North African Texts to Europe in Late Antiquity', in *Medieval Manuscripts, Their Makers and Users* (Turnhout, 2011), pp. 151–67.
32 J. P. Migne, *Patrologia Latina*, 221 vols (Paris, 1844–1903), vol. CI, col. 745; A. F. West, *Alcuin and the Rise of the Christian Schools* (London, 1892), p. 72.
33 Migne, *Patrologia Latina*, vol. CI, col. 745 verse 67; Peter Godman, *Poetry of the Carolingian Renaissance* (Norman, OK, 1985), p. 139.
34 Claire Breay and Joanna Story, eds, *Anglo-Saxon Kingdoms: Art, Word, War* (London, 2018), p. 159.
35 Robin J. H. Clark and Jaap van der Weerd, 'Identification of Pigments and Gemstones on the Tours Gospel: The Early 9th Century Carolingian Palette', *Journal of Raman Spectroscopy*, XXXV/4 (2004), pp. 279–83, at p. 283.
36 Julia Crick, 'English Vernacular Script', in *The Cambridge History of the Book in Britain*, vol. I: *c. 400–1100*, ed. Richard Gameson (Cambridge, 2011), pp. 174–86, at p. 175.
37 The answer is 'key' (*Old and Middle English, c. 890–c. 1400: An Anthology*, ed. Elaine Treharne, 2nd edn (Oxford, 2004), p. 73).
38 Crick, 'English Vernacular Script', pp. 182–4.
39 David Ganz, Rebecca Rushforth and Teresa Webber, 'Latin Script in England, *c.* 900–1100', in *Cambridge History of the Book in Britain*, vol. I: *c. 400–1100*, ed. Gameson, pp. 187–224.

Three *Locus Scribendi* – The Place of Writing

1 Walter Horn and Ernest Born, *The Plan of St. Gall: A Study of the Architecture and Economy of and Life in a Paradigmatic Carolingian Monastery*, 3 vols (Berkeley, CA, 1979), vol. I, p. 147.
2 *Monumenta Germaniae Historica Inde Ab Anno Christi Quingentesimo Usque Ad Annum Millesimum et Quingentesimum Scriptorium*, ed. Georgius Pertz (Hannover, 1829), vol. II, pp. 95, 132.
3 Erik Kwakkel, *Books before Print* (Leeds, 2018), pp. 211–14.
4 Erik Kwakkel, 'Where are the Scriptoria?', 5 November 2013, https://medievalfragments.wordpress.com.
5 A twelfth-century manuscript shows another version, which is easier to see (Morgan Library, MS M.429, fol. 183r), www.themorgan.org.
6 Saint Gallen, Stiftsbibliothek, Cod. Sang. 904, pp. 203–4, www.e-codices.unifr.ch. Translation by Ciaran Carson, https://creativecritical.net.
7 Luc d'Achery, *Spicilegium; Sive, Collectio Veterum Aliquot Scriptorum Qui in Galliae Bibliothecis Delituerant*, 3 vols (Paris, 1723), vol. II, p. 913. Translated in Thomas Duffus Hardy, *Descriptive Catalogue of Materials Relating to the History of Great Britain and Ireland, to the End of the Reign of Henry VII*, 3 vols (London, 1862), vol. III, p. xxiii.

8 CCCC, MS 371, fol. 223v, https://parker.stanford.edu; André Wilmart, 'Edmeri Cantuariensis Cantoris Nova Opuscula de Sanctorum Veneratione et Obsecratione', *Revue des sciences religieuses*, XV/3 (1935), pp. 354–79, at p. 367.

9 It has been suggested that 'cloister' could just refer to anywhere in the wider complex, but as other locations in the customary are given specific names, it seems likely that they do mean the square cloister leading to the abbey.

10 Luc Jocqué and Louis Milis, eds, *Liber Ordinis Sancti Victoris Parisiensis* (Turnhout, 1984), p. 80.

11 BL, Harley MS 3601, fol. 191r; Clark, *Observances in Use*, p. 65.

12 Ibid.

13 '*neque aliqui fratres, nisi in scribendo, vel illuminando, aut tantum notation*', E. Thompson, ed., *Customary of the Benedictine Monasteries of Saint Augustine, Canterbury, and Saint Peter, Westminster*, 2 vols (London, 1902), vol. I, p. 211; vol. II, p. 165.

14 William Claxton, *The Rites of Durham* , ed. Margaret Harvey and Lynda Rollason (Woodbridge, 2021), pp. 300–301, 543–4.

15 H. E. Salter, 'A Chronicle Roll of the Abbots of Abingdon', *English Historical Review*, 26 (1911), pp. 727–38, at p. 733; M. B. Parkes, *Their Hands before Our Eyes: A Closer Look at Scribes* (Aldershot, 2008), p. 23.

16 Cambridge University Library, Hh.6.11, fol. 69v. My thanks to James Freeman for tracking down the folio reference.

17 Marjorie Chibnall, ed., *The Ecclesiastical History of Orderic Vitalis*, vol. II, Bks. 3 and 4 (Oxford, 1983), p. 361.

18 *Patrologia Latina*, ed. J. P. Mign, 221 vols (Paris, 1844–1903), vol. CLIII, cols 651–2, 693–4.

19 *The Letter Collections of Nicholas of Clairvaux*, ed. Lena Wahlgren-Smith (Oxford, 2018), letter 35, pp. 132–5.

20 BL, Cotton MS Nero D I, fols 35r–v, www.bl.uk/manuscripts; *Deeds of the Abbots of St Albans: Gesta Abbatum Monasterii Sancti Alban*, ed. James G. Clark and David Preest (Woodbridge, 2019), pp. 132–3.

21 BL, Harley MS 3601, fol. 190v; Clark, *Observances in Use*, p. 63.

22 *Deeds of the Abbots of St Albans*, p. 300.

23 Ibid., p. 903.

24 DCL, MS B.IV.12, fol. 38r and R.A.B. Mynors, *Durham Cathedral Manuscripts to the End of the Twelfth Century* (London, 1939), p. 9.

25 Cologne, Erzbischöfliche Diözesan- und Dombibliothek, Cod. 63: Girbalda (fol. 86v), Gislildis (fol. 174v), Agleberta (fol. 263v); Cod. 65: Adruhic (fol. 73v), Altildis (fol. 151v), Gisledrudis (fol. 224v), Eusebia (fol. 289v), last folio missing with another name; Cod. 67, all available at https://digital.dombibliothek-koeln.de.

26 Rosamond McKitterick, 'Nuns' Scriptoria in England and Francia in the

Eighth Century', in *Books, Scribes, and Learning in the Frankish Kingdoms, 6th–9th Centuries* (Aldershot, 1994), VII, pp. 1–36, at p. 2.
27 Aliza Cohen-Mushlin, 'The Twelfth-Century Scriptorium at Frankenthal', in *Medieval Book Production: Assessing the Evidence*, ed. Linda L. Brownrigg (Oxford, 1990), pp. 85–101.
28 Ibid., p. 86.
29 Christine Franzen, *The Tremulous Hand of Worcester: A Study of Old English in the Thirteenth Century* (Oxford, 1991); Deborah E. Thorpe and Jane E. Alty, 'What Type of Tremor Did the Medieval "Tremulous Hand of Worcester" Have?', *Brain*, 138 (2015), pp. 3123–7. There is also evidence of manuscript artists with tremors in the fifteenth century (Kathleen E. Kennedy, 'Aging Artists and Impairment in Fifteenth-Century England', *Different Visions: New Perspectives on Medieval Art*, X (2023)).
30 Hugh Feiss, Ronald E. Pepin and Maureen M. O'Brien, eds, *A Benedictine Reader: 530–1530* (Collegeville, MN, 2019), p. xxx.
31 Kimm Curran, '"Through the Keyhole of the Monastic Library Door": Learning and Education in Scottish Medieval Monasteries', in *The Edinburgh History of Education in Scotland*, ed. Robert Anderson, Mark Freeman and Lindsay Paterson (Edinburgh, 2015), pp. 25–38, at p. 27.
32 Timothy O'Neill, *The Irish Hand: Scribes and Their Manuscripts from the Earliest Times to the Seventeenth Century: With an Exemplar of Irish Scripts* (Mountrath, 1984), p. xxvi.
33 Cohen-Mushlin, 'The Twelfth-Century Scriptorium at Frankenthal', pp. 88–94.
34 Rodney M. Thomson, 'Scripts and Scriptoria', in *The European Book in the Twelfth Century*, ed. Erik Kwakkel and Rodney M. Thomson (Cambridge, 2018), pp. 68–84, at p. 69.
35 Berlin Staatsbibliothek, Preußischer Kulturbesitz, Lat. Fol. 270, fol. 10v, http://gutenberg.beic.it.
36 Meyer, 'Neu Aufgefundene Altirische Glossen', p. 176.
37 W. M. Lindsay, *Early Irish Minuscule Script* (Oxford, 1910), p. 42.
38 Richard H. Rouse and Mary A. Rouse, 'Wandering Scribes and Traveling Artists: Raulinus of Fremington and His Bolognese Bible', in *A Distinct Voice. Medieval Studies in Honour of Leonard E. Boyle, OP*, ed. Jacqueline Brown and William Stoneman (Notre Dame, IN, 1997), pp. 32–67.
39 Brussels, Bibliothèque Royale, MS 19607, fol. CCLXXVr, https://medievalbooks.nl.
40 Jochen Bepler, Peter Kidd and Jane Geddes, *The St. Albans Psalter (Albani Psalter): Commentary* (Simbach am Inn, 2008), p. 130.
41 Cambridge, Trinity College, MS R.14.48, https://mss-cat.trin.cam.ac.uk, fol. vii verso.

42 Pamela R. Robinson, 'A Twelfth-Century Scriptrix from Nunnaminster', in *Of the Making of Books: Medieval Manuscripts, Their Scribes and Readers: Essays Presented to M. B. Parkes*, ed. Rivkah Zim and Pamela R. Robinson (Aldershot, 1997), pp. 73–93.

43 Pauline Head, 'Who Is the Nun from Heidenheim? A Study of Hugeburc's *Vita Willibaldi*', *Medium Aevum*, 71 (2002), pp. 29–46; Thijs Porck, 'Anglo-Saxon Cryptography: Secret Writing in Early Medieval England', https://thijsporck.com, 15 May 2017.

44 Inge van Luijtelaar, 'Colofonconventies in Middeleeuwse Handschriften Uit Vrouwenkloosters in de Nederlanden', unpublished PhD thesis, Radboud University, 2015, pp. 26–7.

45 Alison I. Beach et al., 'Guda, a Sinful Woman: A Multi-Scalar Portrait of a Medieval Scribe and Illuminator', forthcoming.

46 Peter Godman, *Poetry of the Carolingian Renaissance* (Norman, OK, 1985), p. 139.

47 Benjamin Thorpe, trans., *The Homilies of the Anglo-Saxon Church: The First Part, Containing the Sermones Catholici, Or Homilies of Ælfric* (London, 1844), p. 9.

48 Brussels, Bibliothèque Royale, MS 2849-51, Erik Kwakkel, 'Getting Personal in the Margin', https://medievalbooks.nl.

49 Marc Drogin, *Anathema!: Medieval Scribes and the History of Book Curses* (Totowa, NJ, 1983), p. 88.

50 Translation by Robin Flower.

51 Cologne, Historisches Archiv, G.B. quarto, 249, fol. 68r; Thijs Porck, 'Paws, Pee and Mice: Cats among Medieval Manuscripts', www.medievalfragments.wordpress.com, 22 February 2013.

52 Emir O. Filipović, 'Of Cats and Manuscripts', http://theappendix.net, 5 March 2013.

53 Jessica Hodgkinson, 'Abbesses and Early Medieval Book Culture', https://jhiblog.org, 23 March 2022.

54 Montpellier, Bibliothèque universitaire de médecine, MS H 51, fol. 138r, https://bvmm.irht.cnrs.fr and BL, Harley MS 5431, fol. 136v, www.bl.uk/manuscripts.

Four Material World: Parchment and Ink

1 *The Leyden and Stockholm Papyri: Greco-Egyptian Chemical Documents from the Early 4th Century AD*, ed. William B. Jensen, trans. Earle Radcliffe Caley (Cincinnati, OH, 2008), https://homepages.uc.edu/~jensenwb/books.

2 Andreas Petzold, 'De Coloribus et Mixtionibus: The Earliest Manuscripts of a Romanesque Illuminator's Handbook', in *Making the Medieval Book: Techniques of Production*, ed. Linda L. Brownrigg (Los Altos Hills, CA, 1995), pp. 59–64.

3 Editions used are Theophilus, *On Divers Arts: The Foremost Medieval Treatise*

on Painting, Glassmaking and Metalwork, ed. Cyril Stanley Smith and John G. Hawthorne (London, 1979); *An Anonymous Fourteenth-Century Treatise, De Arte Illuminandi: The Technique of Manuscript Illumination*, trans. Daniel Varney Thompson and George Heard Hamilton (New Haven, CT, 1933); *Cennino Cennini's Il Libro Dell'arte: A New English Translation and Commentary with Italian Transcription*, trans. Lara Broecke (London, 2015).

4 Hjalmar Hedfors, *Compositiones ad Tingenda Musiva* (Uppsala, 1932), pp. 14–15.

5 Leandro Gottscher, 'Ancient Methods of Parchment Making: Discussion on Recipes and Experimental Essays', in *Ancient and Medieval Book Materials and Techniques: Erice, 18–25 September 1992*, ed. Paola F. Munafò and Marilena Maniaci (Vatican City, 1993), pp. 41–56.

6 Sarah Fiddyment et al., 'Animal Origin of Thirteenth-Century Uterine Vellum Revealed Using Noninvasive Peptide Fingerprinting', *Proceedings of the National Academy of Sciences of the United States of America*, 112 (2015), pp. 15066–71, at p. 15068.

7 *The Account-Book of Beaulieu Abbey*, ed. Stanley Frederick Hockey (London, 1975), p. 195.

8 Jérôme de La Lande, 'The Art of Making Parchment', trans. Gay McAuley, *Art in Translation*, XIII/4 (2021), pp. 326–86, at p. 350.

9 Fiddyment et al., 'Animal Origin of Thirteenth-Century Uterine Vellum'.

10 Sean Paul Doherty et al., 'Scratching the Surface: The Use of Sheepskin Parchment to Deter Textual Erasure in Early Modern Legal Deeds', *Heritage Science*, IX/1 (2021), pp. 1–6.

11 Copenhagen, Royal Library, GKS 4, folio 11, fol. 183r; Stadtbibliothek Nürnberg, Amb. 317.2°; Staatsbibliothek Bamberg Msc.Patr.5, fol. 1v.

12 *The Account-Book of Beaulieu Abbey*, p. 196.

13 Ibid., pp. 169, 195–8.

14 Michael Gullick, ed., *Extracts from The Precentors' Accounts Concerning Books and Bookmaking of Ely Cathedral Priory* (Hitchin, 1985), pp. 12–13.

15 *A Middle English Version of the Circa Instans*, ed. Edurne Garrido-Anes (Heidelberg, 2020), p. 12.

16 Joseph Turney Wood, *The Puering, Bating and Drenching of Skins* (London, 1912), pp. 1–5.

17 Orietta Da Rold, *Paper in Medieval England: From Pulp to Fictions* (Cambridge, 2020).

18 Pliny, *Natural History*, Book 35, ch. 25: Black ink can be made 'from the soot produced by burning resin or pitch, owing to which factories have actually been built with no exit for the smoke produced by this process'.

19 *The Greek Magical Papyri in Translation*, ed. Hans Dieter Betz (Chicago, IL, 1986), p. 167.

20 Yale University Library, 'Medieval Manuscripts: Some Ink and Pigment Recipes', https://travelingscriptorium.files.wordpress.com, 2012.

21 Vlamdimír Karpenko and John Norris, 'Vitriol in the History of Chemistry', *Chemické Listy*, XCVI/12 (2003), pp. 997–1005, at p. 998. Vitriol may be described as blue or green. Green vitriol is from iron, blue vitriol is from copper. There is evidence that early plant inks were made from iron or copper (Tea Ghigo, Ira Rabin and Paola Buzi, 'Black Egyptian Inks in Late Antiquity: New Insights on Their Manufacture and Use', *Archaeological and Anthropological Sciences*, XII/70 (2020), pp. 1–14).

22 *Extracts from The Precentors' Accounts*, p. 8.

23 James E. Thorold Rogers and Arthur George Liddon Rogers, *A History of Agriculture and Prices in England*, 7 vols (Oxford, 1866), vol. III, p. 547.

24 *Account-Book of Beaulieu Abbey*, p. 196; *Extracts from The Precentors' Accounts*, p. 8.

25 *Extracts from The Precentors' Accounts*, p. 6.

26 *Al-Rāzī's Zīnat al-Kataba*, trans. Joumana Medlej (London, 2020), no. 7.

27 Zina Cohen, *Composition Analysis of Writing Materials in Cairo Genizah Documents* (Leiden, 2022), pp. 45–52.

28 See, e.g., BL, Harley MS 2803, fol. 1v; BL, Harley MS 2820, fol. 78r, both available at www.bl.uk/manuscripts; Morgan Library and Museum, MS M.565, fols 13v, 38r, available at http://ica.themorgan.org/manuscript; Prague, Bibliothek des Metropolitankapitels, MS A. XXI/1, fol. 153r.

29 Michelle P. Brown, *The Lindisfarne Gospels: Society, Spirituality and the Scribe* (Toronto and Buffalo, NY, 2003), pp. 224–5.

30 Quoted in Michael Gullick, 'How Fast Did Scribes Write? Evidence from Romanesque Manuscripts', in *Making the Medieval Book*, ed. Brownrigg, pp. 39–58, at p. 43.

31 Ibid.

32 Richard H. Rouse and Mary A. Rouse, 'Wandering Scribes and Traveling Artists: Raulinus of Fremington and His Bolognese Bible', in *A Distinct Voice. Medieval Studies in Honour of Leonard E. Boyle, OP*, ed. Jacqueline Brown and William Stoneman (Notre Dame, IN, 1997), pp. 32–67, at p. 49.

33 Pamela R. Robinson, 'A Twelfth-Century Scriptrix from Nunnaminster', in *Of the Making of Books: Medieval Manuscripts, Their Scribes and Readers: Essays Presented to M. B. Parkes*, ed. Rivkah Zim and Pamela R. Robinson (Aldershot, 1997), pp. 73–93, at p. 76.

Five Illumination and Painting

1 Michelle P. Brown, *The Lindisfarne Gospels: Society, Spirituality and the Scribe* (Torontoand Buffalo, NY, 2003), p. 290.

2 *Cennino Cennini's Il Libro Dell'arte: A New English Translation and Commentary*

with Italian Transcription, trans. Lara Broecke (London, 2015), pp. 45–6.
3 See BL, Add MS 11283, fol. 23v, www.bl.uk/manuscripts, for images of animals with outline pinprick marks.
4 *The Letters of St. Boniface*, trans. Ephraim Emerton (New York, 2000), pp. 42–3.
5 'Medieval Britain in Colour: 500 Years of Illuminated Manuscripts', 2022 exhibition, Fitzwilliam Museum, Cambridge.
6 K. Bickford Berzock, 'Introduction', in *Caravans of Gold, Fragments in Time*, ed. K. Bickford Berzock (Princeton, NJ, 2019), pp. 23–37, at pp. 25–6.
7 Peter Schreiner and Doris Oltrogge, *Byzantinische Tinten-, Tuschen- und Farbrezepte* (Vienna, 2011), pp. 109–11.
8 'Medieval Britain in Colour'.
9 Thomas Arnold, *Memorials of St Edmund's Abbey*, 3 vols (London, 1890), vol. II, p. 289.
10 Stella Panayotova, ed., *The Art and Science of Illuminated Manuscripts: A Handbook* (London, 2020), p. 239.
11 Claire Donovan, *The Winchester Bible* (London, 1993), p. 56.
12 Arnold, *Memorials of St Edmund's Abbey*, vol. II, p. 290.
13 See the work by Team Pigment for more information on this at www.durham.ac.uk/research/institutes-and-centres/medieval-early-modern-studies/research-strands/team-pigment.
14 Andrew Beeby, Richard Gameson and Catherine Nicholson, 'New Light on Old Illuminations', *Archives and Records*, XXXIX/2 (2018), pp. 244–56, at p. 250. Richard Gameson et al., *The Pigments of British Medieval Illuminators: A Scientific and Cultural Study* (London, 2023), pp. 13–14.
15 Cyril Stanley Smith and John G. Hawthorne, 'Mappae Clavicula: A Little Key to the World of Medieval Techniques', *Transactions of the American Philosophical Society*, LXIV/4 (1974), pp. 1–128, at p. 27.
16 Richard Gameson et al., 'Pigments of the Earliest Northumbrian Manuscripts', *Scriptorium*, LXIX (2015), pp. 33–59; Katherine L. Brown and Robin J. H. Clark, 'Three English Manuscripts Post-1066 AD: Pigment Identification and Palette Comparisons by Raman Microscopy', *Journal of Raman Spectroscopy*, XXXV/3 (2004), pp. 217–23.
17 Dioscorides, *De materia medica*, trans. Tess Anne Osbaldeston and Robert P. A. Wood (Johannesburg, 2000), p. 800.
18 Lloyd Tepper, 'Industrial Mercurialism: Agricola to the Danbury Shakes', *Journal of the Society for Industrial Archeology*, XXXVI/1 (2010), pp. 47–63, at p. 49.
19 Smith and Hawthorne, 'Mappae Clavicula', p. 26.
20 S. Kubersky-Piredda, 'The Market for Painters' Materials in Renaissance Florence', in *Trade in Artists' Materials: Markets and Commerce in Europe to 1700*, ed. J. Kirby, S. Nash and J. Cannon (London, 2010), pp. 223–43, at p. 224;

Extracts from The Precentors' Accounts Concerning Books and Bookmaking of Ely Cathedral Priory, ed. Michael Gullick (Hitchin, 1985).

21 Katherine L. Brown and Robin J. H. Clark, 'Analysis of Key Anglo-Saxon Manuscripts (8–11th Centuries) in the British Library: Pigment Identification by Raman Microscopy', *Journal of Raman Spectroscopy*, XXXV/3 (2004), pp. 181–9; Brown and Clark, 'Three English Manuscripts'.

22 Mary P. Merrifield, *Medieval and Renaissance Treatises on the Arts of Painting: Original Texts with English Translations* (Mineola, NY, 1999), p. 51.

23 Lucia Burgio, Dan A. Ciomartan and Robin J. H. Clark, 'Raman Microscopy Study of the Pigments on Three Illuminated Mediaeval Latin Manuscripts', *Journal of Raman Spectroscopy*, XXVIII/2–3 (1997), pp. 79–83; Jo Kirby and Raymond White, 'The Identification of Red Lake Pigment Dyestuffs and a Discussion of Their Use', *National Gallery Technical Bulletin*, 17 (1996), pp. 56–80, at p. 64.

24 Rita Castro, Adelaide Miranda and Maria Melo, 'Interpreting Lac Dye in Medieval Written Sources: New Knowledge from the Reconstruction of Recipes Relating to Illuminations in Portuguese Manuscripts', in *Sources on Art Technology: Back to Basics*, ed. Sigrid Eyb-Green et al. (London, 2016), pp. 88–99.

25 Aurélie Mounier and Floréal Daniel, 'Pigments and Dyes in a Collection of Medieval Illuminations (14th–16th Century)', *Color Research and Application*, XLVI/6 (2017), pp. 807–22; Maria João Melo et al., 'A Spectroscopic Study of Brazilwood Paints in Medieval Books of Hours', *Applied Spectroscopy*, LXVIII/4 (2014), pp. 434–43.

26 Strabo, Book 12, ch. 3, 40.

27 My thanks to Richard Gameson for sharing this information.

28 Merrifield, *Medieval and Renaissance Treatises*, pp. clxiii, 528.

29 Andrew Beeby, Richard Gameson and Catherine Nicholson, 'Illuminators' Pigments in Lancastrian England', *Manuscripta*, LX/2 (2016), pp. 143–64.

30 Lu-Ch'iang Wu and Tenney L. Davis, 'An Ancient Chinese Alchemical Classic. Ko Hung on the Gold Medicine and on the Yellow and the White: The Fourth and Sixteenth Chapters of Pao-P'u-Tzŭ', *Proceedings of the American Academy of Arts and Sciences*, LXX/6 (1935), pp. 221–84, at pp. 232, 264–5.

31 Identified by the Fitzwilliam Museum, Cambridge.

32 Smith and Hawthorne, 'Mappae Clavicula', p. 27.

33 Merrifield, *Medieval and Renaissance Treatises*, pp. 67, 126, 418.

34 'Medieval Britain in Colour'.

35 Paola Ricciardi, Anuradha Pallipurath and Kristine Rose, '"It's Not Easy Being Green": A Spectroscopic Study of Green Pigments Used in Illuminated Manuscripts', *Analytical Methods*, V/16 (2013), pp. 3819–24.

36 Robin J. H. Clark and Jaap van der Weerd, 'Identification of Pigments and Gemstones on the Tours Gospel: The Early 9th Century Carolingian Palette', *Journal of Raman Spectroscopy*, XXXV/4 (2004), pp. 279–83.

37 H.G.M. Edwards, P. S. Middleton and M. D. Hargreaves, 'Romano-British Wall Paintings: Raman Spectroscopic Analysis of Fragments from Two Urban Sites of Early Military Colonisation', *Raman Spectroscopy Applied to the Earth Sciences – Sensu Latu*, LXXIII/3 (2009), pp. 553–60, at p. 558.

38 A. Radini et al., 'Medieval Women's Early Involvement in Manuscript Production Suggested by Lapis Lazuli Identification in Dental Calculus', *Science Advances*, V/1 (2019), pp. 1–8.

39 Beeby, Gameson and Nicholson, 'New Light on Old Illuminations', pp. 244–56.

40 Gameson et al., *The Pigments of British Medieval Illuminators*, pp. 23–7.

41 'Medieval Britain in Colour'.

42 Ibid.

43 Richard Arnold, *In This Booke Is Conteyned the Names of Ye Baylifs Custos Mairs and Sherefs of the Cite of London from the Tyme of King Richard the Furst* (Antwerp, 1503).

44 Maurizio Aceto et al., 'On the Identification of Folium and Orchil on Illuminated Manuscripts', *Spectrochimica Acta Part A: Molecular and Biomolecular Spectroscopy*, 171 (2017), pp. 461–9.

45 Pliny, *Natural History*, Book 34, ch. 176; Vitruvius, *De architectura*, Book VIII, ch. 6.

46 Glyn Coppack, *Mount Grace Priory: Excavations of 1957–1992* (Oxford, 2019), pp. 139–40, 146–7, 344–5.

47 'The Final Chapter: The Book of Dimma's New Binding', www.tcd.ie/library, 10 October 2016.

48 Due to the fragile nature of surviving manuscripts with Coptic bindings, it is not easy to find images of them. However, there are some later examples at https://library.princeton.edu/visual_materials.

49 J. A. Szirmai, *The Archaeology of Medieval Bookbinding* (Abingdon and New York, 2016), pp. 103, 216–17.

50 Ibid., p. 103.

51 *Extracts from The Precentors' Accounts*, p. 6.

52 BL, Harley MS 3601, fol. 191r; Clark, *Observances in Use*, p. 65.

53 BL, Cotton MS E IV, fol. 243v; *Gesta Abbatum Monasterii Sancti Albani*, ed. Henry T. Riley, 3 vols (London, 1867), vol. II, p. 433.

54 Edward Maunde Thompson, *Customary of the Benedictine Monasteries of Saint Augustine, Canterbury, and Saint Peter, Westminster*, 2 vols (London, 1902), vol. II, pp. 97, 165.

55 *Extracts from The Precentors' Accounts*, pp. 6, 12.

56 Herbert Edward Salter, *Survey of Oxford*, ed. William Abel Pantin (Oxford, 1960), pp. 83, 92.

Six The Twelfth-Century Renaissance

1 N. J. Morgan, *Early Gothic Manuscripts, 1190–1250* (London, 1982), p. 14.
2 J. Canivez, *Statuta Capitulorum Generalium Ordinis Cisterciensis ab Anno 1116 ad Annum 1786*, 8 vols (Louvain, 1933–41), vol. I, p. 15 (cap. 12).
3 Bernard of Clairvaux, *Apology*, https://sourcebooks.fordham.edu.
4 C. Norton, 'Table of Cistercian Legislation on Art and Architecture', in *Cistercian Art and Architecture in the British Isles*, ed. C. Norton and D. Park (Cambridge, 1986), pp. 315–93, at pp. 323, 325, 345.
5 *Patrologia Latina*, ed. J. P. Migne, 221 vols (Paris, 1844–1903), vol. CLIII, cols 651–2, 693–4.
6 Herbert Edward Salter, *Survey of Oxford*, vol. I, ed. William Abel Pantin (Oxford, 1960), pp. 75–99.
7 Richard H. Rouse and Mary A. Rouse, *Manuscripts and Their Makers: Commercial Book Producers in Medieval Paris, 1200–1500*, 2 vols (Turnhout, 2000), vol. I, p. 39.
8 Ibid., p. 48.
9 Ibid., vol. II, pp. 21, 52, 79.
10 Ibid., p. 108.
11 Michael A. Michael, 'Urban Production of Manuscript Books and the Role of the University Towns', in *The Cambridge History of the Book in Britain*, vol. II: *1100–1400*, ed. Nigel J. Morgan and Rodney M. Thomson (Cambridge, 2008), pp. 168–93, at p. 169.
12 Charles Haskins, 'The Life of Medieval Students as Illustrated by Their Letters', *American Historical Review*, III/2 (1898), pp. 203–29, at p. 210.
13 Michael, 'Urban Production', p. 168.
14 Erik Kwakkel and Rodney Thomson, 'Introduction', in *The European Book in the Twelfth Century*, ed. Erik Kwakkel and Rodney Thomson (Cambridge, 2018), pp. 1–6, at p. 2.
15 Richard Gameson, *Manuscript Treasures of Durham Cathedral* (London, 2010), p. 53.
16 See, e.g., BnF, MS Latin 14624, https://manuscrits-france-angleterre.org, Bayerische Staatsbibliothek, Clm 835, https://daten.digitale-sammlungen.de.
17 Cynthia Johnston, 'The Development of Penflourishing in Manuscripts Produced in England between 1180 and 1280', unpublished PhD thesis, Institute of English Studies, University of London, 2014, pp. 115–16.
18 Ibid.
19 Sara Charles, '*Litterae Florissae* in English Manuscripts in the Late Twelfth/Early Thirteenth Century', *Manuscript Studies*, V/1 (2020), pp. 79–119.

20 Walter Oakeshott, *The Artists of the Winchester Bible* (London, 1945).
21 See ch. 5, p. 203. Claire Donovan, *The Winchester Bible* (London, 1993), p. 56.
22 Charles Reginald Dodwell, *The Pictorial Arts of the West, 800–1200* (New Haven, CT, 1993), p. 368.
23 See Rodney M. Thomson, *Manuscripts from St Albans Abbey, 1066–1235* (Woodbridge, CT, 1982).
24 Walter Oakeshott, *Sigena: Romanesque Paintings in Spain and the Winchester Bible Artists* (London, 1972), pp. 104–5.
25 Thomson, *Manuscripts from St Albans Abbey*.
26 See www.albani-psalter.de/stalbanspsalter.
27 See, e.g., Oxford, Bodleian Library, MS Ashmole 1511, fol. 9r, https://digital.bodleian.ox.ac.uk and BL, Royal MS 12 F XIII, fol. 13r, www.bl.uk/manuscripts.
28 Willene B. Clark, *A Medieval Book of Beasts* (Woodbridge, CT, 2006), pp. 70–71.
29 Ibid., pp. 139, 195.
30 *The Medieval Book of Birds: Hugh of Fouilloy's De Avibus*, ed. Willene B. Clark (Binghamton, NY, 1992), p. 269.
31 See, e.g., BL, Add MS 29301, fol. 25r; BL, Sloane MS 6, fol. 144v; University of Glasgow, MS Hunter 251, fol. 43v.

Seven The End of the Scriptorium

1 Richard H. Rouse and Mary A. Rouse, *Manuscripts and Their Makers: Commercial Book Producers in Medieval Paris, 1200–1500*, 2 vols (Turnhout, 2000), vol. I, pp. 239–40.
2 Alison Ray, 'The Pecia System and Its Use in the Cultural Milieu of Paris, *c.* 1250–1330', unpublished PhD thesis, UCL, 2015.
3 Krista A. Murchison, 'Medieval Minims: The Hidden Meaning of a Medieval Pen-Twister', www.historytoday.com, 2 February 2021.
4 Kathleen E. Kennedy, 'Hunting the Corpus *Troilus*: Illuminating Textura', *Studies in the Age of Chaucer*, XLIX/1 (2022), pp. 133–63.
5 John Rylands Library, French MS 1, fol. 212r; BL, Add MS 49622, fol. 82r; Beinecke MS 229, fol. 31r; BL, Royal MS 10 E IV, fol. 49v; Walters MS W.102, fol. 78r.
6 Michael Camille, *Image on the Edge: The Margins of Medieval Art* (London, 1992), p. 30.
7 Koninklijke Bibliotheek, MS D. 40, www.wga.hu.
8 Camille, *Image on the Edge*, p. 26.
9 For a girdle book, see BnF, MS Lat. 10533, fol. 24v, https://gallica.bnf.fr.
10 Chiara Ruzzier, 'The Miniaturisation of Bible Manuscripts in the Thirteenth Century: A Comparative Study', in *Form and Function in the Late*

Medieval Bible, ed. Eyal Poleg and Laura Light (Leiden, 2013), pp. 105–25.

11 Conrad von Soest, 'Brillenapostel' (1403).

12 See https://erikkwakkel.tumblr.com.

13 Ruzzier, 'The Miniaturisation of Bible Manuscripts', pp. 110–12.

14 Estelle Guéville and David Joseph Wrisley, 'What is a Paris Bible?' *Paris Bible Project*, https://parisbible.github.io, 15 June 2021.

15 BL, Kings MS 9, www.bl.uk/manuscripts.

16 Kathryn A. Smith, *The Taymouth Hours: Stories and the Construction of the Self in Late Medieval England* (London, 2012).

17 Ibid., p. 152.

18 Kathryn M. Rudy, 'Kissing Images, Unfurling Rolls, Measuring Wounds, Sewing Badges and Carrying Talismans: Considering Some Harley Manuscripts through the Physical Rituals They Reveal', *Electronic British Library Journal*, 5 (2011), pp. 1–56, at p. 21.

19 See, e.g., Walters Art Museum, W.220, https://art.thewalters.org, compared to BL, Arundel MS 157, https://manuscrits-france-angleterre.org.

20 Richard Bulliet, 'Medieval Arabic Ṭarsh: A Forgotten Chapter in the History of Printing', *Journal of the American Oriental Society*, CVII/3 (1987), pp. 427–38.

21 Johannes Trithemius, *In Praise of Scribes: De Laude Scriptorum*, ed. G. R. Elton, trans. Roland Behrendt (Lawrence, KS, 1974), p. 63.

22 Hannah Ryley, *Re-Using Manuscripts in Late Medieval England: Repairing, Recycling, Sharing* (Woodbridge, 2022), ch. 2.

23 Sinai, St Catherine's Monastery, Greek NF MG 2, fol. 58r.

FURTHER READING

Beach, Alison I., and Isabelle Cochelin, eds, *The Cambridge History of Medieval Monasticism in the Latin West*, 2 vols (Cambridge, 2020)

Breay, Claire, and Joanna Story, eds, *Manuscripts in the Anglo-Saxon Kingdoms: Cultures and Connections* (Dublin, 2021)

Broecke, Lara, trans., *Cennino Cennini's Il Libro Dell'Arte: A New English Translation and Commentary with Italian Transcription* (London, 2015)

Brown, Michelle P., *A Guide to Western Historical Scripts from Antiquity to 1600* (London, 1990)

Brownrigg, Linda L., ed., *Medieval Book Production: Assessing the Evidence: Proceedings of the Second Conference of the Seminar in the History of the Book to 1500, Oxford, July 1988* (Los Altos Hills, CA, 1990)

——, *Making the Medieval Book: Techniques of Production: Proceedings of the Fourth Conference of the Seminar in the History of the Book to 1500, Oxford, July 1992* (Los Altos Hills, CA, and Oxford, 1995)

Clayton, Ewan, ed., *Writing: Making Your Mark* (London, 2019)

Clemens, Raymond, and Timothy Graham, *Introduction to Manuscript Studies* (Ithaca, NY, and London, 2007)

Da Rold, Orietta, *Paper in Medieval England: From Pulp to Fictions* (Cambridge, 2020)

Gameson, Richard, ed., *The Cambridge History of the Book in Britain*, vol. I: *c. 400–1100* (Cambridge, 2011)

——, et al., *The Pigments of British Medieval Illuminators: A Scientific and Cultural Study* (London, 2023)

Hamel, Christopher de, *A History of Illuminated Manuscripts*, 2nd edn (London, 1994)

——, *Meetings with Remarkable Manuscripts* (London, 2016)

Hawthorne, John G., and Cyril Stanley Smith, eds and trans., *Theophilus On Divers Arts: The Foremost Medieval Treatise on Painting, Glassmaking and Metalwork* (New York, 1979)

Holsinger, Bruce, *On Parchment: Animals, Archives, and the Making of Culture from Herodotus to the Digital Age* (New Haven, CT, and London, 2023)
Kwakkel, Erik, *Books before Print* (Leeds, 2018)
Lovett, Patricia, *The Art and History of Calligraphy* (London, 2017)
Medlej, Joumana, *Inks and Paints of the Middle East: A Handbook of Abbasid Art Technology* (London, 2020)
Merrifield, Mary P., *Medieval and Renaissance Treatises on the Arts of Painting: Original Texts with English Translations* (Mineola, NY, 1999)
Morgan, Nigel J., and Rodney M. Thomson, eds, *The Cambridge History of the Book in Britain*, vol. II: *1100–1400* (Cambridge, 2008)
Panayotova, Stella, ed., *The Art and Science of Illuminated Manuscripts: A Handbook* (London, 2020)
Rouse, Richard H., and Mary A. Rouse, *Manuscripts and Their Makers: Commercial Book Producers in Medieval Paris, 1200–1500* (Turnhout, 2000)
Ryley, Hannah, *Re-Using Manuscripts in Late Medieval England: Repairing, Recycling, Sharing* (Woodbridge, 2022)
Szirmai, J. A., *The Archaeology of Medieval Bookbinding* (Abingdon and New York, 2016)

ACKNOWLEDGEMENTS

My thanks to the libraries and institutions that generously make their manuscript collections and catalogues available, in particular the British Library and the Bibliothèque nationale de France. Special thanks to all the cataloguers, who are much undervalued but provide a vital service. Thank you to the Society of Authors, who kindly funded research trips to Jerusalem, Bethlehem, Lindisfarne and Iona. Thank you to Anna Dorofeeva, Anuschka Fux, Steve Lawes and Hannah Ryley for their feedback and to Jamie Miller for the diagrams. Personal thanks to all the women whose knowledge and enthusiasm for manuscripts is truly inspiring, including Alison Beach, Elaine Treharne, Joanna Storey, Cynthia Johnston, Stephanie Lahey and Eleanor Baker. Thanks to fellow medievalist colleagues Catherine Clarke and Adam Chapman, and to Claire Langhamer, Philip Carter, Gillian Neale and Louisa Charles for their encouragement. Lastly, thanks go to the editors at Reaktion, particularly Dave Watkins, who initiated the whole project.

PHOTO ACKNOWLEDGEMENTS

The author and publishers wish to express their thanks to the sources listed below for illustrative material and/or permission to reproduce it. Some locations of manuscripts are also given below, in the interest of brevity:

© S. Ballard 2023: pp. 6, 7; Bayerische Staatsbibliothek, Munich: p. 231 (Clm 14000); Biblioteca Medicea Laurenziana, Florence, photo World Digital Library: p. 88 (MS Amiatino 1, fol. 5r); Bibliothèque nationale de France, Paris: pp. 279 (MS Fr. 25526, fol. 77r), 282 (MS Lat. 919, fol. 8v), 297 (MS Lat. 10426, fol. 1r); British Library, London: pp. 44 (Add MS 43725, fol. 251v), 80 (Cotton MS Nero D IV, fol. 18v), 84 (Cotton MS Nero D IV, fol. 25v), 98 (Harley MS 2788, fol. 71v), 101 (Add MS 11848, fol. 1v), 103 (Harley MS 647, fol. 12r), 184 (Royal MS 10 A XIII/1, fol. 2v), 201 (Add MS 42555, fol 30v), 227 (*bottom*; Add MS 89000), 256 (Harley MS 5102, fol. 1r), 263 (Add MS 62925, fol. 1r), 266 (Egerton MS 1139, fol. 12v), 267 (Egerton MS 1139), 289 (Add MS 49999, fol. 5v), 292 (Yates Thompson MS 8, fol. 7r), 293 (Add MS 42130, fol. 62v), 300 (Yates Thompson MS 13, fol. 71r), 301 (Add MS 35313, fol. 77r); Sara J. Charles: pp. 41, 127, 173, 174, 180, 187, 200, 219, 230; Corpus Christi College, University of Cambridge: pp. 68 (MS 286, fol. 129v), 144 (MS 004, fol. 242v), 205 (MS 00211, fol. 147v); Durham Cathedral Library: p. 248 (MS A.II.4, fol 2r); Exeter Cathedral Library (MS 5183), reproduced with permission of the Dean and Chapter of Exeter Cathedral (photo Sara J. Charles): p. 227 (*top*); The Fitzwilliam Museum, University of Cambridge: p. 107 (MS McClean 30, fol. 10r); The J. Paul Getty Museum, Los Angeles: pp. 252 (MS 64, fol. 85v), 286 (MS Ludwig XIII 7, fol. 274v); The John Rylands Research Institute and Library, University of Manchester: p. 33 (Greek P 457); Lincoln Cathedral, reproduced with permission of the Dean and Chapter of Lincoln Cathedral: p. 258 (MS 147, fol. 158r); National Art Library, London: p. 287 (MSL/1902/1707, fol. 103r); Real Biblioteca del Monasterio de San Lorenzo de El Escorial, photo courtesy

Patrimonio Nacional: p. 122 (MS T-I-6, fol. 1v); Royal Irish Academy, Dublin: p. 72 (MS 12 R 33, fol. 21r); Staatsbibliothek Bamberg (CC BY-SA 4.0): p. 189 (Msc.Patr.5, fol. 1v); Staats- und Universitätsbibliothek Bremen: p. 119 (msb 0021, fol. 124v); Stadtbibliothek Nürnberg: p. 169 (Amb. 317.2° (Mendel 1), fol. 34v); Stiftsbibliothek, St Gallen: p. 114 (Cod. Sang. 1092, recto); Trinity College Dublin: p. 85 (IE TCD MS 58, fol. 34r); University of Aberdeen Library (CC BY 4.0): p. 270 (MS 24, fol. 66r); Winchester Cathedral: p. 253 (fol. 148r).

INDEX